POVERTY MONITORING AND ALLEVIATION IN EAST ASIA

POVERTY MONITORING AND ALLEVIATION IN EAST ASIA

KWONG-LEUNG TANG AND CHACK-KIE WONG, EDITORS

Nova Science Publishers, Inc.
New York

Senior Editors: Susan Boriotti and Donna Dennis
Coordinating Editor: Tatiana Shohov
Office Manager: Annette Hellinger
Graphics: Wanda Serrano
Editorial Production: Maya Columbus, Vladimir Klestov,
         Matthew Kozlowski and Tom Moceri
Circulation: Ave Maria Gonzalez, Vera Popovic, Raymond Davis, Melissa Diaz,
         Magdalena Nuñez, Marlene Nuñez and Jeannie Pappas
Marketing: Cathy DeGregory

Library of Congress Cataloging-in-Publication Data

Poverty Monitoring and Alleviation in East Asia / Kwong-leung Tang and Chack-kie Wong, editors.
     p. cm.
Includes bibliographical references and index.
    ISBN 1-59033-828-6 (hardcover)
     1. Poverty—East Asia.   2. Income distribution—East Asia.   3. Equality—East Asia.
   4. East Asia—Economic policy. 5. East Asia—Social policy. I. Wang, Zhuoqi.

HC460.5.Z9P624 2003
362.5'095—dc21   2003016219

CONTENTS

PREFACE

This book deals with poverty monitoring and alleviation in East Asia. This is an area of current and great interest to scholars, activists, policy-makers and the public. Prior to the onset of the Asian financial crisis in 1997, many were optimistic that the problem of poverty would be tempered in the short run. They predicted the crisis would be short-lived and the whole region would get back on track towards rapid economic development. Yet, the impacts of the crisis endure and in many of the East Asian countries, poverty, along with income inequality, has emerged as a serious social problem.

In this book, we emphasize an important role for the state in poverty monitoring and alleviation efforts, contrary to the prevalent belief in small government and unbridled economic growth as a solution to poverty. We believe that in order to wage a successful "war on poverty," resources from the state must be there. Above all, we believe some hard thinking must go into the contents and direction of anti-poverty programs.

We would like to acknowledge all the contributors who helped to make this book possible: Sammy Chiu, Glenn Drover, Xinping Guan, Arlene Herman, Meegon Kim, Sunwoo Lee, James Midgley, Yuki Sekine, Kate Yeong-Tsyr Wang and Mui Teng Yap. We are most grateful to them for the wealth of research experience and understanding that is reflected in their contributions. They are not, however, responsible for any errors that may remain, nor for any omissions.

We would like to thank Vicki Bartell for carefully typing and preparing the manuscript. Furthermore Jacqueline Cheung deserves thanks for proofreading some of the contributions. Special thanks go to Terry McBride who has given us timely and prompt editing assistance. Finally, we would like to thank the staff at Nova Science Press for their careful production of the book.

In: *Poverty Monitoring and Alleviation in East Asia*
K. Tang and C. Wong, editors pp. 1-13

ISBN: 1-59033-828-6
© 2003 Nova Science Publishers, Inc.

INTRODUCTION:
POVERTY MONITORING AND
ALLEVIATION IN EAST ASIA: AN OVERVIEW

Kwong-leung Tang and Chack-kie Wong

DEVELOPMENTAL IDEOLOGY AND POVERTY

In East Asia, the adoption of an export-led, industrialization approach to economic development produced rapid rates of economic growth in the region which resulted in significant increases in per capita incomes. After the Second World War, Japan rapidly grew to become the economic giant of Asia. Since the 1960s, GDP per capita increases in the East Asian economies have been spectacular. GDP per capita rose in Hong Kong from around US $2,400 in 1965 to US $12,000 in the early 1990s. During the same period, GDP per capita income in South Korea increased from about US $600 to more than US $5,000, and in Taiwan, it increased from less than US $3,000 to US $11,500. The most rapid GDP growth occurred in Singapore where per capita income rose from about US $1,600 to more than US $13,000. This rapid rate of growth continued during the first half of the 1990s when average annual rates of GDP growth consistently exceeded 5% per annum, exceeding the growth records of the world's industrial nations such as the UK, Canada, Sweden and the United States (Tang and Midgley, 2002). China, after years of economic stagnation, has seen very impressive growth rates since the 1980s. Ramesh and Asher (2000) report similar trends for other East Asian countries such as Malaysia, Indonesia and Thailand, although here the growth spurt occurred somewhat later. Nevertheless, from the early 1970s to the mid-1990s, these countries recorded average annual growth rates in excess of 6%.

For a long time after the Second World War, there was complacency among East Asian countries that economic development would ultimately eliminate all forms of poverty and income inequality. All post-war developing countries were grappling with the question of economic development. In the post-war period, the most influential approach was modernization theory which saw developing societies as social systems undergoing social changes consequent upon the impact of technological/western institutions. A well-known conception of the process was given by Rostow (1960) who viewed development as a linear process of economic growth passing through five stages, from the "traditional" to the "mass consumption" society. He claimed that economic growth would raise income and improve levels of welfare in a given society.

Thus, the main thrust of development theory after the Second World War was based on a trickle-down model. It focused on the dynamics of national economic development, often indexed by GNP per capita or change in GNP over some specifiable period of time. The policy was on infrastructure development, in the expectation that benefits would flow throughout the population in the developing countries. Some theorists contended that the benefits of continuing economic growth would eventually trickle down to even the poorest people. There was a strong conviction that economic growth would raise incomes through real growth. Government intervention to meet social needs would be unnecessary: social needs would be met by rising national income. East Asian states are ardent followers of this doctrine. They have often defended their relatively low levels of social spending using this perspective (Tang, 2000b).

With the onset of the welfare state crisis in the mid-1970s, a neo-liberal paradigm has become increasingly dominant in many advanced industrialized countries, including the United States, UK and Canada (Midgley, 1997; 1999). This ideology accuses welfare states of having failed and gives primacy to the marketplace as the determinant of individual choice, freedom and wellbeing. Followers of neo-liberalism (in particular international organizations like the World Bank and International Monetary Fund) argue that government spending, especially on welfare, undermines the market, drains the economy and reduces individual initiative. This ideology has found its way into the Asian countries, which have adopted an adverse attitude toward social welfare – an attitude that blends well with the dominant ideology of modernization in the 1960s. The result is that there has been an apology for modest state intervention (or even non-action) in the social sphere in many Asian countries.

Not surprisingly, proponents of neo-liberalism are convinced that alleviation of poverty would take place through economic growth. Drawing from empirical data, they contend that there has been a significant drop in absolute poverty in the last decade. They believe that poverty studies carried out by international organizations like the World Bank provide the evidence for this. Often, East Asia is cited as a success story whereby economic growth has greatly eliminated the number of poorest people in the last two decades. On an optimistic note, Collier and Dollar of the World Bank (2001) predict that poverty in the developing world will have almost halved by 2015 if the trends of the 1990s persist. They believe that most of this poverty reduction will occur in Asia.

Another large-scale empirical study done by Chen and Ravallian (2001) comes to similar conclusions. In a study of 88 countries using national household survey information, they determine that there was a net decrease in the overall incidence of both absolute and relative consumption poverty between 1988 and 1997. Using an absolute poverty line of US $1.08 per day, they find that the incidence of poor people in East Asia fell between 1985 and 1998 (from 26.60% to 14.71%). In absolute terms, the number of poor people dropped from 417.53 million to 267.30 million. If a higher absolute poverty line is used (i.e. US $2.15 per day), the number of poor people fell less dramatically, from 1,052.32 million to 885.29 million in East Asia.

Obviously, there are several limitations of this study. First, it uses an international poverty line of $1.08 per day in 1993 dollars based on purchasing power parity exchange rates, which ignores regional or country-by-country differences (Weller et al., 2001). The inclusion of China is a significant contributing factor affecting the level of poverty assessed. With its impressive growth, China's rural poverty has been reduced substantially, thus lowering the world's poverty figures in their study.

Further, their estimate is based on household income surveys from only eight countries (China, South Korea, Mongolia, Thailand, Malaysia, Philippines, Indonesia and Laos). The study draws on data that was collected primarily before the Asian financial crisis and the full impact of the crisis on poverty is not gauged. One could note that the study done by Chen and Ravallian (2001) focuses on the poorest people in these societies. Thus, one must question whether other measures should be used to measure the extent of poverty in richer economies like Japan, Hong Kong, Singapore and Taiwan. Even the authors give a caveat: taking the world as a whole, it is not enough to measure the reduction in the total number of poor using a universal definition.

Admittedly, there has been remarkable and unprecedented economic development in Asia in the last few decades. Yet it is distressing to see that Asia still accounts for three quarters of the world's poor (Asian Development Bank, 2002). The problem of absolute poverty has always haunted East Asian countries such as India, Malaysia, Philippines, Indonesia and China. The clear lesson of the past five decades is that economic growth, though necessary, is by no means sufficient to eliminate the problem of severe poverty.

The financial crisis that hit Asia in 1997 made many people in the richer East Asian countries (Hong Kong, Taiwan, Singapore and South Korea) slip back into poverty, while millions of others never managed to escape. Thus, the Asian economic crisis has exacerbated a growing problem in these countries – poverty amid abundance. Unemployment, underemployment and poverty emerge as serious social problems in these developed economies. Two other East Asian countries, China and Japan, are not free from these economic and social woes. China, an emerging economic powerhouse, has faced the thorny problem of unemployment and underemployment since its dismantling of the state-owned enterprises. The liberalization of its market has led to rapidly rising unemployment (hence poverty) in urban areas. On the other hand, Japan, the most economically developed country in Asia, has been mired in adverse economic conditions for the last ten years. Its unemployment rate stood at an alarming 5.5% at the end of 2002.

POVERTY IN EAST ASIA: SIX COUNTRY REPORTS

The lingering of poverty in East Asia calls for some urgent scrutiny and intervention. In the literature, there is no universally agreed upon definition (working and conceptual) of poverty. Poverty can be defined in various ways, focusing on absolute or relative poverty, income or consumption poverty, or "human capabilities." The problem in East Asia is that many governments have not devised reliable means of monitoring the problem of poverty. Neither do they collect feedback from the poor in order to keep track of results from policy interventions or provide strong support. Some Asian governments may not even be aware of poor people's situation. A few simply deny the existence of persistent poverty. In short, poverty monitoring systems are modestly developed in most Asian countries. Without such a system, it is difficult to gauge the extent of the poverty problem over time.

We turn now to highlight the major arguments of the contributors in this volume. Six country studies are conducted by local academics. The countries under examination include: China, Hong Kong, South Korea, Taiwan, Singapore and Japan. Each contributor examines the magnitude of poverty and extent of poverty monitoring in their countries, and discusses the intervention of the states (and their effectiveness) in poverty alleviation.

First of all, Guan, examining the newly emerging urban poverty in post-market reform China, observes that despite impressive economic development in the last decade, the Chinese government has to deal with this social problem that has arisen from the dismantling of the state-owned enterprises. This is a unique social problem for the current government to tackle since economic and social policies worked quite well in the socialist planned economy in the past and prevented urban people from slipping into poverty. Guan points out that in China there is no national poverty line. The poverty lines used by the government's departments and most academics are usually based on the data from specific cities.

The Chinese government has done a lot to address this problem. According to Guan, China's anti-poverty strategy is multi-pronged: to increase per capita income and create more job opportunities by a higher economic growth rate; to help the urban poor take the job opportunities by an employment-led economic policy system and greater efforts to provide retraining programs; and to provide more forms of social protection for the urban poor. In particular, Guan draws our attention to the new program of Minimum Living Security. This program was designed to provide cash benefits for all households with urban resident registration whose household per capita income fell below a certain standard. Pioneered in the early 1990s, this new anti-poverty program had been established in all 668 cities before the end of 1999. Guan praises this program as the most stable anti-poverty intervention that is targeted directly at the urban poorest. But he argues that current social assistance can only provide the urban poor with partial relief since the money they receive is insufficient to pay for education, health services and housing. In the end, Guan identifies several problems to be tackled in China's long-term anti-poverty strategy: how to include floating labor in the urban social protection system; how to deal with the problem of social exclusion; and what form will China's anti-poverty strategy take after its entrance into the WTO.

In his chapter, Chiu argues that poverty has always existed in Hong Kong at different stages of its development. The present SAR administration and its preceding colonial governments have persistently engaged in an endeavor to construct and maintain a personalized discourse of poverty, so as to strengthen the conception of personal responsibility for its alleviation. It has been so successful that there is a weak association between poverty, income disparity and social inequality in Hong Kong. In terms of poverty alleviation, the author suggests that there are only scattered social programs for that purpose in Hong Kong. The primary strategy of the government is to contain poverty through a social assistance program called Comprehensive Social Security Assistance (CSSA). However, serious doubts have been raised about the use of CSSA as an unofficial poverty line and, according to estimates by local academic sources, many non-CSSA households are excluded from government assistance despite being in a state of 'abject' poverty. The government has also used active market measures to encourage exit from CSSA. Albeit that the new Chief Executive of the SAR has stated the administration's intention of helping those in need, Chiu argues that the overall policy framework for poverty alleviation has remained unchanged despite the transfer of sovereignty after 1997.

In their chapter, Lee and Kim report that the Korean government has closely monitored the problem of poverty and devised various means to deal with it. South Korea has an elaborate system to monitor and assess the problem of poverty. The economic crisis in 1997 almost brought down the Korean economy. Unsurprisingly, Lee and Kim note that unemployment and poverty rose rapidly immediately after the crisis. According to the Korea Institute for Health and Social Affairs, the poverty rate in Korea shot up to 11.9% in the 3rd quarter of 1998. Since then, the poverty rate in the 4th quarter of 2000 has come down to 6.2%. At the same time, the Gini coefficient went up to 0.327 in the 2nd quarter of 1998 and to 0.331 in the 4th quarter of 1999. These numbers are higher than they were before 1997.

In their contribution, Lee and Kim discuss several social programs that aim to alleviate poverty. Essentially, they argue that the traditional social safety nets were unable to take care of all new needy people. To tackle the poverty problem after the crisis, the National Basic Livelihood Security System (NBLSS) was introduced by the government in 2000. It serves two purposes: it acts as a last social safety net for citizens and it is in line with the ideology of "Productive Welfare." This system tries to secure the minimum standard of living for all citizens as well as to promote self-support and self-reliance. Lee and Kim contend that the NBLSS faces a challenge: how to achieve its dual purposes of securing minimum standards of living for all the people and at the same time promoting the self-reliance of low-income people. As an interim measure, the Korean government set up a monitoring center for the NBLSS at the Korea Institute for Health and Social Affairs in the end of 2002. The center will evaluate the effectiveness and the efficiency of the NBLSS and will closely watch the trends of poverty.

Looking at Singapore, an island-nation-state of 680 sq. km with no natural resources, Yap argues that abject poverty has been eradicated through employment creation and a social policy aimed at creating the conditions for self-reliance. However, she draws our attention to the rising income gap and the state of those on the lowest rung of the income distribution. Statistical monitoring of the poor focuses mainly on the bottom 20% of the income spectrum while in practice, no single definition of the poor has been adopted by the government. Yap contends that poverty alleviation measures are highly targeted. This approach has its usefulness but is also rather complicated. A whole range of actors are involved in the monitoring and delivery of services, given the "many helping hands" approach adopted by the government. One distinguishing feature of the Singapore approach is that poverty alleviation measures are aimed at providing temporary relief while enabling those affected (or their children) to achieve self-reliance. She cautions that structural unemployment and the ageing of the population will pose as potential challenges to Singapore's welfare system in the long run.

Turning to Taiwan, Wang's chapter examines the poverty rates, the state's antipoverty policies and their effects on poverty reduction during the past decade. Based upon official statistics and empirical findings, four poverty-related issues are examined by Wang: the rise of unemployment, the economic insecurity of the elderly, the phenomenon of feminization of poverty and the growing income inequality. Wang then critically analyses the effectiveness of current government antipoverty policies (universal health insurance, employment insurance, social allowances for old-age farmers, and different types of means-tested programs). Among these antipoverty policies, she argues that universal health insurance is particularly potent in reducing poverty in Taiwan, while means-tested programs would help reduce poverty, particularly for households with elderly members. In order to alleviate poverty in the future,

Wang suggests four policy directions: protecting the economic security of the elderly; tackling social exclusion and social polarization; redefining family units; and protecting the welfare rights of ethnic minorities.

Many people would expect the disappearance of poverty in Japan, given its very high level of economic development. Sekine emphatically denies that this is the case. She identifies in her chapter several groups of poor people: homeless people, low income people, minorities facing discrimination and people living in under-populated villages. Based on official statistics, Sekine estimates that there are some 25% of households with a level of income less than half the national average after redistribution through tax and social security. On another front, the average monthly number of households receiving public assistance in 2001 was 805,169, among which 46% were families comprising an older member, while 38% had invalid family members. Sekine argues that most Japanese government policies for poverty alleviation are designed at enhancing the capacities on the part of the poor as a long-term goal, while financial assistance is used as an immediate relief.

POVERTY MONITORING AND ALLEVIATION — COMMON THEMES

Despite the strong emphases on economic growth, invariably, all contributors in their country studies note marked improvements in general social conditions in these East Asian countries under review. However, poverty lingers, even in the economically advanced state of Japan. Some of the salient social issues noted in these chapters include the following:

1. After the Asian economic crisis in 1997, the problems of poverty and income inequality are found to be either severe or worsening in countries like Hong Kong, Taiwan, Singapore and South Korea. Rural poverty is noted in countries like China, Japan, Taiwan and South Korea.

2. Unemployment has been on the rise in most East Asian countries. Currently, underemployment and unemployment haunt the governments of Japan, China, Hong Kong, Singapore and South Korea. Further, research reports tell of suffering among specific groups of people (for instance women and children). With a number of East Asian countries now either in recession or experiencing zero growth, a prolonged period of adversity with high unemployment, rising poverty and greater income disparity is a real possibility.

3. There is a relatively weak poverty monitoring mechanism in place in most parts of East Asia. In fact, some governments (for instance, Hong Kong and Singapore) have not devised an official poverty line to measure the extent of their poverty.

4. Some countries like Singapore, Taiwan, Japan and the Special Administrative Region of Hong Kong, have used the number of social assistance recipients as a means of gauging the extent of poverty. Interestingly, many of these countries also use social assistance as the main form of policy tool to deal with the problem of poverty. There is a caveat if one is to rely solely on this policy tool. Of particular note is post-colonial Hong Kong. Since the end of 1998, there has been a strong public backlash

against welfare recipients in Hong Kong, which is partly due to the worsening economic conditions.

5. Since the early 1990s, there have been some new social policy initiatives which aim at bettering human development and capacities and enhancing social protection of the people: National Health Insurance in Taiwan, a Mandatory Provident Fund in Hong Kong, Unemployment Insurance in South Korea and reform of the social security system in China.

6. Unique political and economic contexts in each East Asian country have engendered different pathways of social initiatives against poverty.

COMPETING APPROACHES TO POVERTY ALLEVIATION

Granted the persistence of poverty in East Asia, one would agree that poverty alleviation and eradication deserve more attention. But poverty alleviation is a very complex and challenging task. This collection of papers explores some approaches that could address the problem of poverty in East Asia.

These approaches should be seen in the context of the dominant approach prevailing in the world. As noted earlier, there is the influential neo-liberal solution to poverty alleviation that puts strong emphasis on means-tested social assistance programs and a return to the market. To this end, neo-liberal proponents in advanced industrial countries argue that welfare-to-work programs should be implemented. Neo-liberal economists contend that the emergence of huge bureaucracies and state regulations suffocated private investment and distorted prices, making developing economies extraordinarily inefficient. In their view, the ills of unbalanced growth and welfare dependency are all due to too much government intervention.

Much of the criticism in the developing world that has been leveled at neo-liberalism centers on its policy inadequacies. People are disappointed with the structural adjustment policies that neo-liberal proponents have introduced in many developing countries. There have been documented cases of failures. Unsurprisingly, international organizations like the World Bank, the IMF and World Trade Organization that used to espouse a neo-liberal agenda of development have modified their neo-liberal pursuits. Since the 1990s, they have supplemented their neoclassical economic doctrine with a declared commitment to poverty reduction, gender equity, participation, pluralism, human rights and partnership.

The Asian financial crisis has also shown the limitations of an approach that relies exclusively on economic growth and social austerity measures. Thus, the IMF began to acknowledge the "human dimension" of the crisis and the need for limited, short-term social programs to assist the unemployed and others who had been affected by the events of 1997 (IMF, 1999a). Because of the serious political and social ramifications of the crisis, these organizations endorsed the introduction of programs that would alleviate the worst social excesses of the crisis (Tang and Midgley, 2002).

Parallel to this development, the ideas of Amartya Sen on development have captured much attention. Academics like Sandbrook (2000) call his ideas a pragmatic version of neo-liberalism that attempts to rescue neo-liberal ideas from its critics. Sen (1999) deems the expansion of freedom as the goal of development. Importantly, development involves the elimination of "unfreedom." Sen (1999) argues that social services like education, health and social safety nets provided through the state, complement individual economic and political participation and eliminate deprivation. However, he does see a limited role for the state: it should not provide these services without sufficient resources and means testing and it must avoid welfare dependency. Overall, he argues for a world of "reasoned social progress" in which citizens, through informed and rational discussion in the context of free speech and free markets, may select policies to promote a just and prosperous society. Sandbrook (2000: 1072) is critical of Sen's approach, saying: "The false promise of Sen's neo-liberalism is to offer a harmonious route to the expansion of freedom, merely by expanding personal liberties and humanely adjusting individuals to the exigencies of global market competition."

Granted that the neo-liberal framework should not be deemed as the panacea for poverty, five alternative approaches to the reduction and elimination of poverty are explored in this text by our contributors: rights-based, institutional, ILO, social development and social activism.

First of all, Drover, in his contribution, argues that the affirmation of a rights-based approach to poverty alleviation is on the rise at a time when poverty is growing across nations. At the start, Drover notes that: "Part of the reason for the increased appeal of a rights-based approach results from the violation of human rights and the oppression of the poor which accompanies globalization." He then provides three normative justifications for a rights-based approach: liberal, Confucian and feminist. Interestingly, in the context of Asia, Drover finds that the Confucian philosophy may not be incompatible with a notion of rights (in the western sense). In the end, he draws our attention to an issue related to this approach: there is no consensus about the meaning and definition of a basic minimum as a way of fighting poverty.

In his chapter on the role of the International Labour Organization (ILO) in poverty alleviation, Tang argues that this international organization has a long history of tackling poverty among industrial workers across nations. The ILO has always considered access to earned income critical in the abolition of poverty. Central to the issue of poverty is whether employment provides workers with sufficient income to keep them and their dependants out of poverty.

In this contribution, Tang argues that ILO standards have played an important role in protecting fundamental human rights, including the right from want and hunger. Many ILO standards that define acceptable levels of working conditions and worker protection have an indirect impact on poverty. Since 1999, the ILO has participated with other international organizations such as the World Bank and the International Monetary Fund in their poverty reduction efforts. The most notable activity involves the Poverty Reduction Strategy Paper (PRSP) whereby all financing decisions at the country level are subject to the preparation of an acceptable PRSP by the countries concerned and the international organizations. Tang cautions at the end of his discussion that even the ILO is under challenge from the overarching influence of neo-liberalism and it has to critically review its future role.

Midgley, in his contribution, argues for the relevance of a social development approach to the alleviation of poverty. He first describes the social development approach by examining its key conceptual features and relating the interventions that have been adopted over the years to address the poverty issue. The social development approach has been advocated by the United Nations for many years. This approach originated in the developing nations in the middle decades of the 20th century when many newly independent states sought to adopt economic policies that would promote rapid industrialization, employment and improvements in living standards but, at the same, address pressing social problems such as poverty, illiteracy, ill-health, landlessness and urban squalor.

Overall, social development emphasizes the social aspects of the development agenda by harmonizing social interventions and economic development efforts within a wider commitment to social change and progress. It urges governments to assume responsibility for directing economic growth in ways that are sustainable and that promote social well-being for all. Central to its conception of social progress through development, it stresses two key underlying principles: first, economic development should be integrated and sustainable, bringing benefits to all citizens; and second, social welfare should be investment-oriented, seeking to enhance human capacities to participate in the economy. Central programmatic provisions include investments in human capital, employment and self-employment programs, social capital formation, asset development, and the removal of barriers to economic participation.

Midgley believes that these interventions are linked to economic development efforts but they all share a common commitment to raising the standards of living of all the world's people. In the end, however, he cautions us that the current political climate that is dominated by neo-liberal political agenda is not conducive to the successful implementation of social development's anti-poverty efforts.

In his chapter, Wong suggests that very few analyses of poverty have approached the study in relation to institutions. Even among those that have, the distinctive features of an institutional analysis have not been fully appreciated. He attempts to outline the meaning of institutions in the analysis of poverty as an independent or intervening variable that means institutions should be seen as an explanation of poverty, in addition to individualist and structural determinants. The institutional approach provides the meso-foundations for the macro-analyses of poverty because institutions are where decisions are made about where and how state capacities should be directed or redirected to alleviate poverty. Therefore, it is necessary to look at how institutional changes in the rules of the game for poverty alleviation modify the behavior of the poor.

Admittedly, there are many other approaches to poverty reduction that would put constraints on the pursuit of a global neo-liberal agenda. To social activists, the current global social (grassroots) protests against capitalism and globalizing capital (since the "Battle in Seattle" in 1999) serve to put a curb on the overarching influences of neo-liberal economic policies. In the final contribution, Herman and Tang examine the potentials and limitations of global social protests as a variable in tempering neo-liberal globalization and world poverty. They draw extensively from the works of Karl Polanyi (particularly his concept of "double movement"), concluding that social activism is an important variable forcing international organizations to seriously address the issue of world poverty.

POVERTY ALLEVIATION: SOME CONSIDERATIONS

The East Asian countries under examination are now encountering the problem of "poverty amidst affluence." The reaction of their governments to this problem is critical. Studies have shown that advanced industrialized countries (for instance the United States) historically have increased their social spending in times of acute social or economic crisis (Piven and Cloward, 1971). Adversity resulting in greater social and political tensions generates these changes. To some extent, South Korea, Hong Kong, Taiwan, Japan and Singapore have responded at different times to the Asian economic crisis and intervened to help the poor and the unemployed in different ways. China, which is relatively less affected by the crisis, has responded to its poverty and unemployment problems. Critics of these interventions would argue that the governments of East Asia have not done enough (e.g. there is a need to devise an official poverty line etc.) and their measures are too ad hoc, reactive and untimely.

In the wake of the Asian economic crisis in 1997, international organizations like the International Labour Organization have called on governments to be attentive to social conditions that have been rapidly deteriorating since the crisis (Tang, 2000b). These governments are urged to introduce or expand their social protection provisions to alleviate human suffering and enhance social stability. At the time of writing, there is no sign that these East Asian countries (with the exception of South Korea) are seriously heeding this advice.

Currently, one might note a degree of apathy or inattention toward the problem of poverty on the part of some East Asian governments (Hong Kong and Taiwan, for instance) in the aftermath of the economic crisis. Their governments have to pay greater attention to other more pressing economic or political issues. Thus, there is no telling whether Asian governments, with the exception of China and South Korea, will look at their poverty and inequality problems in great earnest in the near future. Despite this, the academics in this volume who study the problems of poverty and income inequality see a clear role on the part of their governments to intervene and alleviate poverty. They must also curb the worsening problem of inequality. Their suggestion goes against the main tenets of neo-liberalism that call for minimum state intervention.

Should the governments react slowly or not at all, it is important and pertinent for researchers and concerned groups to keep track of how the problems of poverty and inequality impact on the marginalized and vulnerable groups. Also, there is a need to monitor efforts undertaken by the governments, non-profit sectors and international organizations in East Asia to assess whether they are effective against poverty and income inequality.

For those countries (China and South Korea, for instance) that pay more attention to poverty, there is need for an overview of existing poverty monitoring exercises at the national level that covers the following areas: (1) a review and evaluation of the existing poverty monitoring system that generates data on employment and poverty; (2) an assessment of the quality, timeliness and use given to the data; and (3) an exploration of alternative and reliable mechanisms to develop poverty information for policy making.

Ideally, the primary goal of poverty/inequality reduction efforts would be to increase the wellbeing of East Asian people living in poverty – through projects, programs, policy level interventions and institution building that will systematically reduce poverty and eliminate the root causes of poverty. All of these efforts can lead to poverty reduction if governments can identify and articulate the root causes of poverty, make the links between what they are doing to ameliorate the situation and who will benefit, understand how and why poor people make decisions and ensure that stakeholders are involved in local planning processes.

Pragmatically, East Asian countries should broaden their notion of "development" and critically review the relevance and efficacy of trickle-down economics. In academic circles, Seers (1971) broke the growth fetishism of development theory some decades ago when he argued that development was a social phenomenon that involved more than increasing per capita output. To him, development meant the elimination of poverty, unemployment and inequality as well. Influential economists such as Myrdal and Adelman acknowledged the validity of Seers's (1971) analysis. Parallel to this, trickle-down economics has been challenged by many empirical studies in the last few decades (Goulet, 1977; Adelman and Morris, 1984). In the context of Asia, Donnison (1997) has challenged this economic view, arguing that the hardships of poverty are only tolerated when the economy is growing so fast that people have hope in the future. In effect, Donnison (1997) argues that hope for many people fades as they fail to improve their incomes.

Finally, another important consideration for the East Asian governments is the relevance of a participatory approach in poverty alleviation. This idea is predicated upon the fact that the poor can define what wellbeing means in their own communities and regions. According to this view, development that is sustainable must go beyond band-aid solutions. There is a need to develop strategies that address the root causes of poverty. This can best be done by involving poor people in the selection, design and evaluation of the anti-poverty projects. Ultimately, this approach demands the poor themselves to be involved in strategies for change.

REFERENCES

Adelman, I. and Morris, C.T. (1984). Economic Development and the Distribution of Income. In M. Seligson (Ed.), *The Gap Between Rich and Poor* (pp. 151-55). Boulder, Colorado: Westview Press.

Asian Development Bank (2002). *Fighting Poverty in Asia and the Pacific*. http://www.adb.org/.

Appelbaum, R. and Henderson, J. (Eds.), *States and Development in the Asia Pacific Rim*. Thousand Oaks, CA: Sage Publications.

Chen, S. H. and Ravallion, M. (2001). How Did the World's Poorest Fare in the 1990s? *Review of Income and Wealth*, 47(3): 283-300.

Collier, P. and Dollar, D. (2001). Can the World Cut Poverty in Half? How Policy Reform and Effective Aid Can Meet International Development Goals. *World Development*, 29(11): 1787-1802.

Donnison, D. (1997). Foreword. In Kim W. J. *Economic Growth, Low Income and Housing in South Korea* (pp. xi-xii). London: Macmillan.

Goulet, D. (1977). *The Cruel Choice: A New Concept in the Theory of Development*. New York: Atheneum.

Ha, Y, C. (2001). South Korea in 2000. *Asian Survey*, January/February, pp. 30-39.

Holtz, T. H. (1999). Labour Rights are Human Rights. *Lancet*, Vol. 353, Issue 9156, p.923.

International Labor Organization (1999a). The ILO Governing Board to examine response to Asian Crisis. Press Statement, March 16. http://www.ilo.org/public/english/bureau/inf/pr/1999/6.htm.

_____ . (1999b). *The ILO's Response to the Financial Crisis in East and South-East Asia. Evolution of the Asian Financial Crisis and Determination of Policy Needs and Response. Governing Body, 274th Session (GB.274/4/2)*. Geneva, March.

_____ . (1999c) *Social Issues Arising from the East Asia Economic Crisis and Policy Implications for the Future*. Discussion Summary Prepared by Katherine Hagen, ILO.

International Monetary Fund (1999a). Economic and Financial Situation in Asia: Latest Developments, January 16. Website: http://imf.org/External/np/speeches/1999/011699. HTM.

_____ . (1999b). *The IMF's Response to the Asian Crisis. A Factsheet, January 17, 1999*. http://imf.org/External/np/exr/facts/asia. HTM.

Johnson, C. A. (1982). *MTTI and the Japanese Miracle: The growth of industrial policy 1925-1975*. Stanford, CA: Stanford University Press.

Leftwich, A. (1995). Bringing Politics Back In: Towards a Model of the Developmental State. *Journal of Development Studies*, 31 (3), 400-427.

Midgley, J. (1986). Industrialization and Welfare: The Case of the Four Little Tigers. *Social Policy and Administration*. 20 (4): 225-238.

_____ . (1995). *Social Development: The Developmental Perspective in Social Welfare*. Thousand Oaks, California: Sage.

_____ . (1997). *Social Welfare in Global Context*. Thousand Oaks, California: Sage.

_____ . (1999). Growth, Redistribution and Welfare: Towards Social Investment. *Social Service Review*, 77 (1): 3-2.

Midgley, J. and Sherraden, M. (2000). The Social Development Perspective in Social Policy. In J. Midgley, J., Tracy, M. B. and Livermore, M. (Eds.), *The Handbook of Social Policy* (pp.435-446). Thousand Oaks, CA: Sage Publications.

Midgley, J. and Tang, K. L. (2001). Introduction: Social Policy, Economic Growth and Developmental Welfare. *International Journal of Social Welfare*, 10 (4) 244-252.

Organization of Economic Co-operation and Development (2000). *Pushing Ahead with Reform in Korea: Labour Market and Social Safety Net Policies*. Paris: OECD.

Piven, F. F. and Cloward, R. A. (1971). *Regulating the Poor*. New York: Vintage.

Ramesh, M. with Asher, M. G. (2000). *Welfare Capitalism in Southeast Asia*. New York: St. Martin's Press.

Rostow, W. (1960). *The Stages of Economic Growth*. Cambridge: Cambridge University Press.

Sandbrook, R. (2000). Globalization and the Limits of Neoliberal Development Doctrine. *Third World Quarterly*, 21(6): 1071-1080.

Seers, D. (1971). *Development in a Divided World*. Harmondsworth: Penguin.

Sen, A. (1999). *Development as Freedom*. New York: Alfred Knopf.

Sherraden, M. (1991). *Assets and the Poor: A New American Welfare Policy*. Armonk, NY: M. E. Sharpe.

Tang, K. L. (2000a). *Social Welfare Development in East Asia*. New York: St. Martin's Press.

_____ . (2000b) (Ed). *Social Development in Asia*. Boston: Kluwer Academic Press.

Tang, K.L. and Midgley, J. (2002). Social Policy after the East Asian Crisis: Forging a Normative Basis for Welfare. *Journal of Asian Comparative Development*, Winter.

Taylor, L. (1997). The Revival of the Liberal Creed: the IMF and the World Bank in a Globalized Economy. *World Development*, 25(2): 145-152.

Weller, C. E., Scott, R. E. and Hersh, A. S. (2001). *The Unremarkable Record of Liberalized Trade. After 20 Years of Global Economic Deregulation, Poverty and Inequality are as Pervasive as Ever*. New York: Economic Policy Unit Paper. Available at http://www.epinet.org/briefingpapers/sept01inequality.html

World Bank (1999). *Statement from the International Labour Organization Deputy Director-General (Ms Katherine Hagen).* Regional Meeting on Social Issues Arising from the East Asian Economic Crisis and Policy Implications for the Future, January 21-22, Bangkok. Available at http://www.worldbank.org/eapsocial/meeting/ilo.htm

In: *Poverty Monitoring and Alleviation in East Asia* ISBN: 1-59033-828-6
K. Tang and C. Wong, editors pp. 15-37 © 2003 Nova Science Publishers, Inc.

Chapter 1

POVERTY AND ANTIPOVERTY POLICIES IN URBAN CHINA

Xinping Guan

PATTERNS OF URBAN POVERTY WORLDWIDE AND CHINA'S CHARACTERISTICS: A THEORETICAL MODEL

There are various patterns of urban poverty in the contemporary world as far as their main socio-economic factors are concerned.

Pattern one: Urban Poverty in an Underdevelopment Environment

This pattern of urban poverty occurs mainly in the underdeveloped economies of African, Asian and Latin American cities, as a result of their lower GDP and income per capita. Many research data show, for example, that there is a negative correlation between economic development and the poverty rate in Asian developing countries (Pernia, 1994) and China's regional rural poverty is an example of this pattern.

Pattern Two: Urban Poverty in Affluent Societies

It is universally acknowledged that economic affluence cannot automatically cure the problem of poverty. This is evidenced by the high urban poverty rates in, for instance, North America and Europe. In these developed economies, a high percentage of urban people remain confined in chronic poverty, even hereditarily, although in most cases the poverty is relative, as a result of unequal wealth distribution, social exclusion and lower motivation of poor people to improve their circumstances, together with some other harmful factors in the social structure, culture and economic and social policies.

Pattern Three: Urban Poverty in Circumstances of Rapid Economic Growth

Rapid economic growth is a key factor enabling most people in developing countries to escape from poverty, but higher-level social inequality and poverty may exist or even become more serious during, and even as a result of, rapid economic growth. The experiences of Latin American and Asian developing countries show that many socio-economic factors may cause this problem. First of all, many developing countries, especially Latin American countries, experienced increasing social inequality and higher poverty rates in the period of rapid economic growth as a result of their intrinsically unequal wealth distribution system. Secondly, rapid economic growth may encourage high numbers of rural laborers to migrate to the cities, thus giving rise to such problems as fewer job opportunities and insufficient infrastructure in urban areas etc., which may cause more severe poverty in the cities. Thirdly, recent experience shows that economic and political instability in both Latin American and Asian rapidly growing economies is a significant factor causing urban poverty. Fourthly, as they have become more involved in the globalization process since the 1960s, the developing economies have faced increasing risks in the globalizing world economy, which are the main causes of their economic and political instabilities.

Pattern Four: Urban Poverty in Transitional Economies

As the former Soviet Union's republics and Eastern European countries experienced poverty rates rapidly increased during the transitional period from a planned to a market economy. According to some researches (Milanovic, 1998), economic decline and other fundamental economic, political and social changes in countries undergoing transition are the main causes of increasing poverty rates.

As some studies have shown (Xiao, 1997; Guan, 1999), urban poverty in contemporary China does not conform to any one of the above-mentioned patterns. Firstly, patterns one and two are far removed from China's urban situation, although the first can be used to explain China's rural poverty. Secondly, although China's urban poverty includes some features of patterns three and four, it cannot be fully explained by either of them. As a developing country, China's urban poverty shares some features in common with other developing countries, but at the same time it is also caused by factors related to its economic and social transition, which are similar to those of the transitional societies in the former Soviet Union and Eastern Europe. Secondly, unlike pattern four, i.e. the poverty in transitional economies which occurred in the declining economies of the former Soviet republics and some Eastern European countries, the urban poverty problem in China has arisen in a rapidly growing economy. Therefore, urban poverty in China is quite unique, and can only be summarized as a new pattern, pattern five: urban poverty in a transitional-developing economy, which should be explained by some significant economic, political and social factors related to both economic transition and rapid economic growth.

THE STUDY OF URBAN POVERTY IN CHINA

Urban poverty is a new topic in China. Before the reform, because of the economic and social characteristics of the "socialist planned economy", poverty was not seen as a big problem in urban China. First and foremost of these characteristics was the full employment policy, under which almost all urban laborers were assigned a job, whether in state-owned or in collective enterprises, and thus enjoyed stable though relatively low-paid work. The second was the comparatively equal salary system, which prevented urban residents from losing out in what would otherwise be a highly unequal income structure in the context of a lower economy as a whole. Third was the universal social welfare system in urban areas, which provided urban residents with basic social security benefits, including retirement pensions and medical insurance for state workers, public education, health care and housing, and social relief for poor people who could not get support from other sources. These institutional economic and social policies functioned quite well under the "socialist planned economic system", and effectively prevented the urban population from experiencing poverty.

The effective antipoverty policies reflected a basic economic goal of the socialist system and one of the Communist Party's main political and ideological objectives. As far as its economic goals were concerned, to implement the government's ambitious industrializing strategy, more resources were put into urban areas, thus enabling urban laborers and residents to enjoy higher incomes and better welfare benefits compared with rural people. With regard to its political and ideological aspirations, the Party hoped to show that poverty was an evil of the "old society", which the new "socialist society", led by the Communist Party, was definitely able to cure. In order to achieve these goals, the Party and government tried, by every means possible, to balance the industrialization strategy with the policy of controlling social inequality and eliminating poverty. In official documents, moreover, the term "poverty" was never referred to. Such concepts as "life difficulty" and "handicapped households" were used to replace the term "poverty".

In practice the socialist strategy proved to be a half success, as its anti-inequality and antipoverty goals were quite successful, but its strategy for economic development was not. As a result, poverty was not seen as a problem, in urban areas at least, while average income and standards of living were still very low compared with developed countries and regions. To accelerate economic development and increase the nation's wealth and average per capita income, the Reform and Open Door strategy was initiated in the late 1970s. China has enjoyed a high-rate of economic growth for more than two decades as a consequence of the Reform and Open Door Policy, and the people's average income has increased a lot. But, on the other hand, social inequality and poverty are becoming a serious problem.

China's poverty problem occurred in rural rather than urban areas in the early stages of the Reform. From the mid-1980s, rural poverty was seen as a serious problem as some remote areas remained underdeveloped while most parts of the country had seen great economic achievements as a result of the first stage of the Reform. The rural antipoverty strategy was thus mainly targeted at these rural poverty regions. Since the late-1980s, however, as the main "battleground" of the Reform strategy shifted from rural to urban areas, and especially after the Reform and Open Door strategy entered its second stage in the early 1990s, urban poverty has become a major problem. Since then, and especially since the mid-1990s as the situation worsened, the government has gradually come to accept the fact that urban poverty is becoming a big social problem in cities. The official terminology has also changed to accept such concepts as "urban poverty", "poor households" and the "poverty problem", in academic publications first and later in official documents.

Nowadays, faced with the severity of the urban poverty problem, the various levels of government are reinforcing their antipoverty actions, and more academic efforts are also being directed towards this issue. Although there have been some achievements in the governmental antipoverty measures, there are still many problems to be overcome. As more attention and resources are being concentrated on this issue, it has become a "hot topic" in government policies, academic publications and public opinion. This chapter first summarizes the current urban poverty problem and antipoverty policies, then analyzes the characteristics of urban poverty in contemporary China, and the current problems in the related policies.

POVERTY IN CONTEMPORARY URBAN CHINA: THE DEFINITION AND MEASUREMENT OF URBAN POVERTY

In its general meaning, poverty is a difficult life situation in which a household cannot maintain a normal standard of living because of low income or other disadvantages. Because multiple factors feature in poverty and the boundaries of its definition are blurred, however, the primary issue in the study of poverty is to develop an operational definition and a proper measurement of urban poverty.

Indicators Measuring Urban Poverty

From the early stages of poverty study in China, for researchers and policy-makers alike, the question of what set of indicators should be applied to measure poverty has aroused heated debate. Although most researchers agree that household cash income is the most important and simplest indicator for measuring poverty, some insist that other economic indicators such as unemployment, in-kind income and housing conditions should be taken into account, and some social indicators such as educational opportunity and health care should also be applied in measuring poverty (Liu, 1986; Guan, 1999). In the government's social relief system, however, only household cash income, the simplest indicator, is universally used to measure urban poverty.

Operational Definition of Urban Poverty: Absolute vs. Relative Concepts

Another problem in poverty measurement is how to develop an operational poverty definition. Since the distribution of household cash income is a continuum without a statistically observable dividing point, the poverty line cannot be defined simply by objective statistical data, and the operational poverty definition either becomes a policy-related issue, or a value-involved academic issue. Unlike the definition in the rural poverty study and the rural antipoverty strategy, in which an absolute measurement is simply applied, e.g. by measuring and calculating the minimal consumption necessary to maintain subsistence, an operational definition for urban poverty is more complex. At the beginning stages of urban poverty studies in the early-1990s, the concept of relative poverty was proposed by some researchers (Li, 1989), but without an objective means of defining the poverty line the researchers suggested various methods for defining urban poverty, reflecting their different value orientations, theoretical perspectives and different methods of collecting empirical data. In governmental antipoverty practices, poverty definition is more policy-related, i.e. the urban poverty line is calculated primarily according to the available financial resources for social relief and other antipoverty measures, although some household survey data are also used in the definition.

Poverty Lines and Poverty Rates

To date there is no national poverty line. The poverty lines in the governmental social assistance system and in most academic studies are based on data from specific cities. Therefore, each city has a specific poverty line, and they are quite different from one city to the next because of large regional inequalities and intercity differences in local governments' financial capabilities.

There are several approaches to estimating poverty rates and the scope of poverty, including:

1. Using a poverty line which is defined by calculating people's minimal consumption on food, clothing etc. for subsistence;

2. Estimating the poverty rate by roughly calculating the numbers of people in specific groups, e.g. the number of workers who have been laid-off, the unemployed, and the traditional beneficiaries of urban social relief;

3. Setting a fixed rate, e.g. the bottom 5% of urban households, and including them in the poverty group;

4. Using the so-called "international poverty line", i.e. a percentage of median income or income per capita, to calculate the poverty rate and scope;

5. Simply taking the standard line of the Minimal Living Security (MLS) system as the poverty line and the beneficiaries of this social assistance program as the poverty group.

Since there are so many different approaches to defining poverty and drawing up poverty lines, various poverty rates, whether national or municipal, and poverty extents have been proposed, which range from the bottom 5% income group to upwards of 15%, the majority being around 7%-8%. In most official documents, the MLS standard is used as the urban poverty line and the percentage and numbers of its beneficiaries are taken as the official poverty rate and scope. In terms of the number of MLS beneficiaries, the urban poverty rate is currently about 2.7% of total urban residents, and the lowest rate is just 0.29% in Zhejiang Province (Hong and Wang, 2002). Many researchers argue, therefore, that measuring the poverty rate in terms of MLS beneficiaries underestimates the true situation because the MLS coverage is too small and excludes many poor people. For example, across 31 provincial capital cities the MLS standard lines currently range from 143 Yuan to 281 Yuan (monthly per capita income), and the national average for all cities is 148 Yuan. The total number of beneficiaries were nearly 6.9 million in October 2001 (Social Relief Section of the Civil Affairs Ministry, 2001; Tang, 2002) Recently, however, more researchers are tending to accept the poverty definition, poverty line and poverty scope in terms of MLS beneficiaries, because it is the simplest way to define the poverty group and, more importantly, the MLS standard has been raised and coverage has been increasing since 2000.

The most recent estimate of the number of China's urban poor is that issued by a research group of the Asian Development Bank (ADB). Using official statistical data provided by the National Statistics Bureau for 1998, and measuring the minimum level of consumption for subsistence in an urban context, the researchers in this group estimated that there were 14.8 million urban people living in poverty, or about 3.3% of the total number of urban residents (Tang, 2002).

THE CONSTITUTION AND FEATURES OF CHINA'S URBAN POVERTY

Constitution of the Urban Poverty Groups

In the pre-reform period, only the "Three Nos", i.e. those with no income, no working ability (e.g. the disabled or the elderly) and no family support, were seen as a poverty group and thus were supported by the government. After the reform, however, the urban poverty group has become more motley, i.e. it has diversified into various subgroups. According to some studies, the current urban poverty population includes three subgroups. The first conforms to the traditional "Three Nos". This group is seen as the traditional urban poor, because they have been treated as the urban poor and been beneficiaries of social welfare since the early stages of the urban social assistance system in the 1950s. The second group includes those who are poor because they do not have stable jobs, or have had low incomes for a long time, or have more dependent family members and thus lower average household income. The members of this group are usually in a state of chronic poverty. They existed even in the pre-reform period, but were neither included in the poverty group nor covered by the governmental social relief system, although some of them could obtain some degree of temporary assistance when their situation became extreme. The third group is termed the "new urban poor", which includes some of the urban unemployed and laid-off workers, low-income workers in state-owned and collective enterprises, and some pensioners. The majority of these people have lost their jobs or salaries as a result of the reform of urban enterprises, which has led to bankruptcies or the laying-off of workers.

Of the three groups, the first is the traditional urban poor of Chinese cities and towns. The second group was not regarded as poor until quite recently, although people experiencing such difficulty have existed for a long time. The third is a new poor group in urban China, resulting from urban economic reform and the transition from a centrally planned to a market economy and from a closed economy to an open one. It is this last group which has become the largest in recent years. According to national statistical data, the urban poor, in terms of the beneficiaries of MLS, can be divided into six subgroups (see Table 1.1).

Table 1.1. The Subgroups of Urban Beneficiaries of MLS, 2000

Employees	The laid-off	Retired people	The unemployed	The "Three Nos"	Others[*]
15%	30%	9%	17%	6%	23%

[*] Including the disabled, those without a stable job, and some students.
Source: Social Relief Section of the Civil Affairs Ministry (cited in Hong and Wang, 2002).

The first four columns in Table 1.1 form the subgroup of new urban poverty, accounting for 71% of the urban poor at the end of 2000. According to another study carried out in Wuhan, a big city in central China, this "new urban poverty" accounts for about two-thirds (64.2%) of all urban poor people, defined in terms of the beneficiaries of the Minimal Living Security allowance in 1997 (Poverty Study Team of Wuhan University, 1999). These statistics indicate that the current urban poverty problem in China can, to a large extent, be attributed to economic reform and the transition process.

Some Features of the New Urban Poor

According to a number of studies (e.g. Zhang et al. 1998; Zhao and Niu, 1998; Yang and Wang, 2001; Poverty Study Team of Wuhan, 1999), the urban poor have the following features.

First of all, the urban poor are a fluctuating population. Most of them, especially the able-bodied laborers, are in state of temporary poverty. They fall into poverty because of some temporary predicament, such as being laid-off or their salary being reduced as a result of their employer running into financial difficulty. Most of them, though having temporarily lost their job, are still motivated to work, and thus may easily improve their circumstances within a short time once they get a new job or their enterprise recovers profitability.

Secondly, the poverty group is quite young, compared with some other countries or with the traditional urban poor in the pre-reform period. According to the above-mentioned research in Wuhan, for example, 58.5% of people in the poverty group are between 30 and 45 years of age (Poverty Study Team of Wuhan University, 1999).

Thirdly, the urban poor are unevenly distributed among different regions, different kinds of enterprises and different industries and trades. Most of the statistical data show that the urban poor are disproportionately concentrated in cities that have some unitary industry, especially declining industries, such as coal, steel, forestry and traditional military industries, most of which are in the state sectors. These uneven features show that the current problem of urban poverty is, to a large extent, a result of the economic reform, the economic structural transition, and uneven regional economic development.

LIFE SITUATION OF THE URBAN POOR

Although much attention has been paid to the poverty issue by the government and in academic circles in recent years, most of the research has focused on quantitative description, such as the measurement of poverty rates etc., and less attention has been paid to the actual conditions of life for the urban poor. Among the few that have, two studies provide some panoramic data and a deeper understanding of this issue. One is by the Center for Social

Policy Studies, Chinese Academy of Social Sciences (CASS), which carried out a survey of 2,500 households in five big Chinese cities – Shanghai, Tianjin, Wuhan, Chongqing and Lanzhou – in 1998 (some significant data are published in Tang, 2002). The other is by the Department of Sociology, Nankai University, which undertook in-depth interviews with the urban poor and vulnerable residents in Chengdu and Shenyang in 2001.[1] Through these two important pieces of research, the reality of life for the urban poor can be roughly summarized.

Family Income

According to the CASS researchers' data, the poverty groups' average monthly family income was only about 21%-31% of the total population's average in 1998. Taking into account the raised standard of poverty in 1999, the gap has narrowed to about 27%-40% in these five cities, far lower than the international poverty standard which is usually 50%-60% of the total population's average income (Tang, 2002). The Nankai University scholars found that almost all MLS beneficiaries, who are regarded as the urban poor, do not have other stable income sources because of lower physical capability, less social support and insufficient job training etc. Most of them, especially the able-bodied, are motivated to increase their income through work, but lack opportunities to get a job, and some of them thus seek additional income by taking on socially stigmatized and low-income work such as collecting garbage. In addition, among those whose family income is just above the MLS line, many have fluctuating and occasionally precariously low incomes because of their job instability, fewer working hours and fewer family members who contribute to household income.

Daily Life

According to the CASS researchers' data (Tang, 2002), the urban poor in the five cities find it difficult even to maintain a normal diet. They usually consume meat only once or twice a week.[2] And in the poorest subgroup of the Lanzhou sample, about two-thirds (64.0%) of respondents reported that they did not eat meat in the week before the interview. In all five cities, more than 80% (81.3%-93.9%) of the respondents reported that they always buy the cheapest vegetables. The Nankai University study reported an extreme case of one interviewee resorting to rummaging through dustbins for vegetables. The CASS researchers' data also show that more than 90% of the poor people in the five cities seldom buy new clothes for the adults in the household, and most of their clothes are gifts from relatives or charitable donations.

---

[1] The Nankai University's research, led by the author of this paper, was funded by the Urban Health and Poverty Project (UHPP), which is a Sino-British joint project to develop Chinese urban community health services and the access of the poor to health services. The report has not been published.

[2] Since the price of meat is much higher than that of vegetables in Chinese cities, the consumption of meat can be used as an indicator of people's living standards, especially for the lower income groups.

Education, Health and Housing

In recent years the cost of education has been rapidly rising. Even within the obligatory education period (9 years) education costs have increased, mainly as a result of various additional expenses, though the official fees are kept at a basic level. The increasing costs of education are especially harmful for the poor. In the Nankai University survey most of the interviewees reported that the higher education costs present the greatest difficulty in their family budget. The CASS researchers' data show that 64.4%-92.6% of the respondents in the five cities cannot afford the education fees, and some – 7.2%-27.1% – may have to curtail their children's education as a result of their inability to pay the fees of various kinds and the lack of support from government and other sources (Tang, 2002).

The health of the poor is another serious issue. The Nankai University interviews reveal that most of the poor have a disease of some kind, which is one of the main causes of their poverty. Currently, practically none of the urban poor can afford the expensive health services provided by the state hospitals, and most of them do not see a doctor before their disease becomes very serious. For minor health problems they usually obtain cheap medicines from drug stores, which is much less expensive than seeing a doctor. In one extreme case an interviewee reported using expired medicine. For serious diseases, especially those needing hospital treatment, the urban poor would fall into serious financial trouble. Some interviewees even said they could do nothing but simply "wait for death". The CASS researchers' data show that among the poor respondents, 33.5%-61.1% have chronic diseases of various kinds, and 50.1%-69.5% do not go to hospital when becoming ill (Tang, 2002).

As far as housing is concerned, the situation seems less critical than the problems of education and health. The Nankai researchers found that almost all the interviewees had some basic housing and no homelessness was reported. In most cases their houses had been provided by their employers many years ago under the welfare housing system in the pre-reform period. However, compared with the general improvement in housing conditions among urban residents, the housing situation of the poor is obviously of a relatively low standard, not only in terms of the average size and number of rooms, but also the quality of their houses. Generally speaking, the urban poor resident's houses are more likely to be small and dilapidated with poor sanitary facilities and badly furnished.

Social Life

As a result of their low income and disadvantages in other respects, the urban poor often face difficulties in social life. The CASS researchers' data show that 34.0%-45.5% of the poor respondents in the five cities prefer not to communicate with neighbors or former colleagues, and 39.6%-64.5% do not visit relatives and friends even during festivals (Tang, 2002). Both the CASS research and the Nankai University research show that the urban poor's weaker social networks are a result of their lower economic situation and the discrimination they are subject to.

EXPLANATIONS FOR THE URBAN POVERTY PROBLEM

Urban poverty is more complex and harder to account for than rural poverty. As mentioned earlier, urban poverty in China has some specific characteristics that can be summarized as a transitional-developing pattern. In this section, the growing urban poverty problem is accounted for, and its transitional-developing background will be illustrated and analyzed by reference to a series of economic and social factors.

Economic Factors

The economic factors can be analyzed on three different levels:

The Micro Level

At the immediate level, it is obvious that the current urban poverty in China is caused, to a large extent, by the high unemployment rate and increasing income inequality. Many studies show that most urban poor families are poor because of the household head's (mainly the husband's) unemployment or low income. There are two kinds of unemployment in China's urban economy. The first is registered unemployment, including those who are fired by their employers and then register with the government unemployment services (some qualify for benefits from the official unemployment insurance program). This kind of "registered unemployment rate" has been quite low, about 3% in the 1990s. However, there is another kind of unemployment affecting "laid-off workers", which means that although the workers have lost their jobs, they are still members of their enterprises so are entitled to some living subsidy and welfare benefits from their employers. According to official sources (National Statistics Bureau, 2000), the total number of laid-off workers was 6.5 million at the end of 1999. Up to the end of 1999, according to some researchers, the cumulative number of laid-off workers was about 20 million, of whom about 7 million had not been re-employed to date (Yang and Wang, 2001). The true number of laid-off workers may be underestimated by official statistics, because many workers are not registered with the "re-employment service centers", and have not been officially counted. Due to the complex and fluctuating nature of the situation, there are no accurate official statistics or academic estimates available on the actual rate of lay-offs at the national level. Nevertheless, putting the two kinds of unemployment together, i.e. the laid-off and the registered unemployed, the true urban unemployment rate should be roughly 5%-8% in recent years.

The Meso Level

At an intermediate level, the rising unemployment and increasing income inequality are seen as a result of a series of changes in the economic sphere, including changes in economic systems, the development of a foreign-oriented economy, and changes in the urban industrial structure and urban-rural economic relations.

Changes in Economic Systems

The following changes are seen as having the most significant impacts on urban poverty:

- *Employment policies*: from the former full employment policy, under which all urban laborers were guaranteed a job, to the current labor market policy, under which governments no longer take responsibility for securing jobs.

- *Enterprises policy:* before the reform, the state-owned enterprises were required to undertake some important social functions, such as providing stable employment and welfare for their employees, and government provided financial support for the enterprises. Following the reform, however, the enterprises are treated as independent economic bodies which the government no longer provides financial support for, but agrees to or even encourages them to lay off workers to improve their performance in the market and to meet their objectives.

Development of a Foreign-oriented Economy

The increasing investments from overseas and higher percentage of international trade have contributed a great deal to China's economic development as a whole and to the rapid increase in urban residents' per capita income. However, these developments have also played a part in increasing income inequality and urban poverty, because the price for more overseas investments and higher exports is lower domestic labor costs, i.e. wages and the provision of welfare have to be relatively constrained.

Changes in Urban Industrial Structures and Urban-rural Economic Relations

With the relocation of traditional industries outside metropolitan areas, the development of rural industries and the influx of rural laborers into the cities in search of work, urban laborers have been facing severe competition for jobs, either because of the high number of job-seekers within cities or the number of jobs flowing from cities to villages, and more urban workers have lost their job as a result.

The Macro Level

At the macro-level, the general situation of market transition and globalization forms the fundamental backdrop to the increasing inequality and poverty in contemporary urban China. As a result of the transition to a market economy and the open-door policy, many urban enterprises have encountered strong competition from two quarters: newly developing foreign-invested companies and rural industry. Some less-efficient urban enterprises, mainly the state- and collectively-owned enterprises, have thus fallen into bankruptcy. In order to survive in the face of stronger market competition, those that have not been bankrupted have to increase their efficiency and reinforce their competitiveness by cutting down on their payroll of redundant employees, and many urban laborers have lost their job as a result. Although being unemployed does not necessarily mean having fallen into poverty, it is definitely a significant causal factor for poverty among the current urban poor, since the unemployment rate among the poor, if one includes the laid-off workers, is much higher than the national average (for example among MLS beneficiaries the unemployment rate, including the laid-off, was 47% at the end of 2000 – see Table 1.1).

The urban poverty problem, especially the regional differences in this issue, also derives from the transition in China's economic system and uneven regional economic development.

This feature can clearly be seen in the negative correlation between the variables of poverty rates and economic development. If a unified nationwide measurement, i.e. a nationwide poverty line, were applied, the uneven feature would stand out more. Regional inequality and the higher poverty rate in some less developed regions are also a result of the economic reform and the impacts of globalization.

The economic explanations of the current urban poverty in China are summarized briefly in Figure 1.1.

Figure 1.1. Economic Explanations of Urban Poverty

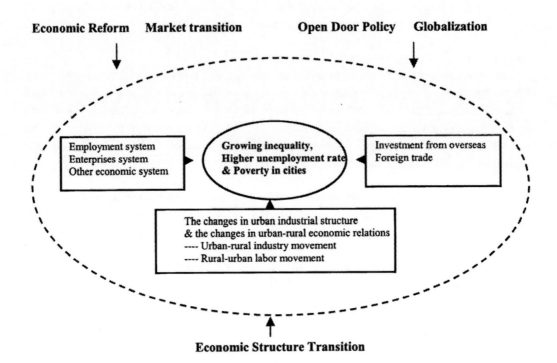

ECONOMIC STRUCTURE TRANSITION

Social Factors

The growing poverty problem and the difficulties faced by the urban poor have also been caused or aggravated by some changes in social policy. The universal social protection system in urban areas, established in the early 1950s, played a significant role in preventing urban people from falling into poverty in a context of underdevelopment and relatively low per capita income in the pre-reform period. After the reform, however, the degree of social protection has changed a lot. Although the current urban poverty can mainly be explained by the above-mentioned economic factors, the decline of social protection puts the urban poor in a more precarious situation.

Changes in the Social Policy Systems

Changes have occurred in almost all areas of so-called social policy: social insurance, social assistance, health care, education, housing and welfare services.

Basic Goods Provision for Subsistence

From the mid-1950s a quota system was applied in urban areas for basic goods for subsistence, including food, clothing, cooking oil etc., which guaranteed all urban residents basic living conditions in the shortage period on the one hand, and especially guaranteed that lower income families could afford the basic supplies within the quota on the other, since the price of these goods was controlled by the government and kept very cheap. After the reform, the quota system and the government's control over prices have been abolished, and all basic goods are now sold at market price. While most urban residents are able to enjoy the sufficiency of supply in the market, the urban poor are worried about the higher prices of basic goods. Some similar issues troubling the urban poor are the costs of electricity, piped water and heating etc., which were partly subsidized or even free of charge in the pre-reform period, but are now at market prices that the urban poor in many cases cannot afford.

Pensions

Before the reform there was a nationwide stable pension system for state workers, in which the government and the state-enterprises took full responsibility for providing pensions for retired workers. After the reform the old state pension system was replaced by social insurance, which is funded by contributions from both the employees and employers. For many less-prosperous enterprises such additional costs will be making their business more difficult and some employers try to escape the responsibility of paying for the insurance, with the result that some retirees may not get pension benefits in the future (Zhang, 2000).

Health Care

Prior to the reform there was a public health service system in urban areas, which was run by public expenditure and thus provided low-cost health services for urban residents. At the same time, state workers and government staff were entitled to non-contributory free medical services. Since the reform, urban health services have become much more commercial and health care costs and charges have risen dramatically, with the result that lower income families cannot afford medicine or health services. On the other hand, the former free medical care has been replaced by a social insurance system, which is also a contributory scheme with payments made by both employees and employers. As a result of the higher contribution rates, the new medical insurance's coverage is so far very small in many cities and most urban residents, especially the poor, are still excluded. Furthermore, for the purpose of controlling costs, strict regulations are universally applied and only part of the medical costs can be reimbursed for those who are fortunate enough to be covered. As a result, the urban poor cannot benefit from the new system. Moreover, since many municipal governments have not yet implemented the new medical insurance program, which was designed by the central government in 1998, many employees in these cities cannot have their medical bills reimbursed and have to pay themselves for the spiraling medical costs. In this situation, medical costs are a significant factor precipitating the fall of some people in low-income groups into poverty.

Education

Similar changes have occurred in the urban education system, although not to such a serious extent as in health care. Firstly, the former free access to higher education has been abolished, and university and college students now have to pay tuition fees of at least several thousand Yuan per year. Secondly, while most of the primary and middle education schools have so far remained public education institutions, and the standard fees for compulsory education (9 years) should be very low under official regulations, the actual education costs for urban families have been increasing. According to a survey in three big cities, 54.3% of the respondents complained that education fees are increasing too fast (Yang, 2002). At the same time, in some cities a few good schools have become private institutions and the fees have increased even more.

Housing

In the pre-reform period, there was a welfare housing system in urban areas, and state workers were provided with basic housing. As a result of the housing reform, which began in the early 1980s, the welfare housing system has been replaced by a commercialized housing system in which urban residents have to buy their houses on the property market, although many employees may receive a cash subsidy from their employers for their house purchase. Obviously, the urban poor cannot afford the high prices of urban houses, especially in the big cities. A low-rent housing system is in place for the urban poor as part of the housing reform, but so far only a very small number have participated in it.

Social Assistance

To deal with the growing problem of poverty in Chinese cities, the urban social assistance system has been rebuilt and the traditional governmental social relief program for the "Three Nos" has been replaced by the more wide-reaching Minimal Living Security (MLS) system. It is the only welfare program in Chinese cities that is enlarging, although there are still some problems with its development as will be discussed in the next section.

General Trends in Social Protection

From the above-mentioned changes, some general trends can be summarized as follows.

1. The market principle has been more widely introduced and there is less welfare provision. In almost all areas of co-called social policy, except for social assistance, some degree of marketization has occurred, and the principle of a general level of welfare has declined. This trend is true of social insurance, health services, housing, education and other public and personal support services, which were traditionally welfare services, but which have now become, to different extents, commercial or semi-commercial services.

2. Societalization of the social welfare system. Since the reform, the government has taken less responsibility for the provision of welfare services and other social actors are being encouraged to participate instead. As a result of the moves to reform social security and the welfare system, the government has abandoned its previous full responsibility for guaranteeing stable employment, pensions and health services for state workers. Although some new patterns of social insurance have been designed to replace the old arrangements for these social protections, employees now have to

share the costs of these with their employers to obtain the benefits. Social welfare reform of this kind is doubtless helpful for improving economic efficiency, but may be more harmful for the urban poor, since it is difficult for them to pay or pre-pay for the services. Another approach in the welfare societalization process is to encourage the local community and NGOs to take on a bigger role in delivering social welfare. Although it may be a promising development in the future, and there have so far been some inspiring achievements, especially in some economically flourishing cities such as Shanghai and Beijing, the NGOs lower ability to mobilize financial resources is still a big problem affecting their development in most Chinese cities.

3. From a universal model to a selective model of the welfare system. Instead of pursuing a universal model, the governmental welfare programs have been turning to a selective model, i.e. targeted directly to poor people and those in most need. While more targeted antipoverty programs have been introduced in urban areas, such as MLS, the government has made big changes to its traditional universal welfare provision (free services) for ordinary urban residents. A more targeted social protection system is good for curing the current problem of poverty in a more efficient way, but less good for creating a wide preventive social protection system.

The Changed Philosophical Basis and Goals of the Welfare System

The changes have not only taken place in particular arrangements, but have also been made in the basic philosophy and the general goals of welfare development. The changes at these fundamental levels are summarized in Table 1.2.

Table 1.2. Changes in the Philosophy and Goals of China's Social Policy since the Reform

	Traditionally	After the reform
Philosophical basis	Pursuing "socialist ideology", in which social protection and social equality are paramount	Prioritizing economic efficiency, and putting social justice in second place
Main economic goals	To increase employees work motivation by providing them with good social services	To reduce labor costs, in order to have a "more efficient economy", by cutting down on social welfare provision
Main social goals	To maintain social justice by a "redistribution mechanism" To improve people's quality of life by relatively high public expenditure	To maintain social stability by providing minimal social relief to the poor.

Briefly, the main task of the Chinese government's current social policy is therefore mainly to provide a basic "safety net" for the people in order to avoid social unrest, while cutting down on social expenditure in order to strengthen economic competition.

ANTIPOVERTY POLICIES IN URBAN CHINA

It is widely acknowledged that urban poverty cannot automatically be eliminated as a result of economic growth. To alleviate urban poverty, some comprehensive strategies are necessary, including economic and social policies to deal with a variety of issues on various levels. In urban China, as well as in many other countries, the antipoverty strategy includes several joint approaches: to increase per capita income and create more job opportunities through a higher economic growth rate; to help the urban poor take the job opportunities by an employment-led economic policy system and more effective re-training programs; to provide more social protection for the urban poor etc.

Since urban poverty and antipoverty issues are still a new topic for both the government and scholars in China, there has not been a precisely planned long-term antipoverty strategy. However, some specific antipoverty actions in urban China began as long ago as the early 1990s, and have been reinforced recently. So far, specific antipoverty measures have been taken mainly in the areas of employment services, social insurance, social assistance and some other related areas.

Employment Services

Although the traditional government policy of assigning all urban laborers a job was abolished in the 1980s, the government still has a policy of helping urban laborers, especially laid-off workers, to secure new jobs in the labor market by providing services for job seekers. There are various programs in operation in cities and towns, including creating more job centers in urban areas and investing in information systems, providing training programs for laid-off workers, encouraging the laid-off to accept informal employment, e.g. self-employment and working in "community services" etc. However, the achievements are still limited, especially as regards providing training programs for laid-off workers. Although re-employment rates are higher in cities with a booming economy – mainly as a result of their higher economic growth rates – laid-off workers are still very difficult to place in employment in most other cities.

The Three "Security Lines"

To alleviate urban poverty, certain social security projects have been established, among which the three "basic security lines" – unemployment insurance, living allowances for laid-off workers and the Minimal Living Security System – are the most important.

Unemployment Insurance

Initiated in the late-1980s, this project was set up to provide benefits to the registered urban unemployed. Based on contributions from both employers and employees, the unemployed – once registered with a social insurance agency – are entitled to unemployment benefit for from 3 to 24 months, according to the number of years the claimant has paid the insurance. However, since most urban job-losers choose not to register as unemployed, the official "registered unemployment" rate is quite low, and the actual coverage has so far remained small.

Living Allowance for Laid-Off Workers

This is a temporary benefit for laid-off workers, mainly of the state-enterprises. After being laid off most of the workers are organized into "re-employment service centers", which help them secure new jobs by providing job information and training and also by providing them with a basic living allowance. However, because the enterprises are required to share the costs of this allowance, some badly placed enterprises find it impossible to contribute to a re-employment service center, or fail to provide all their laid-off workers with the living allowance. According to official statistics, about 95% of laid-off workers registered with the re-employment centers, of whom about 95% received a living allowance averaging 323 Yuan per month in the first half of 2000 (Lue, 2000). More recent data shows that there were in total 6.32 million laid-off workers in the first half of 2001, of whom 91.6%, i.e. 5.79 million, were registered in the re-employment service centers, and 93.5% received basic living allowance in the form of a cash benefit (Tang, 2002; Wang, 2002) But, according to some researchers and reporters, the actual beneficiaries are far fewer than official statistics would suggest. According to a report by the Xinhua News Agency, for instance, some laid-off workers in a city in Anhui Province were only receiving 100 Yuan per month, less than half the local official standard of 207 Yuan (Huang and Zhou, 2000).

Minimal Living Security (MLS)

Because the old urban relief program could not deal with the growing poverty problem due to its very small coverage, the MLS program was designed to replace it. Whereas the old social relief program just covered the "Three Nos", the new MLS provides cash benefits for all households with urban resident registration whose per capita income falls below a certain standard. Pioneered in some big cities, such as Shanghai, in the early 1990s, this new antipoverty program had been established in all 668 cities before the end of 1999. It is so far the most stable antipoverty program, targeted directly at the poorest urban residents. Yet, because it was until recently financially supported mainly by local (municipal and district) governments, the coverage was very small due to fiscal difficulties at local level and many of the urban poor were still not receiving benefits. In 2000, the total number of beneficiaries in all Chinese cities was just 3.82 million, less than 1% of all urban residents. In 2001, thanks to the stronger participation of central and provincial governments, the number of beneficiaries rapidly increased. Up until October 2001, the beneficiaries numbered 7.15 million (about 1.6% of the total urban residents). This number may have reached 11.89 million by the end of 2001, or about 2.7% of the total urban residents. In the first 10 months of 2000, total governmental expenditure on the MLS was about 3.2 billion Yuan. The central government plans to enlarge the coverage of the urban MLS to about 15 million, or about 3.4% of the urban population by the end of 2002 (figures in this paragraph are derived from Social Relief Section of the Civil Affairs Ministry, 2001; Hong and Wang, 2002).

Although it would be a big achievement if this goal could be reached, there remains another problem to be resolved, namely the lower benefits level. Currently, the average standard for all the cities' MLS lines is just 146 Yuan per capita, and in the first 10 months of 2001 the national average monthly benefit was just 66 Yuan per capita (Social Relief Section of the Civil Affairs Ministry, 2001).[3] Moreover, no plan has so far been proposed to raise the MLS standards in China's cities. Without a rise in the MLS criteria and an increase in average benefit levels, the MLS cannot do much to help poor people out of poverty. It can only provide rudimentary living standards for beneficiaries, i.e. basic food and clothes. Their needs with respect to education, health and other departments will continue to go unmet.

ANTIPOVERTY ACTIONS IN EDUCATION, HEALTH CARE AND HOUSING

As mentioned above, the commercialization trends in such fundamental social services as education, health and housing have had serious effects on the urban poor, and the difficulties they face in paying for these are part of their life predicament. Since the current social assistance scheme can only provide the urban poor with very low benefits, which are not sufficient to cover the costs of these services, additional assistance is badly needed. There have been no nationwide social assistance programs in education, health and housing, but in many cities the local governments have taken some measures, although these are mainly discretionary, temporary and less institutionalized.

Education

In most cities, the municipal or district government has some policies to exempt poor families from paying school fees for children in the nine-year compulsory education stage. To help with the costs of higher education, there is a National Education Loan project to which students from poor families can apply for a loan. Moreover, there are a number of different NGO projects to support the education costs of poor families. In many universities there are tuition fee exemptions and other education assistance projects for poor students.

Generally speaking, formal education costs for urban families are not so high, because under the "one child" policy there is just one child in most urban families. In the Chinese value system, moreover, children's education takes a very important place in family financial arrangements, government agenda and public opinion. Those experiencing difficulty paying school fees can usually get support from the government or other sources. However, the real problem is that so far only school fees are covered by the various means of educational assistance, which is just a part of the total expenses for a child's education. Other costs, such as for school uniform, for various extra educational and special skill training projects and for occasional social and entertainment activities inside and outside school, impose a heavy financial burden on poor families. Another problem is how to provide assistance to children without stigmatizing them. Being labeled as "poor" may be a more sensitive issue for children and young people than for adults, and some anti-stigma measures should be taken with respect to educational assistance. Recently, in some cities, schools and education administrators have begun to pay attention to this issue, although it is still underemphasized in the education assistance system in this country.

---

[3] The amount a beneficiary is paid by the MLS is between his/her existing income and the MLS standard. For example, in a city with an MLS standard of 200 Yuan per capita, a family of three with a total family income of 500 Yuan will just get another 100 Yuan paid by the MLS.

Health Services

How to improve the urban poor's access to the health service is one of the most problematic issues for the urban antipoverty strategy. Since the medical costs in hospitals are very high, medical insurance coverage is still very limited and for the most part does not cover the urban poor. Moreover, government social assistance, e.g. the MLS, is insufficient to pay for medical costs. Thus, many of the urban poor cannot access health services and special assistance to enable them to do so is necessary. However, because the financial burden may be very high for medical assistance projects as a result of the high medical costs and the magnitude of demand coming from the urban poor, so far there has not been a nationwide medical assistance project, although nobody would deny that it is badly needed. To date, there are some medical assistance projects only in a few cities with good fiscal capacity, such as Shanghai and Guangzhou etc., and even in these cities the coverage is still small.

In most cities without medical assistance projects the local governments are trying to meet poor people's basic health needs, although only partially at the moment, by developing community health services (CHS), which can provide cheaper health services for urban residents. In many cities, the CHS are able to offer some special discount prices for the registered poor, mainly the beneficiaries of MLS, although it has not been an institutional regulation and is practicable only in those CHS with a strong antipoverty orientation and adequate financial resources.

Housing

To provide the urban poor with a basic standard of housing, some low-rent housing projects have been developed as part of the reform of the urban housing system. This nationwide regulated project was set up to provide affordable housing to the "double-difficulty" households – i.e. those who are within poverty categories in terms of both income and housing conditions, usually those who are eligible for MLS and without housing that meets basic standards, e.g. their houses are smaller than 4-5 square meters per capita. The financial resources for this project derive from local government, mainly the municipal government, and are subsidized by the state enterprises.

Because of the financial burden, this project has so far been implemented in just a few cities, and only a small proportion of the poor have actually benefited. Although the eligibility criteria are already very strict, the number of applicants is still far in excess of the available budgetary resources, and some kind of random allocation is universally practiced in deciding the final beneficiaries.

SOME FURTHER PROBLEMS IN ANTIPOVERTY POLICIES

Although many measures have been taken in the antipoverty strategy, most of them are still short-term responses to current problems. Some further problems need to be addressed for an effective long-term antipoverty strategy.

How to Include Floating Labor in the Urban Social Protection System

The floating population from rural areas is so far excluded from the urban social protection system. Virtually none of the current antipoverty measures cover this group, although many researchers have pointed out that this group of people is obviously a vulnerable group in cities. However, with more rural laborers coming into cities, their poverty problems, as well as other problems, have to be solved within cities. If the floating population is included, the urban antipoverty programs will become much more complicated and financially burdensome.

How to Deal with Social Exclusion

Although most of the urban poor are in a situation of temporary poverty, and phenomena such as poverty trap, poverty inheritance and poverty culture have rarely been observed in urban China, it is possible that social exclusion will become a serious problem in the near future. A recent study in two big cities found that some interviewees reported experiencing social discrimination just because they are poor and vulnerable.[4] If the poverty group is reduced in size, the possibility of their being institutionally and culturally excluded may become higher. Therefore, how to prevent marginalization and social exclusion will be a big issue for future antipoverty policies.

Antipoverty Strategy after Entry into the WTO

Most of the antipoverty programs in urban China were designed before it became a member of the World Trade Organization (WTO). Possible changes in the problem of poverty and proper measures to deal with such changes after China's entry into the WTO have not been well studied and prepared. In the coming years, the negative effects on urban poverty from globalization will be more serious as a result of becoming a member of the WTO. The problem exists on three levels: how to predict the possible changes in urban poverty issues, including poverty rates, features and causes; how to coordinate domestic policies with international standards, e.g. how to deal with such issues as labor standards in the WTO; and how to accept joint international efforts to develop some basic standards of social protection for the poor in different countries, even if only minimal standards.

CONCLUSION

The current alleviation approach to urban poverty in China can be conceptualized as a "top-down statist model", which has three characteristics. First and foremost, the governments have responsibility for and play a core role in providing basic benefits. Secondly, the MLS system is designed, promoted and regulated by the central government, although the financial responsibility was borne by local governments in its early stage. Thirdly, from 2001 the central government began to share financial responsibility with local

---

[4]   The research for UHPP in Chengdu and Shenyang, September 2001.

governments for the provision of MLS, and now its financial commitments are from both local and central governments.

In the near future, the central government will need to play a more active role in developing a long term urban antipoverty strategy. First of all, it should develop centralized regulation systems for the antipoverty programs. On the one hand, to reinforce the basic social relief system, an "urban social relief law" is needed to replace the current "MLS regulations" which have been devised by an administrative body. On the other hand, central government needs to establish some basic regulation frameworks for social protection in employment, education and health services. Secondly, it should put more financial resources into the antipoverty programs. The main factor accounting for the small coverage of MLS before 2001, especially in the less-developed regions, was that the central government did not provide financial resources. From late 2001, with the central government promising to provide funds, nationwide coverage has almost doubled. The central government also needs to play a more active role in providing public assistance for the urban poor's health and education etc. Finally, and most importantly, it must make more efforts to foster a pro-poor social-ideological environment by further emphasizing such ideologies as social equity, social compensation and social care. Only in a more "socialist" ideological environment can the poverty problem be more effectively solved in the long run.

In its development of antipoverty practices in the urban context, China has learnt a lot from other countries. In return, the Chinese antipoverty programs in this area, although still at an early stage, can also make some contributions to antipoverty theories and practices worldwide. The following characteristics of the Chinese urban antipoverty experience can be instructive for other countries. Firstly, in developing countries it is necessary to have a statist antipoverty model in which governments take the core responsibility for and play a central role in regulating and financing antipoverty programs, while social resources of various kinds are also mobilized for poverty alleviation. Secondly, it is important in such a big country to have a centralized regulation framework and a reasonable shared-responsibility model between central and local governments in order to have an efficient nationwide redistribution function and, at the same time, to mobilize local resources more effectively. Thirdly, for an effective antipoverty strategy, a stable and well-financed basic social relief system is necessary as a final "safety net", while a comprehensive social protection system, including antipoverty arrangements in employment, education, health and housing etc, should also be reinforced.

Nevertheless, the Chinese government and researchers are now thinking about some more basic issues in the development of China's urban antipoverty strategy, including:

1. What the main social goal of the antipoverty strategy should be – social equity or simply social-political stability, or something else?

2. How to devise a proper measurement for the definition of eligibility and the level of benefit in order to maximize concurrently both the efficiency and the efficacy of the public antipoverty programs.

3. How to minimize the possible negative effects of dependency of able-bodied beneficiaries while enabling more poor people to get help when they are in real need.

4. How to have an effective administrative system through which both the "stigma effect" for beneficiaries and the "leakage" of public funds can be minimized.

These concerns are also among the key issues in the antipoverty programs of most other countries. Only by more international joint work can these issues be solved at both theoretical and practical levels in the future.

REFERENCES

Duoji, Cairang (2001). *The Researches and Practices of China's Minimal Living Security Systems*. People's Press.

Fan, Xinmin (1999). A Review of China's Urban Inequality Studies. *Social Studies*, 3.

Guan, Xinping (1999). *Urban Poverty in China*. Hunan People's Press.

_____ . (2000). China's Social Policy: Reform and Development in the Context of Marketization and Globalization. *Social Policy and Administration*, 34, 1.

_____ . (2001). Globalization, Inequality and Social Policy: Social Protection in China on the Threshold into the WTO. *Social Policy and Administration*, 35, 2.

Hong, Dayong and Wang, Hui (2002). *Reform of Minimal Social Security in Urban Areas*. In Ru Xin, et al. (Eds.) *Analysis and Foreseeing of China's Social Situation*. Social Sciences Documentation Public House.

Huang, Quanquan and Zhou, Limin (Xinhua News Agency) (2000). *Security is Just a Book Value*, January 13.

Li, Peilin (Ed.) (1995). *Social Stratification in the Market Transition in China*. Liaoning People's Press.

Li, Qiang (1989). *Two Kinds of Poverty and their Causes*. Research Papers in Sociology and Social Reform.

_____ . (1993). *Social Stratification and Mobility in Contemporary China*, China Economics Press.

Liu, Changhua (Ed.) (1986). *Poverty and Development: A Workshop Summary, Information in Economics,* 6/1986.

Lue, Zuxian (2000). The Average Living Allowance for the Laid-Off Workers in State-Enterprises Increased to 323 Yuan Per Month. *Guangming Daily*, Sept. 1, 2000.

Milanovic, Rrank (1998). *Income, Inequality and Poverty during the Transition from Planned to Market Economy*. World Bank Regional and Sectoral Studies, The World Bank.

National Statistics Bureau (2000). *Statistical Bulletin of Economic and Social Development in the People's Republic of China –1999*. February 28, 2000.

Pernia, Ernesto M.   (Ed.) (1994). *Urban Poverty in Asia: A Survey of Critical Issues*. Oxford: Oxford University Press.

Poverty Study Team of Wuhan University (1999). Urban Poverty and Antipoverty Policies: Wuhan's Case. *Economic Review*, No. 4.

Social Relief Section of the Civil Affairs Ministry (2001). *Current Situation of the Urban Minimal Living Security*. Workshop Paper, Nov. 15.

Tang, Jun (2002). *Poverty and Antipoverty*. In Ru Xin, et al. (Eds.) *Analysis and Foreseeing of China's Social Situation*. Social Sciences Documentation Public House.

Wang, Fayun (2002). Progress in Social Security Reform. In Ru Xin, et al. (Eds.) *Analysis and Foreseeing of China's Social Situation*. Social Sciences Documentation Public House.

Wong, Chack Kie (1995). Measuring Third World Poverty by the International Poverty Line: The Case of Reform in China. *Social Policy and Administration*, 29: 189-203.

Xiao, Wentao (1997). *China's Urban Poverty in the Social Transition Period.* Sociology Research, No.5.

Yang, Dongping (2002). Educational Development and its Problems. In Ru Xin et al. (Eds.) *Analysis and Foreseeing of China's Social Situation.* Social Sciences Documentation Public House.

Yang, Gang and Wang, Lijuan (2001). *New Century and New Poverty: Urban Poverty in China.* Economic Reform, No. 1.

Zhang, Jianguo et al. (1998). *To Support the Poor, No Forgetting the Urban Poor Group,* Economic Forum, 6/1998.

Zhang, Yongqing (2000). An Analysis of the Financial Gap Between the Basic Pension Insurance Foundations. *China Labor*, No.3.

Zhao, Xiaobiao and Niu, Cunyong, (1998). An Analysis of the Urban Poverty Problem. *Academic Journal of Yunnan Normal University-Philosophy and Social Sciences*, Vol. 30, No. 3, June.

In: *Poverty Monitoring and Alleviation in East Asia*
K. Tang and C. Wong, editors pp. 39-56
ISBN: 1-59033-828-6
© 2003 Nova Science Publishers, Inc.

Chapter 2

POVERTY MONITORING AND ALLEVIATION: THE CASE OF TAIWAN

Kate Yeong-Tsyr Wang

ABSTRACT

This chapter focuses on the phenomenon of poverty and the role of government in reducing poverty in Taiwan during the past decade. The discussion is organized in four sections. Section one reviews the changes in poverty rates according to official statistics as well as related empirical findings. Section two describes the development of antipoverty policies and government expenditures. Section three analyzes the effects of antipoverty policies on poverty reduction. The final section presents policy discussions on current problems and future policy directions for poverty alleviation in Taiwan.

CHANGES IN POVERTY RATES DURING THE PAST TEN YEARS

Official Statistics

The official minimum living standard for determining the eligibility of social assistance programs changed in Taiwan in the late 1990s. Before the amendment to the Social Assistance Law in 1997, the official minimum living standard was set at 40% of total household expenditure per capita in Taipei City and one third of average annual income per capita in Kaohsiung City and Taiwan Province. Because the Social Assistance Law had been implemented in 1980 and the economic and social contexts had changed over the years, the government amended this law at the close of 1997. It now stipulates that the new minimum living standard is 60% of average consumption expenditure per capita. This change not only raised the level of the minimum living standard, but also required governments at the various levels to use the same definition for the minimum living standard. Owing to the different levels of average consumption expenditure per capita in the three areas, the minimum living standard in 2002 was NT $13,288 (US $381) in Taipei City, NT $9,559 (US $274) in Kaohsiung City and NT $8,433 (US $242) in Taiwan Province.

Under the social assistance system, recipients can be divided into three categories and are entitled to different levels of welfare payments. Category 1 refers to a family with no members who are able to work, no income and no assets. Category 2 refers to a family with less than one third of members who are able to work and with an income which is less than two thirds of the official minimum living standard. A family with less than one third of persons who are able to work and with an income which exceeds two thirds of the official minimum living standard (but is still below the official minimum living standard) belongs to Category 3. A slightly different classification for low-income families in Taipei City was introduced in 1998, which classifies low-income families into five categories, i.e. class zero to class four. In Tables 2.1 and 2.2, Category 1 includes class zero, Category 2 includes class one and two, and Category 3 includes class three and four. In addition to income and the number of members who are able to work, the eligibility requirements for social assistance also take into account the value of applicants' movable and immovable property. For example, the value of movable property should be below NT $150,000 (US $4,298) per person in a household and that of immovable property should be below NT $5,000,000 (US $143,267) per household in Taipei City.

Table 2.1. The Number and Percentage of
Households on Social Assistance in Taiwan, 1991 – 2002

Year	Category 1	Category 2	Category 3	Total	As % of Total Households
1991	12012(28%)	14818(35%)	15835(37%)	42665(100%)	0.82
1992	12216(28%)	14598(33%)	16966(39%)	43780(100%)	0.82
1993	11649(25%)	15266(33%)	19364(42%)	46279(100%)	0.84
1994	9983(21%)	16114(33%)	22085(46%)	48182(100%)	0.85
1995	8755(18%)	17160(35%)	22665(47%)	48580(100%)	0.83
1996	7855(16%)	17884(36%)	23568(48%)	49307(100%)	0.82
1997	6544(13%)	18486(37%)	24750(50%)	49780(100%)	0.80
1998	5795(11%)	20696(38%)	28460(52%)	54951(100%)	0.86
1999	4980(9%)	21357(37%)	31973(55%)	58310(100%)	0.89
2000	4983(7%)	24470(37%)	37014(56%	66467(100%)	0.99
2001	4132(6%)	22461(33%)	40598(60%)	67191(100%)	0.99
2002					
1st quarter	3592(6%)	20324(31%)	40619(63%)	64535(100%)	0.95
2nd quarter	3579(6%)	20610(31%)	42733(64%)	66922(100%)	0.98

Source: Ministry of Interior, Retrieved June 20, 2003 from the World Wide Web: http://www.moi.gov.tw/W3/stat.
Note: Percentages do not add to 100 due to rounding.

Table 2.1 shows that low-income households have remained at a stable level of nearly 1% of total households for the past ten years, although the percentage has slightly increased since 1998. Critics argue that the proportion of poor households has stayed at such a low level because of the low minimum living standard and strict eligibility requirements, as well as the involvement of caseworkers' subjective judgments in the means-testing process (Lin and Wang, 2000: 94-5). As regards the composition of low-income households, in the second quarter of 2002 64% of the households were in Category 3, 31% in Category 2, and 6% in Category 1. The number and percentage of households in Category 3 continue to increase while those in Category 1 indicate the opposite trend. Table 2.2 shows that in the second quarter of 2002 about 0.72% of the total population are low-income individuals. In terms of the composition of low-income individuals, the number and the percentage of claimants in Category 3 are similarly increasing while those in Category 1 indicate the opposite trend over this ten-year period.

Table 2.2. The Number and Percentage of
Individuals on Social Assistance in Taiwan, 1991 – 2002

Year	Category 1	Category 2	Category 3	Total	As % of Total Population
1991	15326(13%)	48089(41%)	52810(45%)	116225(100%)	0.56
1992	15729(14%)	46890(41%)	52665(46%)	115284(100%)	0.55
1993	14636(12%)	46436(39%)	56598(48%)	117603(100%)	0.56
1994	12336(11%)	44204(38%)	59208(51%)	115748(100%)	0.55
1995	10794(9%)	42824(37%)	61089(53%)	114707(100%)	0.54
1996	9533(8%)	42738(37%)	63271(55%)	115542(100%)	0.54
1997	7906(7%)	42852(37%)	65298((56%)	116056(100%)	0.53
1998	6767(5%)	45658(36%)	73001(58%)	125426(100%)	0.57
1999	5769(4%)	47064(34%)	83858(61%)	136691(100%)	0.62
2000	5778(4%)	52630(34%)	97726(63%)	156134(100%)	0.70
2001	4761(3%)	49876(31%)	108062(66%)	162699(100%)	0.73
2002					
1st Quarter	3988(3%)	43331(28%)	106018(69%)	153337(100%)	0.68
2nd Quarter	3988(2%)	44317(28%)	112577(70%)	160882(100%)	0.72

Source: Ministry of Interior, Retrieved June 20, 2003 from the World Wide Web: http://www.moi.gov.tw/W3/stat.
Note: Percentages do not add to 100 due to rounding.

Two main factors can explain the changing trend in the composition of low-income individuals and households after the mid-1990s. One is the amendment to the Social Assistance Law, which raised the minimum living standard and therefore increased the number of recipients, particularly in Category 3. The other factor is the growing rate of unemployment, which also led to an increase in Category 3. As for the unemployment problem,[1] Table 2.3 indicates that after 1996 the unemployment rate kept increasing, reaching over 5% in 2002. At the same time, the average number of weeks experienced in unemployment has also been extended. In 2001 it took 26 weeks on average to find a new job.

---

[1] The official definition of the unemployed population refers to persons who, during the reference week, are 15 years of age or over and fall under the following conditions: (1) no job; (2) available for work; (3) seeking a job, or have applied for work and are now waiting for results. In addition, the unemployed also include people who are waiting to be recalled or are starting a new job but are not yet working and have not received any pay (DGBAS, Executive Yuan, 2001, Monthly Bulletin of Statistics: 60). Statistics on unemployment, derived from the Manpower Resource Survey, are compiled once a month by the Directorate-General of Budget, Accounting and Statistics (DGBAS), Executive Yuan. The coverage of this survey includes all the population aged 15 or over who are engaged in economic activities in Taiwan, excluding those in military service or in prison.

**Table 2.3. Unemployment Rates and Average Weeks
Duration of Unemployment in Taiwan, 1991 – 2002**

Year	Unemployment Rates	Average Weeks of Unemployment
1991	1.51	15.13
1992	1.51	15.52
1993	1.45	15.15
1994	1.56	15.68
1995	1.79	17.20
1996	2.60	20.45
1997	2.72	21.36
1998	2.69	21.79
1999	2.92	22.52
2000	2.99	23.70
2001	4.57	26.13
2002		
March	5.16	
June	5.11	
September	5.32	

Source: (1) DGBAS, Social Indicators(2001): 268-271. (2) DGBAS, Retrieved Dec. 4, 2002 from the World Wide Web: http://www.dgbas.gov.tw

Relative Poverty and Income Inequality

Poverty and income inequality are the two main issues involved in analyzing income distribution. Poverty in relative terms relates to income inequality. In other words, poverty is concerned with the lower range of the income distribution, while income inequality concerns the population as a whole. In this section we discuss three types of measure widely used for analyzing the distribution of income: (1) relative poverty rates; (2) the proportion of aggregate income received by households in the bottom and top income deciles or quintiles; and (3) Gini coefficients. Statistics from the Luxembourg Income Study (LIS), one of the most important data sources for comparative income studies, will be used for analyzing relative poverty rates. The second and third measures are income inequality measures. The second measure concentrates more on the income at the extremes of the distribution range, while Gini coefficients are more sensitive to inequality changes around the median and less sensitive to either the top or the bottom of the income distribution.

LIS provides relative poverty rates for the total population, children and the elderly in Taiwan. The poverty line is 50% of median adjusted disposable income for all persons (from the LIS website). Based upon the LIS analyses, the poverty rate for the total population was 5.5% in 1981 and 6.7% in 1995 (see Table 2.4-1). Referring to Table 2.2, which shows low income individuals in Taiwan, the 1995 relative poverty rate is about 12 times the total number of social assistance recipients in that same year. As for the poverty rates for children, it is close to that of the total population. For instance, the child poverty rate in 1995 was 6.2%. However, the poverty problem is more serious for the elderly: 13.3% of the elderly were poor in 1981 and 21.7% in 1995. This is mainly because Taiwan lacks a comprehensive social safety net for the elderly.

Table 2.4-1. Poverty Rates for the Total Population,
Children and the Elderly in Taiwan, 1981 – 1995

Year	Total Population Poverty Line (% of Median)			Children Poverty Line (% of Median)			Elderly Poverty Line (% of Median)		
	40	50	60	40	50	60	40	50	60
1981	1.8	5.5	11.8	2.1	6.7	14.2	6.5	13.3	22.4
1986	1.8	5.2	11.3	1.8	5.9	13.4	6.8	13.0	21.2
1991	2.3	6.5	12.5	2.1	6.9	14.3	9.7	18.4	26.4
1995	2.8	6.7	13.4	2.0	6.2	14.6	12.7	21.7	30.9

Source: From LIS, Retrieved December 12, 2002 from the World Wide Web: http://www.lisproject.org/keyfigures/povertytable.htm

Empirical findings show an increasing trend toward feminization of poverty in Taiwan. Lee (1998) used 50% of median disposable income per person as the poverty line to analyze the percentage of female-headed households among the poor. The results reveal that 4% of all poor households in 1976 were female-headed, but by 1995 this figure had increased to 14.25%. The poverty rate for female-headed households was 10.13% in 1976 and 14.41% in 1995, while the poverty rate for male-headed households was 13.86% in 1976 and 14.35% in 1995. Lee (1998) also found that the poverty rates for female-headed households have been higher than those of their male counterparts since 1980. The phenomenon of feminization of poverty is becoming increasingly evident, although the majority of poor households are still male-headed. Table 2.4-2 indicates that the percentage of children living in single-mother families has gradually increased and the poverty rates for children in single-mother families have been above 20% since 1986.

Table 2.4-2. Poverty Rates for Children in
Single-Mother Families in Taiwan, 1981 – 1995

Year	Single Mother	% of Children Living in Single-Mother Families
1981	17.3	3.2
1986	22.8	3.6
1991	26.3	3.9
1995	23.8	4.2

Note: Poverty line is defined as 50% of median adjusted disposable income for all persons; Equivalence scale is the square root of family size; The definition of two parent and single mother households allows other adults to be present.
Source: From LIS, Retrieved December 12, 2002 from the World Wide Web: http://www.lisproject.org/keyfigures/childpovrates.htm.

Table 2.5 shows that the poorest 10% of households shared 4.03% of total household disposable income in 2001. The ratio of income share of the highest 10% income group to that of the lowest 10% was 5.33 in 2001 and it has increased, particularly in the period from 2000 to 2001. Furthermore, the poorest 20% of households shared 6.43% of total household disposal income and the ratio of income share of the highest 20% income group to that of lowest 20% was 6.39 in 2001. The Gini coefficient was 0.350 in 2001. Observing the increasing trend in both inequality measures during the recent decade, it is clear that the income gap between the lowest and the highest income groups is widening. Since Gini coefficients are more sensitive to inequality changes around the median and less sensitive to either the top or the bottom of the income distribution range, Gini coefficients show a slighter increase compared to the ratio of income share of the highest income group to that of the lowest income group.

Table 2.5. Three Measures of Income Inequality in Taiwan, 1991 – 2001

Year	Percent distribution of disposable Income by percentile of households		Ratio of income share of highest 10%to that of lowest 10%	Percent distribution of disposable Income by percentile of households		Ratio of income share of highest 20% to that of lowest 20%	Gini coefficients
	Lowest 10%	Highest 10%		Lowest 20%	Highest 20%		
1991	4.88	20.24	4.15	7.76	38.60	4.97	0.308
1992	4.52	20.60	4.56	7.37	38.66	5.24	0.312
1993	4.38	20.47	4.67	7.13	38.66	5.42	0.316
1994	4.51	20.74	4.60	7.28	39.16	5.38	0.318
1995	4.47	20.74	4.64	7.30	38.99	5.34	0.317
1996	4.45	20.55	4.62	7.23	38.89	5.38	0.317
1997	4.41	20.67	4.69	7.24	39.14	5.41	0.320
1998	4.41	20.56	4.66	7.12	39.26	5.51	0.324
1999	4.38	20.59	4.70	7.13	39.24	5.50	0.325
2000	4.33	20.79	4.80	7.07	39.23	5.55	0.326
2001	4.03	21.48	5.33	6.43	41.11	6.39	0.350

Source: Report on The Survey of Family Income and Expenditure in Taiwan Area of Republic of China, 2001, pp.21& 23.

Official income reports also provide related information on the second measure discussed in this section – the percentage share of distributed factor income by percentile groups of income recipients (DGBAS, 2001). Distributed factor income refers to the sum of employee remuneration, entrepreneurial income and net property income. In other words, distributed factor income focuses on the performance of the labor market and provides indirect information on property. The ratio of income share of the highest 10% to that of the lowest 10% was 23.72 in 1997, 33.07 in 1998, 42.17 in 1999, 38.87 in 2000, and 61.33 in 2001. All these figures imply that the distribution is becoming increasingly unequal in terms of income from the labor market and property.

Explanation of the Trend Towards Income Inequality

Taiwan in fact retained a relatively equitable distribution of income along with economic development from the 1950s to the 1970s. Studies found that the 1949-53 land reform, education expansion, labor-intensive export and small and medium sized enterprises (SMEs) promoted equity (Li, 2000; Sun and Gindling, 2000). Land reform redistributed wealth from the rich to the poor. Educational investment in human capital promoted economic development and raised the income of the working population. Export-led economic development during the 1970s and 1980s created a great demand for domestic labor and even created work opportunities for less skilled workers. The majority of SMEs rather than big firms helped keep income more equitable. In addition, Jacobs (2000) found that low unemployment rates, the persistence of multigenerational households, and the lack of single households and single parent families also contributed to the lower income inequality in Taiwan in 1995, compared to Britain.

However, since the 1980s there has been increasing income inequality. Several important factors can be taken into account to explain the growth of income inequality. Technology-intensive industries have played a more important role in manufacturing than traditional industries. The share of exports in high-tech products, compared to non-high-tech products, has also been increasing. Taiwan's international trade pattern has turned towards hi-tech goods and demands for more skilled labor, which widens wage inequality between skilled and unskilled workers (Liou, 2001; C-H. Lin, 2002). The shift in favor of the service industry also accelerates wage inequality. Evidence shows the earnings structure of the service sector is less egalitarian than that of the industrial sector (Hung, 1996).

Furthermore, the global economic downturn in recent years has hit Taiwan's exports which are essential for the economy. Traditional industries such as manufacturing in Taiwan have been relocated offshore, especially to China. These changes have led to more unemployment problems. Since low-income families usually include members who are laid-off or working in low-wage industries, their incomes are most likely to be affected by this worsening economic situation. This will result in the distribution of income becoming more unequal. Finally, Taiwan's accession to the WTO (World Trade Organization) in January 2002 is also expected to exacerbate the growing unemployment rate in the future due to new regulations on free trade (Wang, 2002).

ANTIPOVERTY POLICIES DURING THE LAST TEN YEARS

The Development of Antipoverty Policies

Government usually uses three kinds of policy instruments for alleviating poverty – social insurance, social allowance and social assistance. These policy instruments can also be regarded as income maintenance (or income transfer) policies (Heidenheimer et al., 1990: 218). Because people pay insurance premiums in advance against the occurrence of income loss due to retirement, death or accident, social insurance can be regarded as a policy tool for preventing poverty. Social allowance usually provides a uniform payment without means-testing to certain categories of persons, for instance, children's allowance or old-age allowance, and can also be used to prevent poverty. In contrast to these two types of policy, social assistance is usually seen as a last resort for reducing poverty because it is means-tested and specifically targets the poor (Gilbert and Terrell, 1998; Dinitto, 2000).

During the past ten years, several antipoverty policies have been introduced (see Table 2.6). Under social insurance policies, health insurance for low-income families was implemented in 1990 and has been integrated into National Health Insurance (NHI) since 1995. NHI is a universal program and covers nearly 97% of the total population. Under the current NHI system, the government pays all the insurance contributions and co-payments of specified medical expenses for low-income people, and subsidizes co-payments of other medical expenses for low-income people. Owing to the worsening condition of the unemployment problem, an unemployment benefit scheme as part of the Labor Insurance

Law has been effective since January 1999. In order to establish a more comprehensive system for dealing with unemployment, the government plans to implement the Employment Insurance Act in January 2003. This act is independent from the current Labor Insurance Law. Under the provision of the new act, workers aged 15-60, with the exception of the self-employed, will be compelled to join the program. In return, unemployed workers will be entitled to unemployment benefits for six months. There will be rewards for the unemployed who find a job quickly. In addition, the act provides living allowances for the laid-off during the period when they are receiving vocational training as well as subsidies for national health insurance premiums.

Table 2.6. Major Antipoverty Policies Introduced in Taiwan Since the Early 1990s

Year	Social Insurance	Social Allowance	Social Assistance
1993			Middle-income & Low-income Living Allowances for the Aged
1995	National Health Insurance		Temporary Act for Provision of Welfare Subsidies to Old-age Farmers
1997			Amendment to Social Assistance Law
1998		Amendment to Temporary Act for Provision of Welfare Subsidies to Old-age Farmers	
1999	Unemployment Benefits		
2000			Family Assistance for Disadvantaged Women
2002			Temporary Act for Provision of Welfare Subsidies to the Elderly and the Aboriginal Elderly.
2003	Employment Insurance		

The Temporary Act for Provision of Welfare Subsidies to Old-age Farmers is the only social allowance scheme for the elderly that is means tested in Taiwan. Since there have been different income protection systems for retired laborers, teachers, civil servants and members of the military since the 1950s, the government extended the income protection to include retired farmers in 1995. The eligibility requirements for this program are: (1) people must be aged 65 or over; and (2) people must have been covered by Farmers' Health Insurance for at least six months, or people who had received old-age benefits from Labor Insurance must have been members of fishermen's associations for at least six months. Although by law this program is not a means-tested one, the Cabinet initially restricted the number of recipients by establishing upper limits of income and assets. After 1998, it became a universal program without means-testing under pressure from the legislators, and by 2002 covered 33.1% of all elderly farmers (DGBAS website).

As for social assistance, one of the major policy changes is the 1997 Amendment to the Social Assistance Law. There are some important policy implications deriving from this amendment, including: (1) it unifies the national minimum living standard; (2) it specifies the principle of lower eligibility, i.e. each recipient's total social assistance payments should not be over the official minimum wage of NT $15,840 (US $454); (3) recipients who are aged 65 or over, pregnant or disabled are entitled to a higher level of payment for living assistance. Under the current social assistance system, the government provides subsidies to low-income families to help with living costs, education, medical care, calamities and emergencies. At the same time, other personal support services for low-income families include work relief, foster care, home help etc.

In addition to the usage of the minimum living standard as the eligibility requirement, several programs use 2.5 times the minimum living standard as the poverty line. These programs have been designed for the elderly, the disabled and disadvantaged women. The government started implementing Middle-Income and Low-Income Living Allowances for the Aged in 1993 and then expanded the program until 1997 when it was curtailed by setting stricter standards of eligibility. The current program provides monthly payments of NT $6,000 (US $172) for persons aged 65 and over with income falling below 1.5 times the local minimum living standard, and NT $3,000 (US $86) for persons with income falling between 1.5 to 2.5 times the local minimum living standard (and still below 1.5 times the national minimum living standard). About 9% of the elderly are covered by this program. In addition, monthly cash payments ranging from NT $2,000 to NT $6,000 (US $57 to US $172) are provided to middle-income and low-income disabled persons according to the level of their income and degree of disability. There are about 170,000 people with disability who receive these cash payments (D-J. Lin, 2002: 178).

Family assistance for disadvantaged women was introduced in 2000 and targeted middle-income and low-income women meeting one of the following six conditions: (1) spouse has died or disappeared; (2) women maliciously abandoned by husband or divorced under a court order due to spouse abuse; (3) victims of family violence, sexual assault or other crimes who cannot afford medical expenses or fees for law suits; (4) unmarried women pregnant by force; (5) single mothers who cannot work due to old age, disability, sickness or care-giving responsibilities; (6) women whose spouses are in prison. This program provides temporary living allowances, children's living allowances, and subsidizes children's educational expenses, medical expenses, fees for law suits as well as loans for starting business. As a matter of fact, this program is the first national policy to focus on women's economic security, although it is a selective one.

The Temporary Act for Provision of Welfare Subsidies to the Elderly was launched in 2002, helping to fulfill President Chen's presidential campaign promise to senior citizens. It provides monthly allowances of NT $3,000 (US $86) for citizens over the age of 65 who are not in institutions or not already covered under existing means-tested or non-means-tested social welfare programs. Those who earn more than NT $500,000 per year or hold more than NT $5 million in assets are also ineligible. In other words, the government wants to target people who are neither poor nor rich and not covered by any other government program. The eligibility of the living allowance for the aboriginal elderly is slightly different in terms of age requirement. The age requirement for Aborigine citizens is 55 or over because of their shorter life expectancy. It is estimated that about 440,000 senior citizens qualify for this program. In

July 2003 the government will broaden this program to include seniors covered by the labor insurance or other government insurance programs.

Government Social Welfare Spending

Table 2.7 shows five types of government social welfare expenditures in the ten-year period from 1991 to 2000. Social insurance represented the greatest amount of government social welfare expenditure in 2000. Since National Health Insurance was inaugurated in 1995, it has remained at 40% of social welfare spending in recent years. Welfare services are another important expenditure item, which mainly provide in-cash and in-kind benefits for the elderly, the disabled and children. Based upon the analyses of DGBAS, Welfare Subsidies to Old-age Farmers, accounting for 24.6% of welfare service expenditures in 2000, is the largest item. The second largest item is subsidies to veterans, which accounted for 20.1% in 2000 (Sheu, 2002: 102-8).

Social assistance as a percentage of total government expenditure has remained within 8-12% in the five years from 1994 to 1999. In 2000 this figure increased significantly, mainly because of the subsidies owing to the September 21 earthquake victims and the change in the fiscal calendar (see the note to Table 2.7 for details). Social assistance expenditures include Middle-Income and Low-Income Living Allowances for the aged, Living Assistance for low-income families (i.e. family and student subsidies for living costs, work relief etc.) and Assistance for medical care, calamities, emergencies and other social services. According to the DGBAS analyses, the major source of social assistance spending is Middle-Income and Low-Income Living Allowances for the aged, which accounted for nearly 32% of the total spending in 1998, 42% in 1999 and 65.6% in 2000 (Sheu, 2002: 102-8). Living Assistance for low-income families is the second-largest social assistance expenditure, accounting for 13%, 16% and 25% of total social assistance expenditure in 1998, 1999 and 2000 respectively.

Table 2.7. Net Expenditure on Social Welfare by General Government

Year	Social Insurance	Social Assistance	Welfare Service	Employment	Health	As % of Total Expenditure	As % of GNP
1991	28.4%	11.5%	39.4%	2.5%	18.3%	9.2	2.5
1992	34.7%	4.7%	39.9%	2.1%	18.8%	8.6	2.6
1993	32.7%	6.6%	39.6%	2.3%	18.8%	8.3	2.5
1994	31.9%	6.1%	41.6%	2.2%	18.2%	8.7	2.5
1995	40.9%	9.1%	36.0%	1.4%	12.6%	12.1	3.4
1996	43.3%	10.4%	34.8%	1.5%	10.0%	15.7	3.9
1997	38.8%	12.2%	37.7%	1.7%	9.6%	15.7	3.7
1998	41.3%	8.8%	38.9%	1.2%	9.7%	14.2	3.2
1999	39.9%	8.4%	40.9%	1.3%	9.6%	13.7	3.0
2000[*]	40.4%	17.8%	33.7%	0.6%	7.5%	16.9	3.6

[*] Due to the change of fiscal calendar, year 2000 figures include July – December 1999 as well as the entire for 2000. Before year 2000, figures are calculated from July of the previous year to June of the following year. For instance, figures of year 1999 represent the percentages calculated from July 1998 to June 1999.

Source: DGBAS, Social Indicators, 2001.

THE EFFECT OF GOVERNMENT TRANSFERS ON POVERTY REDUCTION

Smeeding and Ross (1999) analyzed the effects of income transfers on poverty rates in developed countries. The results show that in general higher spending produces lower poverty rates and different countries use different types of antipoverty policies to combat poverty. Universal and social insurance transfers have the largest impacts on poverty in countries such as Canada, France, Germany, Netherlands, Spain, Sweden and the United States. While Australia mainly relies on social assistance and the United Kingdom mainly uses social assistance, universal programs and social insurance to reduce poverty.

Luo (1998) analyzed the 1996 administrative data of the Taiwanese government and found National Health Insurance made a positive contribution to reducing income inequality. DGBAS (2001: 21) analyzes the effect of government transfers on the ratio of income share of the highest 20% of the population to that of the lowest 20%. In 2001, both social welfare benefits and direct taxes, including social insurance premiums, reduced the inequality gap from a ratio of 7.667 to 6.391. Social welfare benefits were responsible for 89% of this reduction in income inequality, and direct taxes including social insurance premiums contributed 11%. In other words, social welfare benefits play a relatively important role in decreasing the income gap between the wealthy and the poor.

Table 2.8 shows the poverty rates under different definitions of income, and the effect of social welfare benefits on poverty reduction for all households and for households with elderly members in 2001. The data source for the following analyses is Taiwan's Family Income and Expenditure Survey of 2001.[2] Medical benefits from National Health Insurance were particularly potent in reducing poverty rates for all households as well as for households with elderly members. The poverty rates declined by 28.2% (from 11.3% to 7.5%) for all households, and by 28.9% (from 23.4% to 15.6%) for households with elderly members. Moreover, cash benefits from means-tested programs also helped reduce poverty, especially for households with elderly members (i.e. a 15.6% reduction for all households and a 22.2% reduction for households with elderly members). In other words, the universal health insurance program and the means-tested programs are two major policy instruments for reducing poverty. From the public finance point of view, implementing a universal health insurance program also implies the government needs to face a financial burden. Means-tested programs would be more target-efficient for the government. However, social stigma would be attached to those receiving social assistance.

---

[2] Taiwan's Family Income and Expenditure Survey has been undertaken annually by the DGBAS since 1975. Individuals possessing Republic of China nationality and their immediate family residing in the Taiwan area are included in the survey. In 2001 the random sample size was 13,601 (DGBAS, 2001: 149-50).

Table 2.8. Poverty Rates under Alternative Definitions of Income and the Effect of Social Welfare Benefits on Poverty Reduction in Taiwan, 2001

	Money Income From Private Sources Minus Taxes	Plus Subsidies to Social Insurance Contributions	Plus Cash Benefits from Social Insurance	Plus Medical Benefits from Social Insurance	Plus Social Allowances for Old-age Farmers	Plus Cash Benefits from means-tested programs	% Change Due to all
Poverty Rate (%)							
All households	13.5	12.1	11.3	7.5	6.7		4.6
Households w/ the elderly	27.0	24.6	23.4	15.6	12.8		6.8
Percent change							
All households	-10.4	-5.9	-28.2	-5.9	-15.6		-65.9
Households w/ the elderly	-8.9	-4.4	-28.9	-10.4	-22.2		-74.8

Note: (1) Figures are calculated by author. (2) Official minimum living standards in 2001 are used for defining poverty (NT$12,977 (US$ 372) in Taipei city, NT$9,814 (US$281) in Kaohsiung city and NT$8,276 (US$237) in Taiwan province). (3) Cash benefits from means-tested programs include Middle-Income & Low-Income Living Allowances for the Aged, Living Assistance for Low-Income Families, Living Assistance for the Disabled, and Cash Assistance for Calamities and Emergencies, etc.

THE PROSPECTS FOR POVERTY ALLEVIATION

Based on the above discussion, it is clear that Taiwan has faced several poverty-related issues, including: (1) rising unemployment; (2) the economic insecurity of the elderly; (3) the phenomenon of the feminization of poverty; and (4) growing income inequality. Over the past decade the government has responded by adopting different measures to protect people's economic well-being. Social insurance programs focus particularly on health and unemployment problems. In terms of social allowance, retired farmers are covered by the universal income transfer policy. Social assistance programs specifically target women and the elderly, and the poverty line which determines the eligibility of these groups is higher than (i.e. 2.5 times) the local minimum living standard. In addition, the ethnicity issue has also been addressed by lowering the retirement age for aborigines to 55 years of age compared with 65 for the general population.

Although expanding the scope of social protection programs, the government still needs to deal with the emergence of new poverty-related issues. The following discussion focuses on four possible directions for the future development of antipoverty policies.

Protecting Economic Security for the Elderly

Taiwan became an aging society about 10 years ago. It is predicted that the aging of the population will further accelerate in the coming decades. With the increase in divorce rates and the growing number of elderly people living alone, the function of economic support from families has been weakened. Therefore, the elderly cannot completely rely on their families for economic security, and there has been a trend toward the government taking over some of the responsibility.

Under the current system, civil servants, teachers in state schools and members of the military receive the most benefits after retirement. Since the government is also their employer, it is obligated to provide retirement benefits in both capacities, and these employees receive double protection when they retire. In contrast, less than 10% of workers collect retirement payments from employers under the Labor Standard Law, and retired workers receive meager retirement benefits from Labor Insurance (Huang and Lin, 2000). Furthermore, people who are self-employed, housewives, and employees without regular work lack public income protection. Hence, it is necessary to change the unequal treatment between retired public employees and other retirees.

In fact, the government has established some income protection measures for those who are not public employees, such as Middle-Income and Low-Income Living Allowances for the Aged, Welfare Subsidies to Old-age Farmers, and Welfare Subsides to the Elderly and Aboriginal Elderly. These are three provisional programs that will be scrapped after a national pension program comes into effect. The national pension program has been in the planning stages since 1993. Different versions of the program have been debated over the years, such as an individual retirement account, a social insurance system or a system financed by government taxes. Although this is an agenda embraced by the Democratic Progressive Party (DPP), which became the ruling party in May 2000, political opposition has blocked consensus about provisions for this program. It is still unclear when this program will be established.

Furthermore, Legislative Yuan passed the Temporary Act for Provision of Welfare Subsidies to the Elderly and Aboriginal Elderly in 2002, but both the Cabinet and the opposition parties are still proposing various amendments to relax the criteria for eligibility for the stipend. Critics argue that political parties are more concerned about senior citizen votes than they are about a well-established economic security system for the elderly. In fact, ferocious political competition can be traced back to the implementation of the Middle-Income and Low-Income Living Allowances for the Aged in the early 1990s. The central government, controlled by the Nationalist Party (Kuo Ming Tang, KMT), implemented the above program in 1993, and the eligibility requirement was income under 1.5 times the minimum living standard. However, because local governments controlled by the DPP introduced the universal allowance program for the elderly and the local elections were held in 1994, the eligibility requirement for the Middle-Income and Low-Income Living Allowances for the Aged was increased to twice the minimum living standard, and then further increased to 2.5 times. Owing to the financial difficulty of the government, a stricter standard of eligibility was established in 1997. On one hand, the policy change reflects the results of party politics. On the other hand, it also shows that the government did not have a long-term plan for a comprehensive safety net for the elderly (Wang, 1999). Hence, establishing a sustainable and fiscally sound national pension system is critical, which would significantly affect the existing structure of income transfer policies and the economic conditions of the aged.

Tackling Social Exclusion and Social Polarization

In recent years, Taiwan's economic transition from manufacturing industries to technology-intensive industries, the exodus of industries to China, and the global economic downturn have resulted in increasing unemployment. Observing the unemployment trend, one finds not only that the number of the unemployed has grown, but also the characteristics of the employed have changed. There are three factors compounding the current unemployment problem: (1) an increase in involuntary unemployment; (2) an increasing number of middle-aged and experienced workers among the unemployed; and (3) an increase in the duration of unemployment (Wang, 2002). Moreover, it has been found that unemployed workers whose income is just above the minimum living standard are most likely to end up being a recipient of the social assistance system. In other words, the poverty problem is not simply lack of income, it is also related to conditions of the labor market.

In fact, recent literature has expanded the discussion on the concept of poverty. The term 'social exclusion' has been widely used to focus on multiple deprivations resulting from lack of personal, social, political or financial opportunities (Barry, 1998). It has also become the main focus of EU social policy, particularly the issue of labor market exclusion (Percy-Smith, 2000). Therefore, one of the major tasks for the government is not only to protect the economic security of unemployed workers from job losses, but also to help them re-enter the labor market, which will in turn prevent people from being excluded from mainstream society.

Government needs to provide more active support in helping people to become integrated into the labor market as well as mainstream society. This is especially necessary for low-income people of working age. Policies for increasing access to the labor market need to be instituted. These would include mobilizing employment services for the most disadvantaged, job creation in the non-profit sector, financial incentives to employers to hire minimum-income recipients, and helping people to move into employment without loss of income (Schulte, 2002: 119). At the same time, the government also needs to enhance the human capital of members of low-income families by means of education or vocational training. Finally, the government needs to establish policy mechanisms for facilitating asset-building of low-income families in order to escape poverty in the long run (Sherraden, 1991).

In addition to provisions which increase benefits under Employment Insurance as mentioned above, there are other conditions related to social exclusion which also need to be addressed. Currently, laid-off workers can only receive unemployment benefit for up to six months for each incidence of unemployment. If they still cannot find work, they have to rely on themselves. Due to the strict qualifying conditions, most of them are not eligible for social assistance. If they are middle-aged, they may face even more adverse economic hardships. Thus, bridging the gap between the unemployment benefits program and the social assistance program is another important policy issue.

The rise of unemployment in turn leads to a more unequal distribution of income. This is because low-income families usually include members who are laid-off or working in low-wage industries, and their incomes are most likely to be affected. According to the official income report, it seems that the rich are becoming richer and the poor becoming poorer. This is particularly evident from the figures for 2001. This phenomenon can be seen as social polarization (Townsend, 2002: 3-19). On the positive side, current social welfare programs have brought about some reduction in income inequality. Therefore, more government interventions are needed to slow down the trend toward social polarization.

REDEFINING FAMILY UNITS

The breakdown of family structures not only affects the economic support for the elderly, but also that of women and children. Taiwan has seen a rise in single-parent families with children under 18 years of age (Huang, 2000). A recent study shows that single-parent families with children under 18 years of age comprised about 3.54% of total families in 1998. This is mainly due to divorce or widowhood (Hsueh, 2000). The percentage of female-headed single-parent families (52%) is slightly higher than male-headed ones (48%). The study also used the official minimum living standard as the poverty line to analyze the poverty rates for single-parent families and two-parent families. The results show that 10.49% of single-parent families were poor, which was over two times the poverty rate for two-parent families in 1998. The current national program, however, only covers middle-income and low-income single mothers who cannot work due to old-age, disability, sickness or care-giving responsibilities. Hence, a more comprehensive form of social protection for single-parent families with children will be necessary in the future.

Changing family structures have also led to new problems in the operation of means-tested programs. The present regulation of means-tested programs uses a very strict definition of a family unit for counting family financial resources. According to the Social Assistance Law, family members include: (1) people with lineal relation except married children who are not able to work; (2) people with collateral relation who register in the same household or share common living quarters or who have care-taking responsibilities by law; and (3) taxpayers who claim income tax exemption for taking care of their children, aged parents or disabled family members.

The implicit value behind this regulation is the Chinese family, which implies paternalism and a tight-knit family pattern. However, family values have been challenged and family structures have changed over the years. Males are no longer the only breadwinners for their families, and the intra-family or inter-family economic resource allocation does not necessarily exist for some families. For instance, single mothers might not receive any financial resources from their parents but parents' income and assets would be added to a single mother's total financial resources. By law caseworkers need to consider all possible sources of economic resources for social assistance applicants. Sometimes applicants are not eligible simply because caseworkers count their relatives' income or assets even though there is no exchange of financial resources among them. Although caseworkers have discretionary power in the means-testing process, the gap between the law and reality has led to many controversial cases and unfair treatment of social assistance applicants (Cheng, 2000). To ease the current strict restrictions on the definition of family unit would assist people who are in real need.

Concerning Welfare Rights of Ethnic Groups

The aboriginal peoples in Taiwan have been relatively deprived in terms of income level and employment opportunities. The average income of aboriginal workers was about 66% of the national mean and the unemployment rate was about 2.8 times the national unemployment rate in September 2001 (Committee of Aboriginal Affairs, 2001). Owing to these disadvantages and the increasing awareness of their own rights, there is a pressing demand for the government to compensate ethnic minorities as a result of their differential treatment in the past.

The phenomenon of global migration since the end of the twentieth century indicates the following four tendencies: an increasing number of immigrants, an increasing number of countries to and from which people immigrate and emigrate, various types of immigrants (e.g. white-collar professionals, migrant workers or refugees), and the feminization of immigration due to the demand for domestic workers in some wealthy countries, and the developments of sex tourism as well as the occurrence of 'mail order brides' (Giddens, 2001).

These tendencies also can be found in Taiwan. Among various types of immigrants, 'mail order brides' from Mainland China and South-East Asia are more likely to face economic hardship because most of them marry Taiwanese husbands with lower social-economic status (Wang, 2001; Han, 2002). Under the current system, if foreign brides need to apply for social assistance, they must possess permanent residency. Nevertheless, in general it takes at least four years for foreign brides from South-East Asia to qualify for permanent residency, while it takes much longer for brides from Mainland China, i.e. eight to eleven years. Furthermore, the government requires their husbands to be their sponsor when they apply for citizenship except under special circumstances. These regulations put foreign brides in a very vulnerable situation. Since it can be expected that the number of foreign brides will continue to grow, concern about the economic well-being of those without permanent residency will be a new challenge to the government.

In conclusion, with economic, social, demographic and international changes, the government has to address different welfare needs for the elderly, single-parent families, unemployed workers, aboriginal peoples, and new immigrants. At the same time, the phenomenon of social polarization is also a pressing policy concern. In order to deal with these diverse social problems and needs, Taiwan needs a government with strong fiscal capacities. At the same time, the relationship between the Cabinet and the Legislature needs to be more policy-oriented rather than politics-oriented. These are tremendous challenges for the Taiwan government. The current economic downturn and rising unemployment have resulted in the reduction of tax revenues, which in turn have worsened the financial condition of the government. At the same time, these uncertainties are exploited by vicious power struggles within and among political parties, which in turn creates more uncertainties for the future. Therefore, it is imperative that the different political parties look beyond their rivalries to engage in rational policy negotiation for the good of the country. Only then will Taiwan be able to pursue the harmonious balance between economic development and social welfare which is fundamental for the future alleviation of poverty.

REFERENCES

Cheng, Li-Chen (2000). Relatives' Responsibility and Means-Tests in Social Assistance Policy: An Example of Female-Headed Families. *National Cheng Chi University Journal of Sociology*, 30, pp.113-143. (in Chinese)

Committee of Aboriginal Affairs, Executive Yuan, Republic of China (2001). *Report on the Employment Survey of Aborigines in the Third Quarter of 2001.* (in Chinese)

Barry, Monica. (1998). Social Exclusion and Social Work: An Introduction. In Monica Barry and Christine Hallett (Eds.) *Social Exclusion and Social Work: Issues of Theory, Policy and Practice* (pp. 1-12). New York: Russell House Publishing.

Dinnito, Diana M. (2000). *Social Welfare: Politics and Public Policy*. The 5th Edition. New York: Allyn and Bacon.

Directorate-General of Budget, Accounting and Statistics (DGBAS), Executive Yuan, R.O.C. (2001). *Report on the Survey of Family Income and Expenditure in Taiwan Area of Republic of China, 2001*. http://www.dgbas.gov.tw

Giddens, A. (2001). *Sociology*. The 4th Edition. Cambridge: Polity Press.

Gilbert, N. and Terrell, P. (1998). *Dimensions of Social Welfare Policy*. The 5th Edition. New York: Allyn and Bacon.

Han, Chialin (2002). *Global Migration of Women in Taiwan: The Case of Brides from Mainland China*. Bureau of Social Affairs, Taipei City Government. (in Chinese)

Heidenheimer, A. et al. (1990). *Comparative Public Policy*. NY: St. Martin's Press.

Hsueh, Chernt-Tay (2000). Single-Parent Families and the Poverty: The Case of 1998 in Taiwan. *NTU Social Work Review*, No.2, pp.151-189. (in Chinese)

Huang, Chien-Chung (2000). Socioeconomic Trends in Single-Parent Families in Taiwan, 1980-1995. *NTU Social Work Review*, No.2, pp. 217-248.

Huang, Mei-lin and Lin, Wan-I (2000). The Analyses of National Pension Plans. *Journal of Community Development*, No.91, pp. 16-29. (in Chinese)

Hung, Rudy (1996). The Great U-Turn in Taiwan: Economic Restructuring and a Surge in Inequality. *Journal of Contemporary Asia*, 26(2): 151-63.

Jacobs, Didier (2000). *Low Inequality with Low Redistribution? An Analysis of Income Distribution in Japan, South Korea and Taiwan Compared to Britain*. Center for Analysis of Social Exclusion, London School of Economics, CASEpaper 33.

Lee, Ann-ni (1998). *Gender Differences of the Poor*. Paper presented at the Conference on Family and Allocation of Social Resources. Taipei: Academic Sinica. (in Chinese)

Li, He (2000). Political Economy of Income Distribution: a comparative study of Taiwan and Mexico. *Policy Studies Journal*, 28(2): 275-291.

Lin, Chun-Hung (2002). The Effect of International Trade on the Outcomes of Labor Market: The Case of Taiwan. *Soochow Journal of Economics and Business*, No. 36, pp.23-46. (in Chinese)

Lin, Dah-Jiun (2002). Establishing a Comprehensive Social Security System. *Journal of Community Development*, Special Issue, p.178. (in Chinese)

Lin, Meiling and Wang, T. (2000). The Effect of Poverty Thresholds on Poverty Rates and Poverty Population Compositions. *Taiwanese Journal of Social Welfare*, Vol. 1 pp.93-124. (in Chinese)

Liou, Ruey-Wan (2001). The Effects of Industrial Structural Change on the Employment and Income Distribution. *Taiwan Economic Review*, Vol. 29, No. 2, pp. 203-233. (in Chinese)

Luo, Jih-Chyong (1998). The Effect of National Health Insurance on Income Distribution. *Industry of Free China*, 88(11): 1-41. (in Chinese)

Luxembourg Income Study (LIS) (2002). LIS Study. Retrieved December12, 2002 from the World Wide Web: http://www.lisproject.org

Percy-Smith, Janie (2000). Introduction: The Contours of Social Exclusion. In Janie Percy-Smith (Ed.) *Policy Responses to Social Exclusion towards Inclusion?* (pp. 1-21) London: Open University Press.

Schulte, Bernd (2002). A European Definition of Poverty: The Fight against Poverty and Social Exclusion in the Member States of the European Union. In Townsend, P. and Gordon, D. (Eds.) *World Poverty: New Policies to Defeat An Old Enemy* (pp. 119-145). Bristol: The Policy Press.

Sherraden, M. (1991). *Assets and the Poor: A New American Welfare Policy*. New York: M.E. Sharpe, Inc.

Sheu, Jang-Yau (2002). The Allocation and Finance of Social Welfare Resources in Taiwan. *Journal of Community Development,* Special Issue, pp.102-108. (in Chinese)

Smeeding, T. and Ross, K. (1999). *Social Protection for the Poor in the Developed World: The Evidence from LIS*. LIS Working Paper, No. 204.

Sun, Way and Gindling, T. H. (2000). Educational Expansion and Earnings Inequality in Taiwan: 1978-1995. *Journal of Humanity and Social Sciences*, 12(4): 597-629.

Townsend, Peter (2002). Poverty, Social Exclusion and Social Polarization: The Need to Construct An International Welfare State. In Townsend, P. and Gordon, D. (Eds.) *World Poverty: New Policies to Defeat An Old Enemy* (pp. 3-24). Bristol: The Policy Press.

Wang, Hong-Jen (2001). Social Stratification, Vietnamese Partners Migration and Taiwan Labor Market. *A Radical Quarterly in Social Studies*, No.41, pp.99-127. (in Chinese)

Wang, Yeong-Tsyr (1999). Means-tests in Taiwan's Programs for the Elderly. *Fu-Jen Studies*, Vol. 29, pp. 43-60. (in Chinese)

Wang, Yeong-Tsyr (2002). Taiwan's Social Development in an Age of Uncertainty. *Journal of Comparative Asian Development,* 1(2): 171-193.

In: *Poverty Monitoring and Alleviation in East Asia*
K. Tang and C. Wong, editors pp. 57-73

ISBN: 1-59033-828-6
© 2003 Nova Science Publishers, Inc.

Chapter 3

POVERTY, VULNERABILITY AND THE EXPANSION OF DISCIPLINARY WELFARE IN HONG KONG

Sammy Chiu

INTRODUCTION

Before 1997, Hong Kong was portrayed as an economic miracle. With a population of around 6.5 million in 1997, Hong Kong enjoyed per capita GDP of over US$23,000 a year, an economic performance that was more remarkable than many industrial societies in the world. In addition to the eye-catching economic success demonstrated by the volume of Gross Domestic Product, Hong Kong was also the eighth largest trading community in the world, had the seventh largest foreign exchange reserves, the eighth largest stock market, and was the fifth largest center for foreign exchange dealing. Behind this "success story" celebrated by the last colonial governor (Hong Kong Government, 1996), however, Hong Kong had one of the worst performances in income distribution compared with the leading economies (World Bank, 2001), had no retirement protection for the elderly and had only a meager level of social security allowance for those in need; above all, it appeared to be a society which was well disposed towards the rich but not so caring for the poor. In short, poverty has always been a major problem in Hong Kong.

Severely hit by the Asian financial crisis, the unemployment rate in Hong Kong rose to an unprecedented height in the 2nd quarter of 2002, and the income level of wage earners has also witnessed a significant drop. Coupled with the absence of a comprehensive income protection program, the vulnerable sector of the community is bound to suffer even more severely.

This chapter discusses poverty as a major social problem in Hong Kong. It is argued that poverty does not only appear after the so-called Asian Financial Crisis, nor is it simply a consequence of economic recession. On the contrary, the problem of poverty existed before the change of sovereignty and even during the previous 30 years while Hong Kong was enjoying great economic success. Unfortunately, it was never taken seriously as an important social agenda to address before 1997, and continuous economic success was held to be the most effective solution to the problem. The author maintains that there is no explicit social policy in Hong Kong which addresses the problem of poverty. Instead, there are only scattered social programs which attempt to help those who are poor. Poverty has been construed as a personal rather than a social problem, the alleviation of which is thus primarily viewed as the responsibility of the person in difficulty rather than an issue for the government to tackle. Though the Chief Executive of the SAR might have every good intention to help those in need, the author still argues that the overall policy framework for poverty reduction has remained substantially unchanged.

THE POVERTY DISCOURSE AND ITS LEGACY

Poverty Discourse in the 1960s

The way in which social policy in Hong Kong addresses the problem of poverty depends very much on how this problem has been historically conceived and understood both by the government and the community. Though a topic frequently discussed in the welfare sector since the International Year of the Eradication of Poverty in 1995, the term "poverty" has rarely been seen in government documents, including annual reports and welfare policy papers, nor has it been publicly discussed as a social policy agenda from the 1960s onwards. Before and during the early 1960s, when the territory was recovering from the destruction caused by the 2nd World War and from Japanese occupation, Hong Kong was essentially a small-scale developing economy where the majority of citizens endured unsatisfactory living conditions. Not only were housing and health for some sectors of the population not well protected, even water supply was a major problem for the territory (Hong Kong Government, 1960). The then colonial government for the first time recorded in its annual report that poverty did actually exist in Hong Kong and that the problem was widespread:

> Although there is widespread poverty in Hong Kong, there is virtually no starvation, nor need anyone live at starvation level ... Genuine beggars have ceased to be a problem of any size in Hong Kong (Hong Kong Government, 1960: 181).

The government of the time regarded the problem of poverty as one that was, on the one hand, a legacy of the War and, on the other hand, imported and aggravated by the problem of refugees. In 1960, Professor Eileen Younghusband from the United Kingdom studied the need for social work in Hong Kong in her capacity as a consultant invited by the governor. Her report, which was widely recognized as a landmark in social work development (commonly known as the Younghusband report), recorded that:

> Overshadowing every effort for betterment, yet also acting as the spur, is this mass of humanity, continually sucking down the individual into overcrowding, malnutrition, low earnings for long hours of work, and a life dominated by the fierce competitive struggle for survival ... Yet the children are often full of energy and quick laughter on a diet which is theoretically insufficient for survival. Tuberculosis is widespread ... (Younghusband, 1960: 7).

The life of the people who lived in poverty in the 1960s was vividly portrayed by Younghusband, though poverty itself was not addressed as a social problem, nor as a cause of other social problems such as inadequate child care and delinquency which also deserved social work attention.

Interestingly, though, from 1961 onwards the colonial government seems to have altered its position with regard to the problem of poverty. This is reflected in the official discourse of the Hong Kong colonial government on the problem of poverty and social welfare. First, the reference to "poverty as a widespread problem" disappears from the 1961 Hong Kong annual report, nor does it appear in other social welfare and related documents. Replacing the discourse of "poverty as a widespread problem", poverty is presented in terms of a need to provide "relief for the destitute", which shifts the emphasis onto unfortunate individuals, and the efforts of the government into providing material assistance for the unfortunate few (Hong Kong Government, 1961). Second, through the introduction of professional social work, poverty as a social problem, or at least as a widespread social phenomenon, was given a professional discourse, with the aim of restoring the destitute to self sufficiency. This professional discourse could be seen in an early government document:

"More intensive casework, aimed at rehabilitating and restoring destitutes and others to full or partial economic independence; strict application of present standards of entitlement; and relative improvement in the economic and employment conditions for fit young people in the Colony are all factors that contributed to a further decrease in relief expenditure during the year" (Hong Kong Government, 1964: 139).

The professional discourse of poverty that was first laid down in 1964 was reiterated more clearly in 1965:

The aim of the relief section of the Social Welfare Department is to rehabilitate and restore the destitute and needy to full, or at least partial, economic independence (Hong Kong Government, 1965: 146).

What the above analyses suggest is that there has been a long history, notably since the early 1960s, whereby the problem of poverty, though once recognized by the government as a widespread social problem, has been construed simply as the problems or sufferings of unfortunate, if not maladjusted, individuals. The early colonial government, although it noted the existence of the problem, opted to address it by means of stringent personal relief rather than tackling it with a social strategy such as redistributing social resources through social policies. The poverty discourse of the 1950s and 1960s had a significant impact on the social security schemes developed in the 1970s.

Poverty Discourse in the 1970s

Another important landmark of social welfare development in Hong Kong was the implementation of a non-contributory but means-tested public assistance scheme in Hong Kong in 1971. As stated by the government, the public assistance scheme was to replace the in-kind relief provided in the 1960s and to provide cash assistance for individuals and families who could not manage on their existing resources (Hong Kong Government, 1973).

For the first time the discourse of poverty had changed from a problem confined to the destitute to a problem affecting individuals and families with inadequate resources. This change in the poverty discourse was outlined in a position paper submitted by Hong Kong to the International Conference on Social Welfare held in 1970. The main thrust of the position was that Hong Kong had witnessed significant economic growth, such that the vast majority of the population had been able to benefit and raise their living standards beyond the clutches of destitution. Poverty had largely disappeared, and if it existed at all, remained only with a small section of the population who for reasons beyond their control failed to obtain adequate resources to maintain themselves and their families.

> In Hong Kong, where wages are comparatively low … income may be insufficient for the family needs or loss of income from serious illness, death or imprisonment of the breadwinner may deprive the family of essentials … Since the breadwinner cannot always be certain of full employment other strategies are necessary to maintain family income (Hong Kong Committee of the International Council on Social Welfare, 1970: 23).

In other words, poverty was being understood in terms of inadequate resources caused mainly by the low income of individuals and sometimes by illness of the breadwinners or other family contingencies. The "low income" discourse was well documented in government policy papers and dominated policy discussion until the 1980s:

> The Public Assistance Scheme is designed to provide cash assistance to needy families and individuals whose income falls below a prescribed level (Hong Kong Government, 1974: 105).

It is necessary to point out that the "low income" discourse of poverty had several distinctive features. First, poverty was measured against the income of an individual. Second, it was viewed as absolute and was not discussed in relation to any forms of income disparity, not to mention social inequality in a broader sense. Third, it is primarily gender-based, if not gender-biased, because as long as the traditional division of labor requires women to provide a domestic contribution at home, poverty will remain a predominantly male issue. I shall return to this point at the end of this section.

The Discourse of Vulnerability and Disadvantage in the 1980s and 1990s

Vulnerability can be regarded as a multidimensional construct (Shi, 2001), and its prevalence is associated with a range of personal, social and ecological factors, depending on the nature of the vulnerability. For example, in discussing why single parents are more vulnerable to the threat of violence, Wikstrom and Wikstrom (2001) attempted to relate vulnerability to the risks that lone-parent families are exposed to. The risks that cause vulnerability are mostly identified as external ones. Caserta and Gray (1984) argued in their study of depression that vulnerability to depression is strongly associated with social class background. While vulnerability and risk have been virtually established as a twin-concept, Turner (2001), in a more recent study, further suggests that the inherent risks of modernity have intensified risks and vulnerability in social life.

Though the discussion of vulnerability has penetrated far beyond the scope of poverty, Townsend (1982), in his classical study of poverty in the United Kingdom, began to adopt the concept of vulnerability in his analysis of poverty, arguing that older workers are more prone to risks of low-pay, marginalization and loss of employment, and thus are more vulnerable to poverty. Again, Townsend's thesis also related vulnerability to poverty to social disadvantages caused by social change. Because vulnerability to poverty is external to the persons and families who are in poverty, alleviation measures are called for to remove as far as possible the social disadvantages that put people at risk. Along the same lines, Schervish (1983) studied unemployment in the USA and related vulnerability to unemployment to sets of structural determinants such as social class, industrial sector and economic cycle. One of the major arguments was that the relative powerlessness of people in the marketplace was an important factor which caused vulnerability to unemployment. In short, vulnerability and poverty were demonstrated to be associated with external risks rather than simply personal failure or misfortune.

In the Hong Kong case, the discourse of vulnerability in relation to poverty first appeared in the Social Security Green Paper released in 1977 (Hong Kong Government, 1977), which stated from the outset that public assistance was aimed at offering cash assistance to the vulnerable groups in society. The 1981 Social Welfare White Paper confirmed this objective, stipulating that it is for helping only "recognised vulnerable groups":

> The overall objective [of social security in Hong Kong] is to meet the basic and particular needs of the recognised vulnerable groups in the community who are in need of financial or material assistance, and to this end, to provide a balanced system of social security schemes (Hong Kong Government, 1981: 3).

While public attention was mainly concerned with the level of assistance being defined as meeting a 'basic level of need', it is worth pointing out that the discourse of vulnerable groups had been established almost without being noticed for more than ten years. However, little attention was paid to what was recognized as "vulnerable", and what the external risks were that had caused vulnerability in particular sectors of the community. The same problem arose in the 1990s when the government again announced that social security would be made available to help the disadvantaged groups in society (Social Welfare Department, 1996). The concern of the activists was once more focused on the level of assistance, which was regarded as far below that which could provide a reasonable standard of living, rather than the discourse of poverty itself being created by the government. The important point is that in the government discourse of poverty, vulnerability has been constructed simply as "particular groups in financial trouble", and there is little discussion or association of vulnerability with the external risks that these groups are likely to face. On the contrary, vulnerability and disadvantage were construed more as deriving from personal weakness and circumstantial misfortune and vaguely implied to be personal responsibilities. A notable example was old age. Unlike what Townsend (1982) argued, the Hong Kong government implied that vulnerability to poverty in old age was a natural consequence of ageing exacerbated by lack of support from the family. The way in which older people are socially and structurally disadvantaged in the labor market appeared to be alien to the discourse. Nothing has been mentioned about the risks older people face in the labor market, and the social exclusion thesis (Jordan 1996; Williams 1996; Dowling, 1999), which suggests that older people are socially removed from the labor market, has been almost completely ignored. Constructing vulnerability as solely a personal or family matter has served to preclude almost any measure that the government might be compelled to take to tackle the social as well as structural causes of poverty and disadvantage. This partly explains why in Hong Kong public pressure for the alleviation of poverty has been contained within, if not restricted to, a rather small scope, where only personal and family failures are addressed. What is also important to note is that the production of a poverty discourse is not simply exercised through the operation of state social policy. It is also mediated through the mass media and is strengthened by attitudes to welfare such as the traditional belief that one should not rely on the state unless absolutely necessary (Lau and Kuan, 1988).

Not only has vulnerability not been linked with external social risks in the poverty discourse, but the scope of vulnerability has also been carefully defined to cover only those groups recognized by the government to be vulnerable. These groups include the physically and mentally disabled, the chronically ill, single-parent families, and, to a limited extent, the unemployed. Ironically, the definition of what constitutes vulnerability has been almost solely based on administrative and financial considerations of the government, rather than on the deprivation suffered by vulnerable groups. For example, the appearance of the chronically ill as a "vulnerable group" is a rather recent phenomenon. Their vulnerability was not recognized by the government until the mid-1990s, and they were thus virtually erased from the social security agenda. The rationale for denying the vulnerability of the chronically ill in the Hong Kong case was simply administrative and financial: i.e. it depended on whether the financial situation of the government permitted more spending on social security. In other words, whether a group is regarded as vulnerable to poverty or not rests strongly on the budget of the government. To some extent, the vulnerability thesis constructed in the 1980s and which penetrated into the 1990s can be seen as a "modern" reproduction of the moral discourse of the 1970s.

In sum, I have endeavored to point out that the discourse of poverty in Hong Kong has been constructed in such a way as to imply personal failure and personal misfortune rather than relating the problem to the wider social institutions which distribute social resources and welfare. As Townsend (1982; 1993) has forcefully suggested, poverty should not be viewed simply as a lack of resources to fulfill basic needs; rather, it should be explained in terms of relative deprivation, which "has to be situated through time in relation to social and institutional structures…" (Townsend, 1993: 35). Townsend (1993) further argued that people are relatively deprived if they cannot obtain, whether fully or partially, the conditions of life which allow them to participate in social relationships and to live customarily as fellow citizens. In relation to the Hong Kong case, the poverty discourse of personal failure and vulnerability fails to situate poverty in the wider social institutions which privilege some while denying access to resources to those who are relatively deprived. The Hong Kong poverty discourse also fails to address the fact that denial of social resources for customary social activities is biased against women, because when poverty becomes personal, women's disadvantages in the labor market and the culture of dependency perpetuated by the existing family ideology are overlooked (Williams, 1989; Lister, 1997; Walker and Parker, 1988).

Income Disparity and the Poverty Debate

Notwithstanding government efforts to construct a personal poverty discourse, which has effectively penetrated into the wider community, there was growing concern about poverty and income disparity in the mid-1990s, albeit initiated and legitimized only within a relatively small social welfare circle. This concern helped to draw public attention to the fact that poverty does not just exist among the government recognized "vulnerable groups". Rather, attention was drawn to the problem of poverty experienced by those who are not yet recognized as vulnerable, for example, those whom the Comprehensive Social Security Assistance (CSSA) eligibility standard excludes from being helped. Another concern was related to the fact that the existing CSSA level was too low and was insufficient to enable recipients to maintain a basic but acceptable standard of living. Concerns about poverty and income disparity were actually first vividly voiced by the late Professor Peter Hodge (1977) when he introduced the concept of a divided society, notably "the poor and the people of quality" in the Hong Kong society of that time. Hodge (1977) argued that social policy in Hong Kong must address this division in order to achieve a social objective. Hodge's argument obviously did not win any converts in the colonial government, though there were some echoes in the social welfare community (Chiu, 1991). Concern about this problem was once raised as a matter for the public agenda in the Legislative Council in a motion debate in 1996. Interestingly, the two major political parties in Hong Kong, namely the Democratic Party and the Democratic Alliance for Betterment of Hong Kong (DAB), both accepted the view that income disparity was serious in Hong Kong, but both parties discounted the need for the government to use social policy to redistribute wealth (Hong Kong Hansard, October 9, 1996). As a solution to income disparity, both parties opted for raising the social security allowance level to help the poor. The stance of the two largest political parties was not so different from that of the Liberal Party, which represented the interests of the business sector. The Chairman of the Liberal Party even suggested that tackling income disparity was just like "those grapes beyond reach [that] are sour", and that any attempt to improve income disparity was essentially pulling down the achievers just because the poor themselves were non-achievers (Hong Kong Hansard, October 9, 1996). The attitude of the Liberal Party vividly reflects the self-preservatory logic of the business sector in Hong Kong, and the stance of the Democratic Party and the DAB unequivocally indicates the domination of this mentality and the propensity for local politicians to avoid upsetting the status quo.

The Huge Disparity of Income

As a matter of fact, disparity of income has seldom been associated with the problem of poverty in related policy debates in Hong Kong. In the discourse of the government, income disparity and the grave inequality of wealth distribution are both an incentive to wealth production as well as an inevitable consequence of economic progress. Above all, this is conceived as a matter for 'free market regulation' that government should not take measures to intervene in. Otherwise the 'free market' upon which the prosperity of Hong Kong's economy so much relies will be jeopardized. This was made clear by the last colonial governor in his final policy address to the Legislative Council under British rule:

Quite deliberately, our welfare system does not exist to iron out inequalities. It does not exist to redistribute income. Our welfare programmes have a different purpose. They exist because this community believes that we have a duty to provide a safety net to protect the vulnerable and the disadvantaged members of society, the unfortunate minority who, through no fault of their own, are left behind by the growing prosperity enjoyed by the rest of Hong Kong …We have to keep a firm grip on public spending. We have done so over the last five years. And I am well aware of the need for Hong Kong to avoid the massive problems caused by spiraling welfare costs in Europe (Hong Kong Government, 1996: para. 78 and 80).

The fact is that Hong Kong people have long been indoctrinated with the idea that social welfare in favor of the poor is the antithesis of economic progress. There is a common belief that income disparity has to be accepted if Hong Kong is to maintain its economic prosperity (Hong Kong Policy Viewers, 2000). As a result, in times of economic prosperity when the general public are able to secure some improvements in their living standards, people do not view disparity of income and the unequal distribution of wealth as a genuine problem. Moreover, in times of economic hardship, they tend to blame welfare recipients for worsening the economy because of the increase in social security expenditure. It has been cogently argued by Chiu and Wong (1998) that the Hong Kong government won legitimation, not by democracy, but solely by its ability to generate economic prosperity. In other words, as long as the citizens of Hong Kong were able to benefit from economic prosperity, albeit to various degrees, they would tend to tolerate inequality of wealth as a necessary evil.

In spite of this, it should be noted that income disparity in Hong Kong has been very serious, especially between 1991 and 1996, and has become even more acute since the Asian financial Crisis. Table 3.1 shows that income disparity over the past twenty years has been polarizing towards two extremes, with the richest getting richer and the poorest becoming even poorer. The poorest 10% income group earned only 1.4% of the total income in 1981, and this distribution plummeted to less than 1% in 2001, showing that the poorest suffer even more seriously in times of economic downturn. By contrast, the richest 10% were awarded 41.2% of the total income in 2001, showing that their interests are not adversely affected in times of economic difficulty. On the contrary, while the poorest sector of the community has suffered from serious disadvantages in income distribution since 1986, the privileges of the richest sector have continued to increase. In addition, the Gini-coefficient, which measures disparity of wealth, also indicates this trend towards unequal distribution of wealth. In 2001, the Gini-coefficient reached a new height of 0.525, which is the worst of all the neighboring countries in Asia.

The bare fact is that the kind of wealth distribution pattern in Hong Kong benefits the minority who are rich. As seen in Table 3.1, the top 20% income group took up 56.5% of the total income in 2001. Compared with twenty years ago, the richest 20% of households received even more while the poorest 20% got significantly less. The unequal distribution of income affects not only the very poor. As a matter of fact, 80% households have suffered from a distributive loss compared with twenty years ago.

Table 3.1. Income Distribution by 10 Income Groups, 1981-2001

Income distribution by income group	1981 (%)	1986 (%)	1991 (%)	1996 (%)	2001 (%)
Group 1 (Lowest 10%)	1.4	1.6	1.3	1.1	0.9
Group 2	3.2	3.4	3.0	2.6	2.3
Group 3	4.4	4.4	4.0	3.6	3.4
Group 4	5.4	5.4	5.0	4.6	4.4
Group 5	6.5	6.4	6.1	5.7	5.6
Group 6	7.8	7.6	7.4	7.0	7.0
Group 7	9.4	9.1	9.0	8.5	8.8
Group 8	11.5	11.4	11.4	10.6	11.1
Group 9	15.2	15.2	15.5	14.5	15.3
Group 10 (Highest 10%)	35.2	35.5	37.3	41.8	41.2
Total	100	100	100	100	100
Gini Coefficient	0.451	0.453	0.476	0.518	0.525

Source: Census and Statistics Department, Census Reports of various years.

Although there is still controversy over whether the Gini-coefficient can accurately measure wealth inequality, very few would cast doubt on the huge disparity of wealth in Hong Kong. Compared with developed countries with a similar economic performance, such as Canada, the UK, France and the Netherlands, Hong Kong has the poorest performance in terms of Gini-coefficient (see Table 3.2). Even compared with neighboring Asian countries, its Gini-coefficient is still the highest (Table 3.3). In view of this, Hong Kong has a first world pattern of wealth production, but its distribution of wealth is similar to that of the developing world.

Table 3.2. Gini-coefficient of Selected Countries

Country	Gini-coefficient
Sweden (1992)	0.250
Germany (1994)	0.300
Canada (1994)	0.315
Netherlands (1994)	0.326
France (1995)	0.327
UK (1995)	0.368
USA (1997)	0.408
Nigeria (1997)	0.506
Zambia (1998)	0.526
Mexico (1998)	0.531

Source: World Bank (2001), World Development Report (2000/01).

Table 3.3. Gini-coefficient of Selected Asian Countries

Country	Gini-coefficient
Japan (1993)	0.249
Korean Republic (1993)	0.316
Taiwan (2000)	0.326
India (1997)	0.378
China (1998)	0.403
Thailand (1998)	0.414
Philippines (1997)	0.462
Malaysia (1997)	0.492
Hong Kong (2001)	0.525

Source: World Bank (2001), World Development Report (2000/01); Taiwan Executive Yuan Statistics Department (2001).

Poverty Measurement and Poverty Prevalence

Notwithstanding the fact that there is only a very weak association between poverty, income disparity and social inequality in Hong Kong, there is also disagreement between the government and the welfare sector with regard to the way in which poverty in Hong Kong should be measured. As is commonly known, Hong Kong has not set up an official poverty line to measure poverty. In the absence of an official poverty line, eligibility for Comprehensive Social Security Assistance (CSSA), which is the only public cash assistance to help the eligible poor in Hong Kong, has always been used as a convenient criterion for measuring poverty. But this standard has often been criticized for underestimating the prevalence of poverty and failing to provide adequate support to the poor (Wong, 2000; MacPherson, 2001).

CSSA and the Magnitude of Poverty

CSSA is thus far the only cash assistance provided by the government for the eligible poor. It is a non-contributory and means-tested program, which aims at providing for the basic and special needs of members of the community who are in need of financial or material assistance. CSSA uses a Basic Needs Budget approach to identify the basic needs of recipients, through which a standard rate of cash assistance is set. The components included in the standard budget are food, transportation, clothing and footwear, electricity and fuel, essential household goods and essential personal goods, among which the food budget takes up the largest share of expenditure. The cost of food is calculated by applying the average retail prices of the lowest 50% price range provided by the Census and Statistics Department of the SAR (Liu and Wu, 1998). Other non-food items are calculated by similar methods to ensure the standard rate does not exceed the basic needs level. Essentially, CSSA provides only cash support at a subsistence level (MacPherson and Lo, 1997). Those who receive CSSA are essentially those who have no alternative means of support.

Taking the CSSA eligibility level as an unofficial poverty line, the magnitude of the problem can clearly be gauged. In 1972, when Public Assistance was first initiated, the total number of cases was only 13,509. The cases increased to 45,813 in 1981, gradually rising to 66,675 in 1991. The number of households receiving CSSA has rocketed in the past five years from 136,201 in 1996 to 252,675 in May 2002, representing an increase of 85.5% over a period of just six years (Table 3.4).

Table 3.4. CSSA Cases by Type in Selected Years Since 1971

Category	1972	1981	1991	1996	1998	2000	2002*
Old Age	6,644	29,262	44,806	84,243	112,067	133,070	140,288
	(49.2%)	*(63.9%)*	*(67.2%)*	*(61.9%)*	*(57.3%)*	*(58.4%)*	*(55.5%)*
Single-parent family	1,407	2,188	3,899	8,982	17,161	25,146	30,350
	(10.4%)	*(4.8%)*	*(5.8%)*	*(6.6%)*	*(8.8%)*	*(11.0%)*	*(12.0%)*
Low earnings	1,803	2,495	918	1,814	4,714	8,002	9,557
	(13.3%)	*(5.4%)*	*(1.4%)*	*(1.3%)*	*(2.4%)*	*(3.5%)*	*(3.8%)*
Unemployed	135	283	1,754	10,131	19,108	26,185	34,382
	(1.0%)	*(0.6%)*	*(2.6%)*	*(7.4%)*	*(9.8%)*	*(11.5%)*	*(13.6%)*
Sick and disabled	3,374	10,219	13,324	24,508	34,519	31,693	34,239
	(25.0%)	*(22.3%)*	*(20.0%)*	*(18.0%)*	*(17.6%)*	*(13.9%)*	*(13.5%)*
Others	146	1,366	1,974	6,523	8,076	3,919	3,859
	(1.1%)	*(3.0%)*	*(3.0%)*	*(4.8%)*	*(4.1%)*	*(1.7%)*	*(1.5%)*
Total	13,509	45,813	66,675	136,201	195,645	228,015	252,675

Note: 2002 figures are as at end of April 2002.

Data source: Social Welfare Department Annual Reports of various years; 2002 data is from http://www.info.gov. hk/swd/html_eng/ser_sec/soc_secu/index.html

Judging from CSSA statistics, it is apparent that old age is the most important source of poverty. As a matter of fact, the number of elderly people who rely on CSSA for financial assistance has increased steadily over the past 20 years. In 2002, one in every five people aged 65 or above receives CSSA. Given that it would not normally be granted to elderly people with family support, the extent to which single old people suffer from poverty appears obvious. However, there is a problem of hidden poverty among those elderly people who live with their adult children and are only supported by means of sharing the accommodation and the dinner table. Yet, due to CSSA regulations and the stigma attached to receiving welfare, which family members take pains to avoid, the true poverty situation of these elderly people remains invisible. It is hard to estimate the actual deterrent effect of CSSA on elderly people with a family; nonetheless, poverty among elderly people is quite indisputable.

Apart from old age, unemployment has become the second major reason for people to fall back on the safety net of CSSA in recent years. In 2002 more than 34,000 CSSA cases were under the category of unemployment, showing an increase of 40% over a period of six years. Since Hong Kong has no unemployment insurance scheme, those who lost their jobs either have to lean on their family for support, or have no choice but to resort to CSSA. At present, the standard CSSA rate for an unemployed adult is HK$1,805 a month, which is only 70% of that of an elderly recipient, or 20% of the median income of a wage earner. As a matter of fact, the unemployment rate has increased significantly in the past five years, reaching a new height in the 1st quarter of 2002. According to the most recent statistics revealed by the Census and Statistics Department (2002), the seasonally adjusted unemployment rate rose further, from 7.1% in February-April 2002 to 7.4% (provisional) in March-May 2002, while the underemployment rate also edged up from 3.0% to 3.1% (provisional), meaning that there are 255,300 people unemployed.

Comparing March-May 2002 with February-April 2002, the unemployment rate (not seasonally adjusted) rose across many of the major economic sectors, with more noticeable increases occurring in construction work, the retail trade, restaurants, import/export trades and communications sectors. This more than offset the declines observed in the decoration and maintenance, finance and business services sectors. As regards the underemployment rate, the increase was concentrated in the construction sector. In other words, not only is labor in the non-skilled construction sector vulnerable to unemployment, the problem has spread to the service, trade and communications sectors where semi-skilled and skilled laborers are also affected. Hong Kong has a massive unemployed population, among whom only 13.5% are receiving help from the CSSA, while the rest either live on savings or rely on their family members (or extended family) for support. The extent to which this unemployed section of the population suffers from poverty has not yet been researched. However, in view of the fact that there is no unemployment insurance which protects individuals and families from loss of income, the adults and especially children in families whose breadwinners are without work are very likely to fall into poverty.

Poverty among Non-CSSA Recipients

There have been serious debates for a number of years over the use of CSSA as an unofficial poverty line. For example, Wong and Chua (1996) used the income proxy measure to analyze the expenditure pattern of low-income households in Hong Kong. The aim of the study was to identify the incidence of "abject poverty", defined as a situation in which household income is not adequate to cover basic and necessary expenditure. In other words, the objective was to determine the extent of poverty among poor non-CSSA families. It was found that households in abject poverty lived in extremely poor conditions where money was not adequate to cover even basic food costs. Monthly food expenditure of the lowest 5% to 10% expenditure group of one-person households was 13% less than their CSSA counterparts. It was not only one-person households that suffered from extreme poverty, the food expenditure of the lowest 5% of all sizes of households shared the same problem, that is, the incomes of these households were not adequate to support basic food expenditure. Wong and Chua (1996) further estimated that 141,000 non-CSSA households, amounting to almost half a million Hong Kong citizens, were living in abject poverty (Table 3.5).

Table 3.5. Number of Non-CSSA Households in Abject Poverty

Household Size	% of households in abject poverty	Number of households	Number of people
1	12.5	16,000	16,000
2	7.5	20,000	39,000
3	7.5	24,000	73,000
4	12.5	53,000	213,000
5 or more	7.5	28,000	145,000
Total	141,000	486,000	

Source: Wong and Chua (1996)

According to Wong and Chua's (1996) study, the number of poor households not receiving CSSA was around 27% more than those on CSSA. Based on this formula, they estimated that one in seven households in Hong Kong was living in abject poverty.

Besides Wong and Chua (1996), MacPherson and Lo (1997) used the standard budget approach to assess the poverty situation of low-income families. The findings showed that there were 126,600 non-CSSA households whose living standards had fallen below the minimum acceptable level. Apart from the similarity in the prevalence of poverty above the CSSA eligibility level, both studies similarly found that poor families spent most of their expenditure on foodstuff, which is essential for survival. The consequence of this is that expenditure on other needs, for example normal social activities, is seriously squeezed, leaving household members with extremely limited resources for other purposes. As observed by MacPherson (2001) poor families, especially those with children, are extremely restricted in terms of social activity and participation in the everyday activities enjoyed by ordinary people in Hong Kong. These poor families, however, have not been officially recognized as in poverty and no state support has therefore been given because of their invisibility. The common reason for not taking up CSSA is two-fold: on the one hand the CSSA eligibility level has been set too low and poor families above the eligibility level have therefore been excluded; on the other hand, the stigma of being welfare recipients has also acted as a strong deterrent so that only those who have nowhere to turn end up applying for CSSA.

Besides these studies, the Hong Kong Social Security Society also attempted to arrive at a poverty rate in terms of household income per capita. The method was to calculate the number of people whose household income per capita was below half the median in order to determine the percentage of those in poverty (Mok and Leung, 1997). The findings showed that the poverty rate in 1996 was 14.14%, representing one seventh of all households in Hong Kong, or 0.85 million people living in poverty. The poverty rate calculated by the Social Security Society also unequivocally demonstrates that poverty among non-CSSA recipients is serious.

State Strategy and Poverty Alleviation

As argued in the earlier part of this chapter, the Hong Kong Government before 1997 endeavored to construct a discursive reality that poverty is solely a matter of personal failure and personal misfortune. Although some social elements of poverty, for example social disadvantages and vulnerability, were added to the discourse of poverty in the 1980s and 1990s, this construction of personal responsibility has fundamentally been maintained. The general belief of the public is that disadvantages and vulnerability only happen to those who are disabled, mentally or physically ill, and a few who become temporarily dysfunctional due to contingencies beyond their control. For the rest of the population, it is believed that poverty will not happen to those who are willing to work hard. This belief is especially prevalent in times of economic growth when jobs appear to be easily available, but is also popular in times of economic recession, post 1997. In a territory-wide telephone survey conducted by the Hong Kong Policy Viewers in 2000, it was found that 68.1% of Hong Kong adults believed that poverty was a consequence of people's laziness and unwillingness to work. In addition, about half believed those who were in poverty lacked the confidence to find work and suffered from low self-esteem, while one third (36.6%) believed that they had poor skills in interpersonal relationships (Hong Kong Policy Viewers, 2000). The findings confirmed to a large extent that the thesis of personal failure as a cause of poverty has been firmly established and is still popular under the SAR administration.

As pointed out by Jones and Novak (1999), poverty is not simply a question of low income, though ultimately it is about lacking resources and the command over resources. Poverty is also, equally importantly, a matter of social relations – relations between people, which embody relationships of power, of superiority and inferiority, security and insecurity. Obviously in Hong Kong this view of poverty is not adopted, because recognition of poverty as a set of social relations implies that the solution may involve modifying the distributive mechanism and distributive outcomes. In other words, the distribution of power, social status and material resources such as income and other benefits would have to be modified. Practical policy solutions may include more progressive taxes for high-income earners and enterprises as well as more redistributive rather than disciplinary welfare. This is almost impossible in view of the existing power structure in Hong Kong. Not only did the former colonial government make it clear that social welfare would not be used as a tool to redistribute social resources, this intention has been confirmed by the SAR government as well. For example, in answer to a question concerning government measures to help alleviate poverty at a meeting of the Provisional Legislative Council in September 1997, the Secretary of Financial Services of the SAR government reiterated the importance of activating the market so as to lift up income levels in order to help alleviate poverty:

> The most essential point is that the household income of each and every income group has increased ... As the income level is increasing and also because of the high social mobility, quite a lot of households in Hong Kong have moved to the higher income group ... Therefore, instead of debating on the basis for setting the poverty line, I think we should continue to implement the Government's ongoing policies for helping the poor and providing assistance for those in need in the community (Provisional Legislative Council, Official Record of Proceedings, September 27, 1997).

Again, in a paper submitted to the Welfare Panel of the Legislative Council in November 2001, the SAR government re-emphasized that the best approach to tackling poverty is to foster economic growth, facilitate human investment and increase social investment (Legco Panel on Welfare Services, November 12, 2001). It was stressed in the same paper that the government determined to use the existing CSSA to help vulnerable groups, but "with the purpose of enhancing, not impeding their will to be self-reliant".

The important point here is that the government not only intends to maintain the existing social policy to help the poor, but also to uphold a measure to enforce self-reliance instead of encouraging dependence on social security. The reason underlying this is that the government is very aware of the sharp increase in CSSA cases over the past few years, especially among the unemployed, and if this trend continues government spending on social security might become unsustainable. This led the SAR government to review the implementation of CSSA in 1998, the focus of which was directed towards "support for self-reliance" (Social Welfare Department, 1996). The thrust is to encourage exit from CSSA rather than to encourage use. The main features of "support for self-reliance" are three-fold: providing active employment assistance, requiring able-bodied CSSA recipients to do community service, and providing incentives to work by raising the level of disregarded earnings of CSSA recipients. In a nutshell, the strategy of the government is to use active market measures instead of state provisions to help alleviate poverty. This is supported by the powerful discourse of personal failure and personal responsibility for poverty, which is so prevalent and deeply ingrained in Hong Kong minds.

Apart from adopting the above measures to encourage exit, the government has also been considering reducing the standard rate payment to able-bodied adults and children in larger households (Legco Panel on Welfare Services, December 9, 1998). The rationale behind this is that following the general reduction in wages in the Hong Kong labor market, the income level of larger households claiming benefits, for example households comprising three or more members, has been greater than that of their waged counterparts. So cutting back the CSSA allowance would help to encourage re-entry to the labor market. However, whether the government can help to alleviate poverty by encouraging exit from social security, especially in times of high unemployment, is really doubtful. In the social circumstances of Hong Kong, where people would prefer not to rely on government support if a genuine choice was available, enforcing exit would naturally mean punishing the poor rather than supporting self-reliance. In this light, it would appear only more ironical to suggest that the problem of poverty has been alleviated because the number of CSSA cases has stopped increasing or has even reduced.

CONCLUSION

Poverty has always existed in Hong Kong at different stages of its development. The government, including the former colonial government and the present SAR administration, has endeavored to construct and maintain a discourse of poverty based on personal misfortune and personal failure, so as to strengthen the notion of personal responsibility for its alleviation. The primary strategy of the government is primarily to contain poverty through CSSA and to encourage exit to contain CSSA costs. In this light, it is questionable whether the poor are being punished further or are being more effectively helped. If the government is indeed prepared to build a caring society, an objective which the Chief Executive of the SAR stated his commitment to in his first Policy Address (Tung, 1997), the eradication of poverty must first be included as one of the government's major policy agendas. The problem of poverty also needs to be redefined so as to locate its prevalence within certain institutional contexts, for example distribution of wealth and welfare, social exclusion and deprivation. Strategies which encourage exit from welfare have to be replaced by more empowering measures, including creating opportunities for economic independence. Measures also need to be taken to address age and gender discrimination so that elderly people as well as women engaged in full time domestic labor have access to resources for economic and social independence. Poverty is not a problem that only occurs in times of economic recession. It is a longstanding social phenomenon that the government has to address with due commitment.

REFERENCES

Caserta, M. and Gray, R. (1984). Social Class, Vulnerability, and Depression among Hospitalized Utah Women. *Western Social Science Association Paper.*

Census and Statistics Department (1981). *Census Report,* Hong Kong: Government Printer.

_____ . (1986). *By-Census Report,* Hong Kong: Government Printer.

_____ . (1991). *Census Report,* Hong Kong: Government Printer.

_____ . (1996). *By-Census Report,* Hong Kong: Government Printer.

_____ . (2001). *Census Report,* Hong Kong: SAR Government Printer.

Chiu, S. (1991). Towards a Citizen-Centred Social Policy. *Journal of Policy Viewers,* May 1(1): 3-8 (in Chinese).

Chiu, S. and Wong, V. (1998). Social Policy in Hong Kong: From British Colony to Special Administrative Region of China. *European Journal of Social Work,* 1(2): 231-242.

Dowling, M. (1999). Social Exclusion, Inequality and Social Work. *Social Policy and Administration,* 33(3): 245-61.

Hodge, P. (1977). The Poor and the People of Quality. *Hong Kong Journal of Social Work,* Vol. 11.

Hong Kong Committee of the International Council on Social Welfare (1970). *Hong Kong Report to the 1st International Conference on Social Welfare.* Hong Kong: Hong Kong Council of Social Service.

Hong Kong Government (1960). *Hong Kong Annual Report.* Hong Kong: Government Printer.

_____ . (1964). *Hong Kong Annual Report.* Hong Kong: Government Printer.

_____ . (1973). *Hong Kong Annual Report.* Hong Kong: Government Printer.

_____ . (1974). *The Five Year Plan for Social Welfare Development in Hong Kong: Review.* Hong Kong: Government Printer.

_____ . (1977). *Help for Those Least Able to Help Themselves: A Programme of Social Security Development.* Hong Kong: Government Printer.

_____ . (1981). *Social Welfare into the Nineties.* Hong Kong: Government Printer.

_____ . (1996). *Policy Address.* Hong Kong: Government Printer.

Hong Kong Hansard (1996). 9 October 1996.

Hong Kong Policy Viewers (2000). *A Survey on the Impression of the General Public on People in Poverty in Hong Kong.* Hong Kong: Hong Kong Policy Viewers.

Jones, C. and Novak, T. (1999). *Poverty, Welfare and the Disciplinary State.* London: Routledge.

Jordan, B. (1996). *A Theory of Poverty and Social Exclusion.* Cambridge: Polity Press.

Lau, S.K. and Kuan, H.C. (1988). *The Ethos of Hong Kong Chinese.* Hong Kong: Chinese University Press.

Legco Panel on Welfare Services (2001). *Measures to Address Poverty.* Paper No. CB(2)317/01-02(05), 12 November 2001.

Littlewood, P. et al. (Eds.) (1999). *Social Exclusion in Europe: Problems and Paradigms.* Aldershot: Ashgate.

Lister, R. (1997). *Citizenship: Feminist Perspectives.* N.Y.: New York University Press.

Liu, E. and Wu, J. (1998). *The Measurement of Poverty.* Hong Kong: Research and Library Division, Provisional Legislative Council Secretariat.

MacPherson, S. and Lo, O.Y. (1997). *A Measure of Poverty: Calculating the Number of People in Poverty in Hong Kong*, Hong Kong: City University of Hong Kong.

MacPherson, S. (2001). Hong Kong. In Dixon, J.and D. Macarov (Eds.) *Poverty: A Persistent Global Reality*. London: Routledge.

Mok, T.K. and Leung, S.O. (1997). *Poverty Rate in Hong Kong*. Hong Kong: Hong Kong Social Security in Hong Kong (in Chinese).

Provisional Legislative Council (1997).Official Record of Proceedings, 27 September 1997.

Schervish, P. (1983). *The Structural Determinants of Unemployment: Vulnerability and Power in Market Relations*. New York: Academic Press.

Shi, L. (2001). The Convergence of Vulnerable Characteristics and Health Insurance in the US. *Social Science and Medicine*, 53(4): 519-29.

Social Welfare Department (1996). *Report on Review of Comprehensive Social Security Scheme (CSSA)*. Hong Kong: Government Printer.

Taiwan Executive Yuan Statistics Department (2001). *Statistical Yearbook*. Taiwan: Executive Yuan.

Townsend, P. (1982). *Poverty in the United Kingdom: A Survey of Household Resources and Standard of Living*. CA, Berkeley: University of California Press.

_____ . (1993). *The International Analysis of Poverty*. New York: Harvester Wheatsheaf.

Tung, C.W. (1997). *Policy Address*. Hong Kong: SAR Government Printer.

Turner, B. (2001). The End(s) of Humanity: Vulnerability and the Metaphor of membership. *Hedgehog Review*, 3(2): 7-32.

Walker, R. and Parker, G. (Eds.) (1988). *Money Matters: Income, Wealth and Financial Welfare*. London: Sage Publications.

Witstrom, S. and Witstrom, P. (2001). Why Are Single Parents More Often Threatened with Violence? A Question of Ecological Vulnerability. *International Review of Victimology*, 8(2):183-98.

Williams, F. (1989). *Social Policy: A Critical Introduction: Issue of Race, Gender and Class*. Cambridge: Polity Press.

_____ . (1996). New Thinking on Social Policy Research into Inequality, Social Exclusion and Poverty. *Paper to be published by the Centre for the Analysis of Social Policy, University of Bath, United Kingdom*.

Wong, H. and Chua, H.W. (1996). *The Study of the Spending Pattern of Low Expenditure Households in Hong Kong*. Hong Kong: Hong Kong Council of Social Services and Oxfam Hong Kong.

Wong, H. (2000). The Cause for Poverty in 1990s Hong Kong: Micro, Macro and Metero Analysis. In Mok, H. et al. (eds.) *Poverty and Social Development*, Asian Social Development Series. Hong Kong: Hong Kong Social Security Society and Asia Monitor.

World Bank (2001). *World Development Report, 2000/01*. Washington DC: Oxford University Press.

Younghusband, E. (1960). *Training for Social Workers: A Report Prepared for the Government of Hong Kong,* Hong Kong: Government Printer. http://www.info.gov.hk/censtatd/eng/press/labour2/lb2_latest_index.html.

In: *Poverty Monitoring and Alleviation in East Asia*
K. Tang and C. Wong, editors pp. 75-90

ISBN: 1-59033-828-6
© 2003 Nova Science Publishers, Inc.

Chapter 4

POVERTY MONITORING AND ALLEVIATION IN SINGAPORE

Mui Teng Yap

THE POOR IN SINGAPORE

Singapore, an island-city-state of about 680 sq. km with no natural resources, is generally acknowledged to be an economic success story. The country saw its per capita income (GDP) rise steadily from a mere US $512 in 1965, when it first became an independent nation, to US $22,962 in 2000[1] (Singapore Department of Statistics, 2001). Singapore's GDP continued to grow at an annual rate of 7.7% in the 1990s (Leow, 2001) after more than two decades of growth. More importantly, economic growth has translated into improvements in the wellbeing of the population. Singapore is consistently placed high among the "High Human Development" countries as measured by the United Nations' Human Development Index (UNDP, various years).

Despite these achievements, concern has been raised in recent years over a growing disparity in income, particularly as regards the situation of the lowest income groups (see, for example, Chua Mui Hoong, "Mind the widening income gap", *The Straits Times*, February 11, 2001; Mitton, 2000; Thevarakom, 2001). As Table 4.1 shows, while the average income of the highest earning 10% of households has grown steadily, the bottom 20% have seen their incomes dwindle. Among the lowest earning 10% of households, moreover, monthly income from work averaged only about $500 in 1999 and 2000. The figures dip to $133 and $61, respectively, if households with no income earners are also included. In response to the furore that arose when the $133 figure was highlighted in the media ("Some families lived on $133 a month", *The Straits Times*, May 31, 2000), both the government and labor leaders argued that there was not an "underclass", even among the lowest 10% of Singaporean households (Yeo, 2000; National Trades Union Congress, 2000). This was because these households had assets,

---

[1] US $1 was equivalent, on average, to S $3.06 in 1965 and S $1.72 in 2000. Unless otherwise stated, all the dollars stated in text are in Singaporean dollars.

such as their own homes (typically a public housing flat), consumer durables (color televisions, refrigerators, etc) and savings for old age (their median Central Provident Fund [CPF] savings in 1999 was $20,000). The very low *average* reported, it was explained, was a statistical artifact as a high proportion of the households in this group (amounting to 75% in 1999 and 87% in 2000) had no income earners and therefore no income. These were either households comprised entirely of elderly people (the proportion of retiree households rose from 27% in 1997 to 35% in 1999) or households whose income earners had lost their jobs due to the recession brought on by the Asian financial crisis. According to the Minister for Trade and Industry, George Yeo, the average real income of the bottom 20% of households had actually grown by 0.5% between 1990 and 1998, a rate comparable to that of the United Kingdom and higher than that of the United States and Japan, despite Singapore having a poorer educational profile (Yeo, 2000).

Table 4.1. Average Household Income from Work by Decile among Resident Households

	Average Household Income from Work ($)					Annual Change (%)		
	1990	1007	1998	1999	2000	1998	1999	2000
Total	3,076	4,745	4,822	4,691	4,943	1.6	-2.7	5.4
Lowest 10%	370	327	258	133	61	-21.1	-48.4	-54.1
Excluding Households with No Income Earner	620	716	681	531	459	-4.9	-22.0	-13.6
Next 10%	934	1,352	1,332	1,172	1,145	-1.5	-12.0	-2.3
Next 10%	1,321	2,002	2,005	1,853	1,862	0.1	-7.6	0.5
Next 10%	1,686	2,613	2,647	2,470	2,535	1.3	-6.7	2.6
Next 10%	2,076	3,254	3,305	3,137	3,237	1.6	-5.1	3.2
Next 10%	2,541	4,019	4,097	3,900	4,036	1.9	-4.8	3.5
Next 10%	3,116	4,938	5,034	4,828	5,017	1.9	-4.1	3.9
Next 10%	3,897	6,093	6,271	6,023	6,316	2.9	-4.0	4.9
Next 10%	5,152	7,965	8,221	7,937	8,419	3.2	-3.5	6.1
Top 10%	9,671	14,890	15,053	15,451	16,804	1.1	2.6	8.8

Note: Deciles are based on ranking of all resident households.
Source: Leow (2001).

Be that as it may, Singapore is not without its indigent population. Media reports carry stories of vagrants found begging or sleeping in public places and families found living on beaches, although these are, admittedly, few and far between. Official statistics show that public assistance recipients (comprising the elderly, disabled and destitute who are unable to work and do not have other means of support) number about 2,000 annually in the five years since 1995, down from well over 3,000 in the 1980s and double that number in the 1970s (cf. Lim and Associates, 1988: 423, Table 14C.7). This number is generally regarded to underestimate the number of the needy because of the stringent eligibility criteria used. A Cost Review Committee (CRC), convened in 1996 to look into allegations made by opposition political parties of phenomenal rises in the cost of living, estimated that 41% of households in the lowest quintile in 1992/93 (about 30,000 households) were "genuinely poor" (Ministry of Trade and Industry, 1996). These were households with per capita monthly income of $250 or less that were unable to make ends meet and had no potential to increase their earnings.

The Asian financial crisis hit the lowest 20% of Singaporean households the hardest, although the higher income groups were not spared either (particularly in 1999 – see Table 4.1). Based on a poverty line of $1,040 per month for a family of four or $390 a month for single-person households, the Department of Statistics (DOS) estimated that about 120,000 or 4% of the resident population in 1998 were poor (*The Straits Times*, December 2, 2001). Welfare agencies estimate that there are 100,000 households comprising single people and families with a low level of education, living in the smaller public housing units who earn less than $500 a month and cannot make ends meet (Thevarakom, 2001). Perhaps more than the Asian financial crisis from which Singapore is generally acknowledged to have escaped relatively unscathed, however, the worldwide economic slowdown of 2001, aggravated by the terrorist attack on the US on September 11, is likely to have the greater impact on Singapore (see *Business Times*, December 18, 2001). Currently in its worst recession since independence, Singapore was the first among the Asian economies to go under. Retrenchments are expected to have reached 25,000 by end-2001 and the unemployment rate 4.5%. While economists are optimistic about the prospects for 2002, with some academics forecasting that the growth rate will rise to 6-7%, the business community is less sanguine. In any case, schools and various grassroots and voluntary welfare agencies have reported larger numbers of families coming forward for financial assistance ("Crisis forces 800 more to seek handout", *Today*, December 3, 2001; "Can't pay fees – more ask schools for help" and "Record 3,600 families get Hari Raya cash gifts", *The Straits Times*, December 10, 2001). The total prevalence of the poor is difficult to know, however, given that the affected could have sought assistance from multiple sources. Unlike during the Asian financial crisis, it is mainly middle-class families who have reportedly turned up for assistance as more professionals, managers and executives have lost their jobs. Jobs, retrenchment and social safety nets for the unemployed were hot campaign issues in the most recent general elections held on November 3, 2001.

As mentioned, public assistance in Singapore is targeted at a very specific group – the poorest of the poor who are unable to help themselves and have no other support. In addition, there is a wide range of poverty alleviation measures aimed at providing temporary relief until individuals and families become self-reliant again. There is also a strong emphasis on the role of the family as the first line of support, followed by the community. The economic downturn of 2001, particularly if prolonged, will test the viability of this "Singapore approach" (Chua Mui Hoong, "Are there enough life-boats for the jobless?" *The Straits Times*, July 18, 1998; Yap Chuin Wei, "Need for a rethink on how Govt. helps poor?" *The Straits Times*, May 31, 2001). Looking forward, new groups of the poor are also likely to surface as the Singapore economy restructures to meet the challenges of globalization. One such group, as shown below, would be workers with low education levels, currently in their forties and fifties, who would not be able to compete effectively in the new economy due to lack of the necessary skills. The number of single elderly people who never married and might be without family support is also likely to grow. This is on top of the expected increase in the number of elderly, particularly the very old, as life expectancy rises and people live longer. Being better educated, the future elder generation could be more vocal in making demands on the government to provide for them.

POVERTY MONITORING

Statistical Monitoring[2]

In Singapore, the DOS is the main government agency that publishes statistics on income distribution and generates measures of poverty. Absolute poverty is measured based on the Minimum Household Expenditure (MHE) required for a family of four. Actual expenditure on subsistence items, comprising food, clothing and shelter, obtained from five yearly Household Expenditure Surveys (the last conducted in 1997/98) is computed and then "grossed up with a multiplier of 1.25 to account for the other necessary expenditure for normal living (Ang, 1999: 3). On the other hand, relative poverty is measured "based on a poverty line defined as half of the median per capita household income" (ibid.: 4). Adjustments are made for household size and composition using "OECD equivalence scales … for countries in a similar stage of development" (ibid.).[3]

As Ang (1999) has noted, the income measure used is based only on income from work and thus excludes other forms of income. This has important implications, particularly for elderly households for whom transfer and other incomes are an important source of financial wellbeing. For example, the 1995 National Survey of Senior Citizens in Singapore found that children provided regular cash contributions to 76% of the senior citizens (aged 55 and older) studied, and some had income from assets and investment (Ministry of Health et al., 1996). It should be noted, moreover, that households living in better quality housing, defined as four-room or larger public housing units and private housing are also excluded from poverty study.

As household surveys are the main sources of data for the measurement of poverty, the relevance of the information depends on the frequency of these surveys. Data on income distribution, and thus the income-based measures of poverty, are more readily available as these are based on Labor Force Surveys that are conducted quarterly by the Ministry of Manpower. On the other hand, household expenditure surveys, on which MHEs are based, are conducted only at five-year intervals. This could have an impact on the relevance of data, particularly in periods of rapid change such as at present.

More importantly, however, information on the poverty line or the incidence of poverty is neither widely known nor readily available to the public. Indeed, the label "the poor" is avoided, because of its stigmatizing effect (Indra Chelliah, MCDS, personal communication 2001). Moreover, no single definition of the poor is used in policies towards this group; rather, various ministries study the information on the bottom 20% identified by the DOS to determine groups that might require assistance (ibid.).

---

[2] This section draws heavily on Ang (1999).

[3] In Singapore, equivalence scales are not available as the survey data on household expenditure exclude one-person households. The absolute poverty line is first derived from the MHE for a reference four person household. The poverty lines for households of other sizes are then derived using the OECD equivalence scales which can be used for countries at a similar stage of development that have not established their own equivalence scales. The OECD equivalence scales are: single adult 1.0, second and subsequent adults 0.7, each child 0.5 (Ang, 1999: 4).

Monitoring in Practice

In practice, monitoring and identification of the needy is carried out by a slew of government, grassroots and voluntary agencies and individuals in Singapore. This is because the government has adopted a "many helping hands" approach to welfare provision, and programs and services are run and administered by agencies at multiple levels (see below). In particular, great emphasis has been placed in recent years on community-based self-help schemes, with the establishment of the (electoral) constituency-based Community Development Councils (CDCs) and ethnically-based self-help groups, whereby the better-off members in the community are encouraged to help the weaker members[4]. In this regard, neighbors and grassroots leaders have been asked to act as the "eyes and ears" of the CDCs to identify members of the community who might need assistance but are either too shy or ignorant to seek help (Ng Boon Yian, "Misery Scouts; Scheme to help those who won't help themselves", *Today* August 24, 2001). As another example, grassroots leaders in the Citizens' Consultative Committees (CCCs), whose task is to implement the Economic Downturn Relief Scheme initiated by the government in 2001 to help families in difficulty meet their household expenses, are encouraged to visit applicants to determine the merit of the cases ("CCCs give $1.3m to needy in first month", *The Straits Times* December 6, 2001). This is not to say, however, that the government has relinquished its responsibilities. While the MCDS has, with effect from April 2001, relinquished its role as a direct provider of services and concentrates instead on regulatory and financial support roles, it also seconds its officials to the CDCs to identify cases eligible for government programs. Public officials such as schoolteachers and principals, and medical social workers in public hospitals, also serve as referral points for the needy.

Thus, in summary, there is a wide network of monitors and "monitoring agents" to identify those in need. This is especially important in a culture where dependency on welfare is viewed with embarrassment, if not shame. However, as is evident from media coverage, there remain (mostly isolated) cases that have apparently escaped this net. Some may have done so by choice. However, there could be another problem in that the slew of programs, and the various eligibility criteria adopted, are too confusing and complicated even for the better-educated, not to mention the poor who are usually either quite old or have little education. Ignorance of entitlements is another problem. To assist the public navigate the web of assistance programs and services, one-stop centers have been set up in the CDCs and a single-number nationwide hotline is also available. In the words of the head of a voluntary welfare organization, "There is help for anyone who knows how to pick up the phone and look for help [and the role of the] voluntary welfare organization is to teach and empower people to pick up that phone" (Thevarakom, 2001: 14). However, others have also pointed out

---

[4] CDCs are part of the effort to build community bonds and promote social cohesion. It is also felt that being closer to the ground, they are in a better position to identify and meet the needs of local communities. Services that used to be provided directly by the government are increasingly being devolved to the CDCs. There are currently five CDCs covering the entire island. Ethnically-based self-help groups were introduced on the assumption that members of the same ethnic community would be better able to communicate with their more disadvantaged members, particularly in sensitive areas. There are now five such self-help groups, one each for the Chinese, Indians and Eurasians, and two for Malays/Muslims. It should be noted, however, that programs initiated by self-help groups are not necessarily confined to the respective communities. For example, tuition and financial assistance programs reach out to all ethnic groups.

that low-income families "often get their phone lines and electricity cut off because of inability to pay their bills" (ibid.: 10).

While it is appreciated that the cautious Singapore approach is a response to concern over possible abuse and over-dependence on welfare if it is too readily available, anecdotal evidence also suggests that Singaporeans do not view reliance on welfare positively. A study should be conducted to determine if official perception coincides with reality. The outcome should help shape future policy directions, and perhaps help answer the question of whether the programs and procedures can be simplified. Moreover, under the multi-agency approach to the provision of services, it is also possible for the needy to receive assistance from multiple sources. For this reason, it is rather difficult to assess accurately the number and prevalence of the poor in the country. A national survey on the poor (under whatever label) would also be helpful.

Poverty Alleviation

Singapore's approach to poverty alleviation is built on the adage: "Give me a fish, I eat for a day; Teach me to fish, I eat for a lifetime" (Ministry of Community Development and Sports, n.d). As the Permanent Secretary of the Ministry of Community Development and Sports, Lim Soo Hoon, explained in her statement at the World Summit on Social Development in Geneva in June 2000 (paragraph 17):

> The key thrust of Singapore's social policy is creating the conditions such that every Singaporean has equal opportunities for education, a job and a home. Opportunities and support [are available] to help the disadvantaged level up with the rest of the population ... through education, training, skills upgrading to remain employable and a network of social services.

The government is supported by the labor movement, as Minister without Portfolio and Secretary-General of the National Trades Union Congress, Lim Boon Heng (2000), also noted: "We recognised very early that the best welfare that we can provide for a worker is a job" (see also Lim, 1999). This is probably because of the inauspicious circumstances that prevailed at the time Singapore's first-generation leaders inherited the mantle of government from the British colonial administration in the 1950s. These included rapid population growth (from a high birth rate as well as in-migration), massive unemployment, and the problems of poverty and urban slums. As Goh Keng Swee, one of Singapore's first generation leaders who is also generally recognized as the architect of the Singapore economy, noted: "The PAP (People's Action Party) Government ... decided that the way to help the poor was to provide more work and abolish unemployment" (Goh, 1995c: 197). According to Goh, there was no other choice as the country had no natural wealth to redistribute.

Singapore, moreover, learned from the negative experiences of state welfarism experienced in the more developed countries. According to Senior Minister Lee Kuan Yew, also Singapore's founding Prime Minister:

> Watching the ever increasing costs of the welfare state in Britain and Sweden, we decided to avoid this debilitating system. We noted ... that when governments undertook primary responsibility for the basic duties of the head of a family, the drive in people weakened.

Welfare undermined self-reliance. People did not have to work for their families' wellbeing. The handout became a way of life. The downward spiral was relentless as motivation and productivity went down. People lost the drive to achieve because they paid too much in taxes. They became dependent on the state for their basic needs" (Lee 2000: 126).

Singapore's policies, according to Lee, are aimed at keeping people "keen to achieve their best" (ibid.: 129). Subsidies are given, but only in education, housing and public health as these "improved the earning power of citizens" (ibid.: 116). A cautious approach is adopted otherwise – "We decided each matter in a pragmatic way, always mindful of possible abuse and waste" (ibid.). In Lee's view, however, "there will always be the irresponsible or incapable, some 5 per cent of our population ... [who] will run through any asset, whether a house or shares. We try hard to make them as independent as possible and not end up in welfare homes. More important, we try to rescue their children from repeating the feckless ways of their parents. We have arranged to help them in such a way that only those who have no other choice will seek it" (ibid.: 128-9). This hard-headed, and some may say hard-hearted, view of welfarism continues to be pursued by the current generation of leaders in government. This message was reiterated most recently by the Prime Minister in his annual National Day Rally speech in August 2001 when he said that: "The Government ... will ensure that every Singaporean has equal and maximum opportunity to advance himself, while providing a social safety net to prevent the minority who cannot cope, from falling through" (Goh, 2001). More recently, in January 2002, he also warned that: "While (the government) will increase the resources of the CDCs ... this does not mean that we are moving into becoming more of a welfare state. We must never allow a dependency mentality to be built up among Singaporeans. The premise of all such assistance is that it is temporary in nature. It is lending a hand to help Singaporeans in need to stand up on their own two feet again, not to weaken their spirit to help themselves" (ibid.).

Approach

As mentioned, the Singapore government has adopted a "many helping hands" approach to the delivery of social services. The family has been identified as the first line of support for individuals in need of assistance and, where needed, it will be supported by the community, comprising the CDCs, voluntary welfare organizations, grassroots political organizations, the National Trades Union Congress (NTUC), as well as businesses. The Government's part in the network is that of a planner, provider and regulator. It provides premises, financial and other resources to civic and community groups and acts as a "catalyst" to the voluntary sector (see Ministry of Community Development and Sports, 1997: 3). The government funds 90% of the development expenditure of voluntary welfare organizations and 50% of their recurrent expenditures. Particularly with the establishment of the CDCs in 1997, social service delivery functions have been gradually devolved to these organizations while the MCDS concentrates on policy formulation and regulation. The devolution was completed in April 2001, when the MCDS' Community Action Fund, which supports various financial assistance schemes, was fully transferred to the CDCs. The latter's functions have also grown (as originally envisaged by the Prime Minister who initiated the idea of setting up CDCs) to include job placements, student services, care of the elderly and community security, among others.

MEASURES ON EMPLOYMENT AND EMPLOYABILITY

Given the emphasis on employment and self-reliance in Singapore's social policy, it is no surprise that education has been one of the three most highly subsidized social provisions by the government (the other two being healthcare and housing). The government has assured Singaporeans that no one will be deprived of an education (or healthcare or housing, for that matter) for financial reasons (Goh, 2001). Financial assistance is readily available for children from low-income families and this may take the form of a waiver of school fees, textbook grants and/or bursaries. The Ministry of Education (MOE) gives financial assistance to students whose net monthly family income does not exceed $500 (for families with one or two children) or $600 (for families with three or more children). Fees may be waived fully or partially; textbook grants are provided together with bursaries for higher-level students. Edusave Merit Bursaries, funded by a government endowment fund, are given to the top 25% of students from families earning less than $3,000 a month, as an incentive for them to perform better. Children from families where neither parent has GCE O or N Level passes and each earns below $750 a month at the time of application are eligible for bursaries under the Small Families Improvement Scheme. Introduced in the 1980s as an incentive for lowly-educated, low-income couples to limit their family size to no more than two children, the scheme also provides a housing grant to own HDB flats. The grants can be revoked if the couple exceeds the family size limit. Besides such government-funded schemes, assistance may be obtained from a whole gamut of community-based organizations and, as mentioned, schools often act as referrals. For its part, the NTUC gives a $100 education grant to every school-going child of union members who are strapped for cash to help defray expenses associated with starting school.

Children from low-income families cared for in school-based or community-based childcare centers may also receive fee assistance. The Centre-based Financial Assistance Scheme for Childcare (CFAC) provides low-income families with a monthly subsidy for childcare. Besides helping low-income working mothers put their children into childcare centers, it is also aimed at giving young children whose mothers cannot work outside the home because of household responsibilities a chance to attend a childcare center and benefit from developmental programs. The scheme also provides a one-off cash benefit to meet "start-up" costs (e.g. for deposits, uniforms, the first month's fees and insurance).

For those seeking or in employment, the Skills Development Fund (SDF) under the Productivity and Standards Board (PSB) provides assistance for training and skills upgrading among workers who earn not more than $1,500 monthly and/or have post-secondary ('A' levels) or lower qualifications. In October 2001, the government increased its contribution to the Fund as part of the off-budget package to help tide Singaporeans over the recession. According to Deputy Prime Minister Lee Hsien Loong who announced the package, "with the top-up, the SDF can further intensify its promotion of skills upgrading, particularly in certifiable skills. Efforts in continuing education and training will also be stepped up" (Lee, 2001). At the same time, the government also increased its support to the Skills Redevelopment Programme (SRP), set up by the NTUC in 1996 for the retraining of older workers. With effect from November 1, 2001, the government increased the training allowance for unemployed and temporarily laid-off workers attending full-time and part-time SRP training, while employers who send their workers for training also receive increased absentee payroll support. The objective is to make it more attractive for employers to retain and train their workers and for unemployed workers to upgrade their skills. The Government also injected more funds into the NTUC's Education and Training Fund, on a 3-to-1 matching basis (NTUC, 2000).

To assist job seekers, the Ministry of Manpower runs an employment exchange that provides free services, giving priority to job seekers who are sole breadwinners or have low household incomes. With the current downturn and rise in retrenchment and unemployment, the MOM, together with the CDCs and employers, have organized job fairs and job-matching services for all, including the better educated. The Ministry also provides one-off interest-free loans not exceeding $2,000 through the Self-Employment Assistance Scheme to encourage the needy to be self-reliant. Over and above the loan, a one-off grant from MCDS' charitable fund helps applicants pay for the first month's rental and utilities deposit and purchase of equipment. Reflecting the close tripartite relationship between government, labor and employers in Singapore, labor accepted work freezes and wage and CPF cuts in 1999, while calling on employers to minimize unemployment by retrenching only as a last resort.

SOCIAL ASSISTANCE SCHEMES

Table 4.2 presents a list of assistance schemes available to low-income and, more recently, middle-income families, as well as the elderly. As the table shows, these are wide ranging and cover a range of basic needs.

Table 4.2. Types of Assistance

	For Low-income Families	For Middle-income Families	For the Elderly
Cash	Public assistance scheme provides $230-$670 per month depending on household size	Economic Downturn Relief Scheme gives retrenched workers up to $200/month for 3 months	Public assistance scheme provides $230-$670 per month depending on household size
	Interim (Short-term) Financial Assistance Scheme provides a monthly grant	New Singapore Shares	Interim (Short-term) Financial Assistance scheme gives a monthly grant over a period of time
	Economic Downturn Relief Scheme provides $200 monthly for 3 months Short-term financial help from CDCs New Singapore Shares		New Singapore Shares

Table 4.2. Types of Assistance (Continued)

	For Low-income Families	For Middle-income Families	For the Elderly
Food	Vouchers for groceries and household items at participating shops in the neighborhood through various CDC schemes		Neighborhood Meal Program provides meals several times a week at senior activities centers (NE, CDC) Community Outreach Program for Elderly (COPE) provides meals on wheels, laundry and medical support and help with housekeeping Vouchers for groceries at participating shops in the neighborhood through various CDC schemes
Housing and Utilities	Postpone monthly payment for flat for up to one year Stretch loans to 30 years Make family members joint owners so that their CPF can also be used Get help of $90/month for utilities and $35/month for conservancy fee up to 3 months If renting flat, can apply for more subsidies under the RUAS for 6 months	Postpone monthly payments for flat for up to one year Extend loan repayment to 30 years Make family members joint owners so that their CPF can also be used	If renting a flat, can apply for more subsidies under the RUAS for 6 months
Health	Medical assistance schemes by CDCs 10% off hospital bill if warded in B2 or C class ward or when going for subsidized day surgery If retrenched, a further 40% off	10% off hospital bill if warded in B2 or C class ward or when going for subsidized day surgery If retrenched, a further 40% off	Free clinics Primary Care Partnership Scheme for people who are 65 and above with personal incomes of less than $700 10% off hospital bill if warded in B2 or C class ward or when going for subsidized day surgery If retrenched, a further 40% off

Source: Adapted from Ministry of Manpower (n.d.).

Cash Assistance

The Public Assistance (PA) scheme, as mentioned, provides financial assistance to Singapore citizens who are unable to work because of old age, ill health or disability and have no one to depend on. The grant, currently $230 for a single person household to $670 for a household of four (equivalent to 10% and 18% of median incomes from work in 2000[5]), is provided for meeting household expenses. There is also a parallel scheme for permanent residents, the Special Grant (SG). The majority (80%) currently on PA are the elderly. Other recipients include people with learning or physical disabilities, the medically unfit, abandoned families and widows with young children. Households on PA also receive in-kind assistance as well as assistance with medical care and rent and utilities if they live in rental HDB flats. The Interim Financial Assistance Scheme provides for individuals or families who need short-term financial help to tide them over a difficult period. A monthly grant, given for up to three months in the first instance, is to help meet day-to-day expenses. As mentioned, the Economic Downturn Relief Scheme was introduced as part of the off-budget package in October 2001 to help families whose breadwinners have been retrenched or who have fallen ill. From November 1, 2001, cash assistance of up to $200 a month is given for three months and subject to review thereafter. CDCs and voluntary work organizations also initiated their own short-term financial assistance schemes.

An innovative scheme introduced in 2001 is the New Singapore Shares, a scheme mooted by Prime Minister Goh to "help especially the less well-off" (Goh, 2001). Under this scheme, PA recipients, residents of welfare homes and those earning not more than $1,200 per month receive an allocation of 1,200-1,700 shares (depending on age and national service status) and those earning above $4,000 only 200 shares (housing type is used as a proxy measure for the self-employed and those not in employment). The shares, valued at $1 each, are non-tradable but may be cashed (half immediately upon the scheme coming into effect in November 2001). Shares held earn dividends at a rate depending on the performance of the economy. The scheme matures in 2007. As with all government wealth redistribution schemes, entitlement to receive the shares is conditional on a $100 contribution to the individual's CPF account. In cases where individuals are unable to make the contribution, families and even welfare agencies may assist.

Food

In-kind assistance in the form of groceries and food vouchers are given out by various community-based and voluntary organizations. The elderly may also receive assistance in the form of meals-on-wheels services or at participating stalls at food centers.

Housing and Utilities

While the majority of Singaporeans (except for those with monthly family incomes exceeding $8,000[6]) are entitled to purchase subsidized public housing and apply for low-interest loans from the Housing and Development Board (HDB) under the government's homeownership scheme, there are also special schemes to assist low-income families to own their own homes. These include the sale of three-room flats at subsidized or discounted rates

---

[5] According to the results of the 2000 Census, the median monthly income from work among the resident population aged 15 and over was S $2,234. For households (averaging 3.7 each), the median monthly income was S $3,607.

to families with monthly incomes of less than $1,500; sale of four-room budget flats at lower prices; and larger mortgage loans amounting to 95% of the selling price. Rent is subsidized for households earning $800 or less. The Rents and Utilities Assistance Scheme (RUAS) assists needy families living in HDB 1-3 room rental flats, who are in arrears of rent, utilities and services and conservancy charges. The scheme provides subsidies for payment, subject to a cap. In view of the current recession and rising unemployment, there is also financial assistance for HDB lessees with difficulties servicing mortgage loans as a result of wage cuts, retrenchment or business failure. These include reduced repayments, deferment of monthly mortgages of 6-12 months and extension of loan repayment periods. More than 11,000 homeowners have been helped under the various schemes in the first ten months of 2001, up from about 10,000 for the whole of 2000 ("HDB's lifeline for flat owners", *Today* December 29, 2001). Nearly 6,000 chose to reduce their repayments while about 3,800 had their loans deferred.

Healthcare

In Singapore, the government subsidizes medical care in all public and restructured hospitals, with the size of the subsidy varying from 20% for a class B1 ward to 80% for a C class ward[7]. Those who cannot afford to pay for B2 and C class wards can also apply to the hospital's Medical Social Worker for Medifund, a government endowment fund to help patients who have difficulty paying their hospital bills. The government also heavily subsidizes outpatient services provided at polyclinics, the average subsidy ranging from 50% for adults to 75% for children and senior citizens. Patients who are unable to pay can also apply for remission or waiver of fees. As part of the off-budget package announced in October, the hospitalization fee assistance scheme provides for a 10% rebate on all class B2 and C hospital bills and on subsidized day surgery. Retrenched Singapore citizens and their immediate family members can apply for additional help to cover 40% of their bills. Together with the 10% rebate, retrenched citizens will effectively enjoy a 50% reduction in their hospitalization bills.

Impact of Poverty Alleviation Activities and Prospects

It is quite clear from various indicators cited throughout this paper, that the abject poverty that characterized many developing countries, and even pockets within developed countries, has been eliminated in Singapore. As Lim and his associates (1988) have noted, the government's strategy of employment creation has succeeded in reducing the level of poverty in Singapore over the last three or so decades. Policies on the CPF, health, education and housing have also helped (Low and Aw, 1997). Judging by recent developments, the

---

[6] The ceiling is S $10,000 for applicants of executive condominiums.

[7] Beds in public hospitals are classified into ward classes – A1, A2, B1, B2 and C – depending on the level of physical amenities such as the number of beds in the ward and the availability of telephones, television and air-conditioning. "A" class wards, which are the most luxurious and afford the most privacy, are regarded as "private" wards and patients are charged the full cost of their treatment, while "C" class wards are the cheapest for patients because of government subsidy. Patients have a choice of ward class on admission. Financial counseling is also available to help patients choose the most appropriate ward class.

government has also been flexible and responsive to the changing needs of the population, the retrenched and financially distressed. Indeed, as a veteran journalist Seah Chiang Nee has noted, the government seems to have broken a taboo on providing unemployment benefits (Seah, 2001). According to Seah, it is also returning to its socialist roots after decades of steadily reducing subsidies.[8]

While this approach has worked well in the past, it remains to be seen whether it will continue to work in the future. First, social workers and observers have expressed concern over the "working poor" with incomes corresponding roughly to the second lowest decile and who have no access to assistance (Thevarakom, 2001). Often holding more than one job to make ends meet, they would have difficulty coping with illness, caring for elderly household members and other life emergencies. In recent times, too, some observers have also warned of an emergent "permanent underclass" comprising able-bodied young from low-income families who seem unwilling or unable to break out of their disadvantaged circumstances (Thevarakom, 2001). The extent to which this intergenerational transmission of poverty is prevalent is not known, and respondents interviewed for this study often profess not to be aware of these.

There are limits to a social policy based on employment and family support, especially given the restructuring of the Singapore economy and the ageing of the population. This has been acknowledged indirectly by the Prime Minister as he warned that "in the new economic environment, we do need to do more to support lower-income Singaporeans" (Goh, 2001). New groups of the poor are likely to surface in the future that are unable to cope with the demands of the labor market and who may have no family support.

As Lian (2001a) has noted, there is a large pool of middle-aged Singaporeans with below-secondary education who may lack the skills and qualifications for the new knowledge-based economy. While the government has been promoting training, retraining and lifelong learning, it is not certain to what extent they can be or desire to be retrained. They will have to compete with low-cost foreign workers and will have difficulty staying employed. Further, as the number of elderly increases, and as the old live longer, they are more and more likely to outlive their savings.

In conclusion, the Singapore government has been responsive to the growing need of its citizenry for assistance during the current economic downturn. Increasingly, however, there are also voices that it needs to review the adequacy of the existing safety nets (see Davidson and Drakakis-Smith, 1997: 98; Mukul Asher, cited in Chua, 1998, *The Straits Times* December 6, 2001; Lian, 2001b). As mentioned, structural changes in the population, as well as the economy, are likely to throw up vulnerable groups that will need assistance, and perhaps on a longer term basis than is currently the case. Moreover, some economists have predicted that the economy, unlike in the past, is more likely to be subject to major swings in the future. The corollary is an increased likelihood of unemployment over the life course. This could also have an impact on the ability of Singaporeans to save (either privately or through the Central Provident Fund) for their old age security.

In view of all the uncertainties, the Singapore government has embarked on a major exercise to review existing policies and to identify ways to "remake" Singapore. Among other things, income disparity and social safety nets would also be subject to review (see Remaking

---

[8] The People's Action Party (PAP), which has been in government since 1959 when Singapore was granted internal self-government, was founded as a democratic socialist party in 1954.

Singapore, 2002). According to Seah (2001), the old social contract where government delivered jobs in return for political support no longer works in the new, globally competitive world. This makes the alternative of mitigating the impact of unemployment crucially important (ibid.). Government leaders have promised that no stone will remain unturned in the current review exercises. It remains to be seen whether state welfarism will in the long term be part of Singapore's social policy, given that the government (at least the PAP government) has always adopted a pragmatic approach in responding to changing circumstances.

In the short to medium term, however, one suggestion would be for the introduction of a low-cost, endowment-type unemployment insurance scheme through the CPF. This could be along the lines of the Medishield scheme and the proposed Eldershield scheme whereby an individual's monthly contribution may be used as premiums, respectively, for catastrophic illness and long-term care insurance run by the CPF. While the government has rightly rejected calls for CPF savings to be drawn to tide-over periods of unemployment (on the grounds that the Fund is meant to provide for old age security), a risk-pooling insurance scheme appears sensible. Funds not drawn as well as investment income can be redistributed back to contributors at their retirement, thus fulfilling the fundamental objective of the CPF, i.e. old age security. While the addition of an unemployment insurance function would probably increase the burden on the already complex CPF system in Singapore, it could also draw from the excessive over-investment in housing using CPF savings (see Low and Aw, 1997). Singaporeans may be better served in this way.

Currently, there are also numerous schemes that provide ad hoc financial and training assistance, involving substantial public funds. While the objective of these highly targeted schemes to keep Singaporeans "on their toes" and not be over-reliant on welfare is appreciated, it is suggested that their consolidation into a unified "social development" fund may be useful. This would facilitate the adoption of a holistic approach towards solving the problems of the needy in terms of their training and employment, as well as other social-financial needs, that is long-term and that preserves the dignity of the assisted. This is particularly important given that structural and long-term unemployment could become a reality.

In some ways, it is early days yet in the guessing game of what will unfold in terms of the changes in the world and in Singapore, making predictions difficult. Whatever the outcome, the importance of social cohesion cannot be overemphasized in a small, compact multiracial society such as Singapore. Will Singapore become a welfare state in the name of social cohesion (or solidarity, as in Europe)? It is difficult to say at this point.

REFERENCES

Ang, Seow Long (1999). Country Paper on Poverty Measurement: The Case of Singapore. Seminar on Poverty Statistics, organized by the United Nations Economic and Social Commission for Asia and the Pacific, Bangkok, 21-23 June 1999. (www.unescap.org/stat/povstat/pov7_sig.pdf).

Chua, Mui Hoong (1998). Are There Enough Life-Boats For The Jobless? *The Straits Times* 18 July 1998.

Davidson, Gillian and Drakakis-Smith, David (1997). The Price of Success: Disadvantaged Groups in Singapore. In Chris Dixon and David Drakakis-Smith (Eds.), *Underdevelopment in South East Asia*. Aldershot: Ashgate.

Goh, Chok Tong (2001, 19 August). National Day Rally Speech 2001. Singapore: Ministry of Information and the Arts.

_____ . (2002, 5 January). Speech by Prime Minister Goh Chok Tong at the Swearing-in of the Mayors of Community Development Council Districts on Saturday, January 5, 2002. Retrieved from http://app.internet.gov.sg/data/sprinter/pr/archives/2002010503.htm

Goh, Keng Swee (1995a). Man and Economic Development. In Goh Keng Swee, *The Economics of Modernization*. Singapore: Federal Publications. (Reprinted from Commerce, Journal of the Commerce Society, Nanyang University, Volume 1, No 4, November).

_____ . (1995b). Population Control. In Goh Keng Swee, *The Economics of Modernization*. Singapore: Federal Publications. (Reprinted speech delivered on 1 October 1969 at the International Monetary Fund/International Bank for Reconstruction and Development Annual Meetings in Washington).

_____ . (1995c). Labour in a Technological Society. In Goh Keng Swee, *The Practice of Economic Growth*. Singapore: Federal Publications, 1995. (Reprinted paper delivered at the NTUC Symposium on "Labour in a Technological Society Today – An Action Programme for the Seventies", April 27 –May 1, 1973).

Lee, Hsien Loong (2001). Speech by Deputy Prime Minister Lee Hsien Loong in Parliament, October 12, 2001. Retrieved from http://app.internet.gov.sg/data/sprinter/pr/archives/2001101204.htm

Lee, Kuan Yew (2000). *From Third World to First; The Singapore Story: 1965-2000*. Singapore: Times Media and Straits Times Press.

Leow, Bee Geok (2001). *Census of Population 2000 Advance Data Release*. Singapore: Department of Statistics.

Lian, Daniel (2001a). Structural Unemployment – A Key Challenge. Singapore: Morgan Stanley Dean Witter Equity Research Asia/Pacific (21 August).

_____ . (2001b). Stone Turning Exercise for 2002. Singapore: Morgan Stanley Equity Research Asia/Pacific (14 December).

Lim, Boon Heng (1999). How Unions in Singapore Work with the Government to Establish Social Safety Net. NTUC Speech 5 October 1999. Retrieved from http://www.ntucworld.org.sg/ntuc3/ospeech/19991006162728.htm

Lim, Boon Heng (2000). Speech by Mr. Lim Boon Heng, Secretary General of NTUC and Minister without Portfolio at the Reception for Participants of the 17th Regional Conference of the IFCTU-APRO. Publication date: November 8, 2000. Retrieved from http://www.ntucworld.org.sg/ntuc3/ospeech/20001109092039.htm.

Lim, Chong Yah and Associates (1988). Poverty, Income Distribution and the Less Privileged. In Lim, Chong Yah et al. (Eds.) *Policy Options for the Singapore Economy* (Chapter 14). Singapore: McGraw-Hill.

Lim, Soo Hoon (2000, June). Singapore. Statement by Ms Lim Soo Hoon, Permanent Secretary, Ministry of Community Development and Sports (Head of Delegation for Singapore to the World Summit for Social Development and Beyond: achieving social development for all in a globalising world, UN, Geneva.) Retrieved from http://www.un.org/socialsummit/speeches/286sin.html.

Low, Linda and Tar Choon, Aw (1997). *Housing a Healthy, Educated and Wealthy Nation*. Singapore: Times Academic Press for the Institute of Policy Studies.

Mitton, Roger (2000, 10 November). For Richer or Poorer. *Asiaweek*.

National Trades Union Congress (2000). Income Disparity, Yes. Underclass, No! – Summary of parliamentary discussion on Income Disparity. Publication date: June 29, 2000. Retrieved from http://www.ntucworld.org.sg/ntuc3/ostate/20000703094923.htm.

Remaking Singapore (2002). Retrieved from http://www.remakingsingapore.gov.sg.

Seah Chiang Nee (2001). Socialism Revisited. 20 October. Retrieved from http://www.littlespeck.com/content/economy/CTrendsEconomy-011020.html

Singapore Department of Statistics (2001). Selected Historical Data. Retrieved from http://www.singstat.gov.sg/FACT/HIST/gdp.html

Singapore Ministry of Community Development and Sports (1997). Helping Low Income Families – The Singapore Way. Singapore: The Author.

Singapore Ministry of Community Development and Sports. (n.d.). Social Assistance – Policy. Retrieved from http://www.mcds.gov.sg/HTML/soc_asst/socasst_fr.html.

Singapore Ministry of Health, Ministry of Community Development, Department of Statistics, Ministry of Labour and National Council of Social Service. (1996). *The National Survey of Senior Citizens in Singapore 1995*. Singapore: The Author.

Singapore Ministry of Manpower. (n.d.). Assistance Schemes for Individuals and Families. Retrieved from http://www.employmenttown.gov.sg/ecareer/solutioncontent/1,1380,151,00.html

Singapore Ministry of Trade and Industry (1996). *Report of the Cost Review Committee 1996*.

Thevarakom, Margaret (2001, July-August). *Faces of Poverty Singapore*. Singapore: Singapore International Foundation.

United Nations Development Programme (Various years). *Human Development Report*. New York: Oxford University Press for the UNDP.

Yeo, George (2000). Minister of Trade and Industry, George Yeo's Reply to Questions Relating to Income Disparity. Parliament, 29 June 2000. Retrieved from http://app.internet.gov.sg/data/sprinter/pr/archives/2000062908.htm

In: *Poverty Monitoring and Alleviation in East Asia*
K. Tang and C. Wong, editors pp. 91-103

ISBN: 1-59033-828-6
© 2003 Nova Science Publishers, Inc.

Chapter 5

POVERTY AND ANTI-POVERTY MEASURES IN SOUTH KOREA

Sunwoo Lee and Meegon Kim

INTRODUCTION

The economic crisis in South Korea (Korea) in 1997 has totally changed its socio-economic landscape. The most significant fall-out from the crisis has been high unemployment rates. The Korean economy had been characterized by low unemployment rates and low wages from the 1960s. These were the main impetus for the outstanding economic development in the 1970s and 1980s. However, the Asian financial crisis radically changed this situation in 1997. The unemployment rate leapt from 2.6% (0.6 million) in the 4th quarter of 1997 to 6.9% (1.5 million) in the 2nd quarter of 1998, reaching 8.4% (1.7 million) in the 1st quarter of 1999 (see Table 5.1). The unemployment rate started to go down after peaking in the 1st quarter of 1999, but has never recovered to its low levels before the economic crisis. Table 5.1 shows the number of unemployed increased from 0.56 million in 1997 to 1.5 million in 1998 due to the economic crisis, and decreased to 1.0 million in 1999 due to the availability of social safety nets. However, it should be pointed out that many unemployed people stayed out of the labor market because they could not find jobs. They gave up their job search but were in fact available for work. Moreover, according to government statistics, if a person has worked just one hour during the previous week, he/she is considered "employed". Participants in community work schemes are considered "employed" and participants in job training are categorized as "economically inactive." These official categorizations are expected to lower the unemployment rate. If the true situation were considered, the unemployment rate would be revised upwards by another 1.5% in 1999.

Table 5.1. Indices on Poverty, Inequality and Unemployment

	Gini Coefficient for Salary and Wage Households	Unemployment Rate (Percent)	Number of the Unemployed (1,000 Persons)	Poverty Rate (Percent)
1996				
1st quarter	0.306	2.2	457	8.0
2nd quarter	0.309	1.9	415	6.2
3rd quarter	0.302	1.8	392	5.1
4th quarter	0.318	2.0	438	5.8
1997				
1st quarter	0.308	3.1	645	6.5
2nd quarter	0.297	2.5	549	5.4
3rd quarter	0.297	2.2	470	4.6
4th quarter	0.292	2.6	561	5.3
1998				
1st quarter	0.318	5.7	1,179	9.9
2nd quarter	0.327	6.9	1,481	10.7
3rd quarter	0.321	7.4	1,597	11.9
4th quarter	0.309	7.4	1,587	11.5
1999				
1st quarter	0.337	8.4	1,749	11.5
2nd quarter	0.320	6.6	1,435	10.7
3rd quarter	0.312	5.6	1,220	9.1
4th quarter	0.331	4.6	1,011	8.1
2000				
1st quarter	0.319	5.1	1,092	8.6
2nd quarter	0.320	3.8	840	7.2
3rd quarter	0.312	3.6	809	6.5
4th quarter	0.315	3.7	817	6.2
2001				
1st quarter	N.A.	4.8	1,029	N.A.
2nd quarter	N.A.	3.5	791	N.A.
3rd quarter	N.A.	3.3	732	N.A.
4th quarter	N.A.	3.2	725	N.A.

The high unemployment rates have created serious social problems in Korea, which had been benefiting from a prosperous economy for several decades. First of all, many unemployed workers who are unable to find new jobs have been left with very few resources for themselves and their family members. As a result, the poverty rates are estimated to have more than doubled since the economic crisis.

Korea's poverty rate is estimated through a three-stage process because there is no annual income record for all the households. In the first stage, the Korea Institute for Health and Social Affairs (KIHASA) estimates the minimum cost of living and the poverty line every year. In fact, the Korean government uses a market basket to determine the poverty line. This measure takes into account expenses related to food, housing, health and medical care, culture and recreation, clothing and footwear, commuting, utilities and furniture. The Minister of

Health and Welfare announces the poverty line every December, based on inflation and the results of a market basket survey carried out every five years. The poverty line for 1998, based on the 1994 survey and subsequent increases in the cost of living, was 218,000 Won per month (US $182).

In the second stage, the KIHASA estimates the poverty rate for salary and wage earners' households. In other words, it calculates the proportion of these households that are falling below the poverty line. This assessment is based on data collected by the Korea National Statistical Office (KNSO). This Office publishes an *'Annual Report on the Household Income and Expenditure Survey'*, which includes monthly income and expenditure for salary and wage earners' households, but not monthly expenditure for all other households. Therefore, only the income of salary and wage earners' households is surveyed every year.

Finally, since the salary and wage earners' households only represent a part of the total households in Korea, the KIHASA calculates the ratio between the poverty rate for salary and wage earners and the poverty rate for all households. The annual poverty rate for all households is then drawn up by applying this ratio to the poverty rate for salary and wage earners' households. The KNSO conducts the more comprehensive *'National Survey of Family Income and Expenditure'* every five years, which includes monthly income and expenditure for all households in Korea. Most recently, it was conducted in 1996.

As a result of this three-stage process, the poverty rate in Korea was estimated to be 4.6% in the 3rd quarter of 1997, but it shot up to 11.9% in the 3rd quarter of 1998. The poverty rate has been gradually going down since reaching this peak, descending to 6.2% by the 4th quarter of 2000. The number of the poor who needed support from the Korean government was estimated at 1.3 million in 1998, and 1.5 million in 1999. However, Korean social safety nets were unable to meet the needs of these people. For instance, the proportion of the poor excluded from the social safety nets was 65% in 1998, though this was expected to improve to 39.6% in 1999.

When poverty is examined, there is another statistical measure that is worthy of attention: the Gini coefficient. This measure shows the income distribution of a country. A Gini coefficient of 0 indicates perfect income equality, while 1 would imply that all wealth is concentrated in a single person. Gini coefficients do not show how poor people have become, but they give an indication of how much poorer people are compared to others. In Korea, many people feel they have become poorer than before and feel frustrated that they are poorer than others. Like the poverty rates, the Gini coefficients have gone up in Korea since the economic crisis. The Gini coefficient was 0.292 in the 4th quarter of 1997, but went up to 0.327 in the 2nd quarter of 1998, and 0.331 in the 4th quarter of 1999. It went down a little as the economy recovered from the worst, but for the most part has remained higher than before 1997. The income distribution has become more unequal as the rich are getting richer and the poor become poorer. It cannot be overemphasized that Korea's Gini coefficients are not as bad as those in other Asian countries. When compared with Hong Kong and Singapore (whose coefficients are above 0.5), Korean figures are considered moderate. However, poor Koreans do not compare themselves with Hong Kong or Singapore. They compare themselves with wealthy Koreans.

After the crisis, the Korean government changed the social safety net systems and introduced new measures to deal with the economic problems. The main policy concept is Productive Welfare, which was put forward by the Kim Dae-Jung Administration. Along with democracy and a market economy, productive welfare is one of three main ideological concepts advanced by the Kim Administration. This chapter will discuss Korean policies to combat the economic crisis, which are aimed at strengthening the social safety nets. It will focus in particular on the changes in the public assistance system, the current situation and the future.

SOCIAL INSURANCE IN KOREA

Korea started to set up various social safety nets in the 1960s, but has been vigorously developing social safety nets since the 1980s. At present, policies to alleviate poverty in Korea consist mainly of the following programs: industrial injury insurance, health insurance, national pension, employment insurance and public assistance. However, the economic crisis in 1997 forced the government to establish other temporary measures, such as community work programs and loans for unemployed people. This section will discuss the historical development of the main social safety nets and the current situation.

The social safety nets in Korea currently form a two-layer system. The primary layer comprises social insurance schemes, and the secondary layer consists of public assistance schemes. The former is based on beneficiaries' contributions without any means-tests, while the latter is non-contributory but means-tested.

SOCIAL INSURANCE PROGRAMS

Employment Insurance

Korea introduced employment insurance (EI) in July 1995, marking the completion of its social security system of four social insurance schemes, public assistance and social services. The EI initially started to cover full-time workers in companies with thirty or more employees. Due to high unemployment rates since the late 1997 economic crisis, its coverage was extended to full-time workers in companies with five or more employees in March 1998, and has covered all full-time, temporary and part-time workers, except daily workers, since October 1, 1998. Moreover, the EI's minimum benefit level was increased from 50% of the minimum wage to 90% to stabilize the life of the unemployed.

The payment period was 30-210 days, but was extended to 90-240 days depending on the beneficiary's age and contributing period. Under the EI, the Special Extended Benefit Program (SEBP) was introduced to deal with the 1997 economic crisis. The SEBP gives benefits to the long-term unemployed upon their completion of publicly funded technical and vocational training programs.

National Pension

The national pension was introduced in 1988 to cover workers in companies with ten or more employees. Its coverage was extended to workers in companies with five or more employees in 1991 and to farmers and fishers in 1995. Finally, it has started to cover all waged workers, including self-employed workers, since April 1999. As a result, the number of subscribers jumped from 7.8 million in 1997 to 16.2 million in 2001 as Table 5.2 shows.

**Table 5.2. Change in Number of Beneficiaries by Type of
Social Safety Net after the Economic Crisis in 1997**

Type of Social Safety Net	Number of Beneficiaries (Thousand persons)				
	1997	1998	1999	2000	2001
National Pension subscribers	7,840	7,130	16,260	16,210	16,185
recipients	150	200	310	590	595
Health Insurance* days of coverage	270	300	330	365	365
Employment Insurance subscribers	4280	5270	6060	6750	N.A.
recipients	50	410	460	300	N.A.
Livelihood Protection	370	440	540	1510	

* The whole population is covered.

In 1999, the compulsory contribution period was decreased from 20 years to 10 years to alleviate the plight of the people. Since July 2000 the Special Old Age Pension has been extended to farmers and fishers who are 60 years or older and have contributed for more than 5 years. The total number of recipients for the old age pension was 595,000 in 2001. It will jump up in 2008 as the subscribers will normally start to receive pensions.

Health Insurance

Introduced in 1977, health insurance (HI) has covered all citizens since July 1, 1988. The HI's duration of coverage has been extended from 270 days a year in 1997 to 300 days in 1998, 330 days in 1999 and 365 days in 2000. This move was to relieve the burden of health costs on people. The benefits of coverage were extended to include canes and wheelchairs in 1998, prostheses for disabled people in 1999 and prenatal care in 2000.

As a countermeasure to the economic crisis, the government reduced the contributions by up to 50% from some of the unemployed and the poor, who occupied 2.5% of the total households in Korea. These were the most disadvantaged, such as low-income disabled people, single elderly people, and female-headed household members, farmers, and fishers.

Industrial Accidents Compensation Insurance

Finally, the industrial accidents compensation insurance (IACI), which was introduced in 1964, pays benefits to workers who are sick or injured from work. The IACI is financed by employers' contributions. It has covered all working people including the self-employed since July 2000, and the number of subscribers was nearly 9.5 million in 2001.

PUBLIC ASSISTANCE

Livelihood Protection System

The Livelihood Protection System (LPS) was introduced in 1961, and formed the basis of public assistance until the National Basic Livelihood Security System came into effect in 2000. There were three requirements to be eligible for LPS benefits. First, a beneficiary could not have family members who could support him/her. Second, a beneficiary had to be 65 or older, or younger than 18, a prospective mother, disabled, unemployed or on a low-income. Third, a beneficiary could not have assets and earnings in excess of a yearly standard set by the Minister of Health and Welfare (Lee and Lee, 2000).

There were three kinds of care provided by the LPS: home care, institutional care, and self-support care. Home care was provided at one's own residence, while institutional care was provided at a residential facility. Self-support care was provided to those who were able to work, but were unemployed or on a low-income.

The LPS had six kinds of aid: livelihood aid, medical aid and educational aid, maternity aid, funeral aid and self-support aid. Livelihood aid was provided as cash for food, clothing and other necessities of life. Medical aid and educational aid were provided in kind, while maternity aid and funeral aid were provided in cash. Self-support aid was provided in the form of various types of job training or low-interest loans to assist low-income people to get out of poverty. During the job training period, beneficiaries received allowances, living costs for family members, training preparation fees, and expenses for applying for jobs. A low-interest loan of up to 12 million Won per household was available.

The beneficiaries of self-support care were not eligible for livelihood aid because they were considered to be able to work. In other words, the LPS provided cash benefits only to low-income people who were unable to work. The government officials believed that if a citizen wanted to work and was able to do so, he/she would be able to find a job to earn enough to live. The Korean economy was booming before the crisis, and with companies expanding their workforce the demand for labor was high.

The economic crisis in 1997 created a group of poor people whom the pre-existing livelihood protection system could not protect. The crisis led many companies into bankruptcy, which resulted in mass unemployment. Those who were unemployed or underemployed could not pass the means-test to become beneficiaries of the LPS because many of them had assets as home owners or tenants. In Korea, there is a unique housing system, called *Jeonsei*. It is a system whereby a tenant gives a lump-sum deposit to a home owner on taking up the tenancy, and the owner pays the deposit back when the tenant moves out. The amount of deposit usually ranges from 40% to 60% of the house price. Thus, because of the strict criteria relating to property they were not eligible for livelihood aid in the form of cash benefits. However, without a monthly income they did not have enough resources to survive and usually used up their savings within six months (Kim, 1998).

As a result, the Korean government set up a number of short-term programs after the crisis to help these people, and the Temporary Livelihood Protection System (TLPS), community work for low-income households and general community work programs to help the unemployed and the underemployed came into effect in 1998. The TLPS was very similar to the LPS in that its programs included all six types of aid as the LPS. The level of income criteria for the TLPS was the same as for the LPS, but the TLPS had a higher property level for eligibility than the LPS in order to provide more low-income people with benefits. The number of beneficiaries of the TLPS was 310,000 in 1998 in the immediate aftermath of the economic crisis, rising to 760,000 in 1999. The number reduced to 540,000 in 2000, and most of these became beneficiaries of the National Basic Livelihood Security System (which will be explained below).

Moreover, as a last safety net to help people overcome economic difficulties, the Livelihood Protection System began to provide people in the category of self-support care with a lower level of benefits in 1998. However, the effort was not very successful because the economic crisis created too much demand. Since the LPS had only provided livelihood aid to the poor who were under 18 or over 65, it was not able to deal with mass unemployment. Consequently, low-income people who were able to work could not get livelihood aid under the LPS. The number of beneficiaries of the LPS was 1.92 million in 1999, but the number of the beneficiaries of livelihood aid (cash benefit) was only 0.54 million, which was 28.1% of the total beneficiaries. The vast majority received medical and educational benefits only when they needed them.

NATIONAL BASIC LIVELIHOOD SECURITY SYSTEM

The economic crisis created mass unemployment, which had been unprecedented in Korea since the 1960s. The situation resulted in serious social problems such as high divorce rates, desertion of children and/or the elderly, homelessness, high suicide rates, and malnourishment of children. For example, the divorce rate after the economic crisis in 1998 was 34% higher than before 1997, and the suicide rate was 41% higher. However, the LPS could not deal with these social problems because it was based on an assumption that there were enough jobs for all citizens who wanted to work. Moreover, under the LPS, those who had no income but who owned or rented a property could not become beneficiaries. A new public assistance system was needed to reduce the problems resulting from mass unemployment.

The National Basic Livelihood Security System (NBLSS) replaced the Livelihood Protection System in October 2000. The NBLSS is based on two premises. First, it plays a role as a last safety net for citizens. Second, it fulfills an ideology of productive welfare. In other words, the NBLSS tries to secure a minimum standard of living for all citizens, and to promote self-support and self-reliance.

The NBLSS has the following different features from the LPS: a fundamental paradigm shift from gifts to rights; the abolition of demographic eligibility criteria; rationalization of assets criteria; introduction of a concept of estimated household income; and an emphasis on work incentives and self-reliance.

Change from Gifts to Rights

The NBLSS strengthens people's rights to a moderate standard of living and makes the government more responsible for supporting low-income people to maintain a minimum standard of living. The old LPS benefits were considered as gifts from the government, not as citizens' rights. Therefore, under the LPS the government was not obliged to provide social assistance to low-income citizens and government officials could use their discretion when making decisions on beneficiaries. Moreover, the central government could adjust the number of beneficiaries according to the budget for the year. However, the benefits are considered to be citizens' rights under the NBLSS, which means that people may file a suit against the government if they do not receive the benefits they are entitled to. The government has to provide basic necessities to low-income citizens whose income and assets meet certain criteria.

Abolition of Demographic Eligibility Criteria

The LPS had demographic eligibility criteria stipulating that a beneficiary for livelihood aid must be under 18 or over 65 unless disabled or chronically ill. The NBLSS abolished the demographic eligibility criteria and decides beneficiaries solely on the basis of their own income and assets and those of supporting family members.

Those who have a duty to support a poor family are called support-obligators. They are limited to immediate adult family members such as a spouse, parents, children and any siblings who financially support them. However, different assets and income criteria are applied to siblings as support-obligators. The support-obligators are divided into three groups based on their assets and income: those able to support, those who have difficulty in supporting, and those unable to support. Only in the latter two cases are family members eligible for NBLSS benefits (Park, 2001).[1]

The income criterion of a support-obligator is 120% of the combined income of an applicant's household and his/her support-obligator's household. The property criterion of a support-obligator is 120% of the combined property of an applicant's household and his/her support-obligator's household. If a support-obligator's income is less than 120% of the minimum cost of living, he/she is considered as 'unable to support'. If his/her income is more than 120% of the minimum cost of living, 40% of the income over the 120% threshold (called 'cost of support') is calculated as the income of the applicant. If married daughters and widowed daughters-in-law have income less than 120% of the minimum cost of living, they are regarded as 'unable to support', no matter what their property status is.[2]

Introducing a Concept of Affirmed Household Income
to Rationalize Income and Property Criteria

One of the eligibility criteria for the NBLSS is the minimum cost of living, which is the official poverty line. It was decided solely by the Minister of Health and Welfare under the

---

[1] Income criteria of a support-obligator = (an applicant household's income criteria + a support-obligator household's income criteria) × 120%.
   Property criteria of a support-obligator = (an applicant household's property criteria + a support-obligator household's property criteria) × 120%.
   Cost of support = (real income − minimum cost of living × 120%) × 40%.

[2] The cost of support for married daughters and widowed daughters-in-law is (real income − minimum cost of living × 120%) × 15%.

LPS, but is now jointly decided by the Minister of Health and Welfare and the Central Committee of Livelihood Security (CCLS) under the NBLSS.

The new system works as follows. The Korea Institute for Health and Social Affairs (KIHASA) suggests the minimum cost of living every year. It carries out a national survey on the minimum cost of living once every five years and suggests the minimum cost of living every year based on the survey. In non-survey years, the KIHASA proposes a minimum cost of living which reflects the survey results and inflation rates. The CCLS makes a decision on the minimum cost of living based on the suggestions from the KIHASA. The Minister of Health and Welfare accepts and pronounces the Central Committee's decision as the official minimum cost of living. The minimum cost of living is adjusted based on the size of a household.

The minimum cost of living is calculated on the basis of minimum living costs in a medium-sized city. Residents in large cities may be in a disadvantageous position because there are extra costs of living in large cities. In 1999, the minimum cost of living was calculated as 928,000 Won (approximately US $714) as a result of the national survey (Kim et al., 1999). The minimum costs of living in 2000, 2001 and 2002 were decided based on the minimum cost of living in 1999 and the inflation rates in 1999, 2000 and 2001. The minimum cost of living in 2001 was 956,000 Won, and in 2002 990,000 Won, representing an increase of 3.5%.

The current benefits level of the NBLSS is based on the minimum cost of living. The amount of cash benefits (called the 'standard cash benefit') is the minimum cost of living after subtracting the amount of benefits from other entitlements, such as medical and educational benefits, and assessed income. Livelihood aid under the NBLSS supplements any shortfall in household income that is below the minimum cost of living, the amount of aid being equal to the difference between the two. In 2002, the standard cash benefit for living expenses and housing expenses was 871,000 Won for a four member household. If a household has no income at all, it will receive 871,000 Won. If a household has income, it will receive the difference between that income and 871,000 Won. Other types of aid, such as educational aid and medical aid, are provided in kind.

The NBLSS introduces a concept of Affirmed Household Income to improve the equity of the system. Affirmed Household Income consists of earned income and property-induced income which will be calculated on the basis of the amount of property owned from 2003. If an applicant's affirmed household income is less than the minimum cost of living, they are entitled to be a beneficiary of the NBLSS. The amount of the benefit will be the difference between affirmed household income and the minimum cost of living.

The National Basic Livelihood Security Act, which is the legislative basis for the NBLSS, has a temporary provision regarding affirmed household income. Since affirmed household income is a very new concept, the Ministry of Health and Welfare is currently carrying out a pilot project for a year. The concept of affirmed household income will be utilized in the NBLSS from 2003. Until then, the NBLSS will use income criteria and property criteria. The income criteria in 2002 is 990,000 Won for a four member household, which is the minimum cost of living, and the property criteria is set at 36 million Won for a three or four member household.

Table 5.3. Household's Income and Property

Criteria	Number of Household Members					
	1	2	3	4	5	6
Income						
2001	33	55	76	96	109	123
002	35	57	79	99	113	127
Property						
2001	3,100	3,400	3,800			
2002	3,300	3,600	4,000			

Note: Based on Table 3 income and property criteria of the NBLSS in 2001 and 2002 (Unit: 10,000 Won).
Source: A Plan for the National Basic Livelihood Security in 2002 (Ministry of Health and Welfare).

Introduction of Work Incentives and Self-Reliance

The NBLSS includes a work incentive program, intended to motivate people with work-ability to find jobs and participate in the labor market. While it helps beneficiaries to escape poverty, cash benefits are conditional upon voluntary participation in cooperatives or vocational training.

Prospective beneficiaries of livelihood aid are divided into two groups according to their age, health, level of skills and motivation for self-reliance: the employable and the non-employable. The employable should participate in job searches, job interviews and job training. The non-employable should participate in establishing small businesses, joint businesses for self-reliance, community work for self-reliance, and voluntary activities. Under the NBLSS, the heads of Si, Gun, and Gu (these are administrative units whose heads are elected officials) have to set up a support plan for beneficiaries' self-reliance, taking into consideration their special needs, abilities, educational attainment and level of skills.

First of all, the direction of self-support and the services necessary for self-support are determined, and services such as careers information, vocational training, job sharing programs, and finances for a self-reliance fund are provided. Those who are in the self-support program are eligible for other social welfare services such as day care and/or home-based services (Ministry of Health and Welfare, 2003).

Self-support centers, social welfare centers, religious groups and civil organizations are used as sponsoring institutions for self-support. Community jobs are developed, such as repairing houses for poor people, caring for elderly or disabled people, and maintaining social welfare facilities and educational facilities.

The NBLSS has an income deduction system, which may stem declining motivation to find work by exempting some of the beneficiaries' earned income from income tax. Since the NBLSS abolished the demographic criteria for eligibility, some low-income people who are able to work may choose to receive the NBLSS benefits instead of working. The income deduction system tries to motivate people to work by increasing their total income. In 2001, the proportions of income-deduction are 15% for disabled people in vocational rehabilitation and 10% for beneficiaries participating in self-help groups and training. The model project for Affirmed Household Income will try out several types of income deduction scheme for beneficiaries who are able to work, with different income deduction rates.

SOME ISSUES OF THE NATIONAL BASIC
LIVELIHOOD SECURITY SYSTEM

The NBLSS provides a minimum income to those whose earnings are below the poverty line, regardless of their age or capacity to work. As a result, the number of beneficiaries for livelihood aid has increased dramatically from 370,000 in 1997, to 440,000 in 1998, 504,000 in 1999 and rising to over 1.5 million in 2001. Among the beneficiaries, those participating in self-support groups, who would not have been able to receive livelihood aid under the LPS, number 69,000 in 2001.

Moreover, it should be noted that the amount of benefits per person has increased from 138,000 Won in 1997 to 205,000 Won in 2000. This is because the amount of benefits under the NBLSS reflects the minimum cost of living. Moreover, the NBLSS has introduced an additional type of aid to the range of benefits provided by the LPS: housing benefit. This has been introduced to stabilize housing for the low-income class, and is usually provided in cash. Therefore, the NBLSS has been successful in helping low-income people to survive during the economic crisis, although it is still too early to evaluate its achievements.

Despite the tentative achievements of the new system, there are criticisms of the NBLSS. These criticisms come from two ends of the political spectrum: conservative and progressive. First of all, conservative groups raised serious doubts about the NBLSS even before it began to operate. The main newspapers in Korea ran many stories of 'fraudulent beneficiaries'. One newspaper clip reported that a beneficiary of the old system had a bank account with more than 0.5 billion Won, which was 25 times higher than the threshold of eligibility. A year into the new system, the newspaper also reported that the NBLSS provided 930,000 Won for four family members (a husband and wife with two children), which exceeded the entitlement threshold of 843,000 Won, the minimum wage for two people if both husband and wife are working. The paper quoted a researcher who worked for an industry institute as saying that "the NBLSS may be helpful for social integration, but it may lower work motivation and result in moral hazard because the NBLSS benefit level is higher than the minimum wage" (*Dong-a Ilbo*, December 20, 2000). Another newspaper article, headed "Welfare Policy Must Increase Will for Self-Reliance," argued that work was lost in workfare, and that the NBLSS payments had harmful effects on low-income people. It raised a concern that the NBLSS would result in a vicious cycle of increasing dependence of low-income people on the government, long-term unemployment and a severe strain on public finances (*Hankook Ilbo*, April 2, 2001).

The progressive analysts have raised different issues. After a year of operating the new system, one serious problem is that many low-income people cannot become beneficiaries of the new system because they have children who can in principle support them. Korea has a tradition that children must support their parents. *Hyo*, which means respect for ones parents and ancestors, has long been one of the fundamental values in Korean society. However, there has been a great change in this value. Many Koreans do not expect to be supported by their children when they become old. The tradition of *Hyo* is still a popular value in Korea, but the reality is changing very rapidly. The gap between the value and the true situation has been creating many low-income old people. Generally, people are able to support their parents if they have enough income over and above what they spend on their own living costs and their children. In Korea, private educational costs are notoriously high. In some households, women are working to pay for their children's private education costs even though their husbands have relatively high paying jobs. They would not support their parents if they had to give up their children's private education.

Another issue is related to households that used to receive livelihood aid under the LPS. The amount of livelihood aid provided for the self-reliance group who did not receive any aid under the old system has increased more relative to the entitlements of the residential care group who used to receive livelihood aid under the old system. The latter's cash benefit entitlement was not linked to their income under the LPS. Therefore, if they had a small income which was less than the income criteria of the LPS, their total income would be their earned income plus the cash benefit. However, under the NBLSS, the amount of benefit depends on the income of the household, which means that the beneficiaries' total income cannot be over the minimum cost of living. Therefore, the total income for households with small incomes has decreased compared with the former system. Households with special needs, such as those with a disabled member, suffer most. These households used to receive livelihood aid under the LPS and would usually open a street stall for supplementary income. They generally spend more on transport, medicines, education and other necessities than households with no disabled members. Some low-income people may have to depend on the NBLSS because their medical costs are very high. They would then have to be out of work to continue to be on the list of beneficiaries. In many cases, they lose their medical aid if they work and earn some income, which will result in less disposable income. If these people were provided with medical aid, they would not have to be NBLSS beneficiaries. Therefore, the progressives argue that more benefits should be provided to households with special needs.

Another problem is related to the self-reliance program. The number of self-reliance sponsor institutions is only 70, and the number of public employment offices only 122 in 2000. Moreover, these offices are almost non-existent in rural areas. Therefore, beneficiaries with work-ability cannot find jobs even though they are willing to work. The economic crisis has deprived many people of jobs. The beneficiaries of the NBLSS are the least favored workers despite being available and able to work. Thus, the progressive groups insist that community jobs with a vision of growth must be provided for the self-reliance group.

FUTURE OF THE NATIONAL BASIC LIVELIHOOD SECURITY SYSTEM

The NBLSS needs to be improved in order to achieve its main purposes: to secure a minimum standard of living for all and to promote the self-reliance of low-income people. It is a very difficult task to achieve both goals at the same time. The conservatives attack the NBLSS from the perspective of the latter objective, while the progressives attack it from the point of view of the former. For the Kim Dae-Jung Administration, it is important to balance the two sides. Therefore, the Korean government focuses on totally different policies.

On one hand, the government continually checks for fraudulent beneficiaries, and makes them repay the benefits that they have obtained illegitimately. At the same time, it is expanding its programs for self-reliance. In fact, several self-support centers have begun to make some profits. The government will also introduce the income deduction system from 2003. These policies will motivate low-income people to work rather than to become beneficiaries of the NBLSS.

On the other hand, the government is continuing to expand the NBLSS to support an increasing number of people. Some low-income people are at risk of becoming poor because of medical costs. If they were entitled to medical aid, they would not have to be totally dependent on the NBLSS. The primary target of the expansion is low-income people whose income is over the minimum cost of living, but less than 120% of the minimum cost of living.

Finally, the government will set up a monitoring center for the NBLSS at the Korea Institute for Health and Social Affairs at the end of 2002. The center will evaluate the effectiveness and efficiency of the NBLSS. Moreover, it will closely monitor poverty trends. However, it is not yet clear how effective the center will be.

Like the Welfare Reform in the United States, the fate of the NBLSS is greatly dependent on Korea's politics. In 2002, Korea will have a presidential election. The Kim Dae-Jung Administration is considered progressive compared to past administrations. In fact, implementation of the NBLSS was made possible because the relatively progressive government has been working with progressive non-governmental organizations.

The expenditures on welfare in Korea are still very low compared to those in the developed economies. From now on, the issue will be how the government deals with the pressure from the conservatives. It will certainly become more difficult for the government during the present period of global competition and neo-liberalism. Increased social spending is deemed by neo-liberal economists to be harmful to the economy. It would also reduce the global competitiveness of Korea. It remains to be seen whether the Kim Administration will gather enough public support to bulwark the expanded social insurance program and the newly introduced NBLSS.

REFERENCES

Kim, M. G. (1998). *A Study to Improve and Develop the Livelihood Protection System.* Health and Welfare Policy Forum, May 1998.

Kim, M. G. et al. (1999). *A Study on Measuring the Poverty Line in 1999.* Seoul: The Korea Institute for Health and Social Affairs.

Lee, S. W. and Lee, I. J. (2000). Social Welfare Development in Korea: Past, Present and Future. In K. L. Tang (Ed.), *Social Development in Asia* (pp.61-82). Dordrecht and Boston: Kluwer Academic Publishers.

Ministry of Health and Welfare (2001). *A Guide to the National Basic Livelihood Security.* Seoul: Ministry of Health and Welfare.

_____. (2002). *A Plan for the National Basic Livelihood Security in 2002.* Seoul: Ministry of Health and Welfare. Unpublished Materials.

Ministry of Health and Welfare (2002). *Home Page.* Retrieved on December 16, 2002 at (http://www.mohw.go.kr/english/contents/c7_2_5.html).

National Statistical Office (2002). *Major Statistics of Korea Economy, 1996-2002.* Seoul: NSO.

Park, C. Y. (2001). Productive Welfare: Achievements and Limits. In C. Y. Park (Ed.), *The Way to Productive Welfare: Achievement and Vision.* Seoul: The World Bank and The Korea Institute for Health and Social Affairs, 2001. Retrieved at http://www.mohw.go.kr/english/contents/c7_2_5.html

In: *Poverty Monitoring and Alleviation in East Asia*
K. Tang and C. Wong, editors pp. 105-115

ISBN: 1-59033-828-6
© 2003 Nova Science Publishers, Inc.

Chapter 6

POVERTY MONITORING AND ALLEVIATION IN JAPAN

Yuki Sekine

INTRODUCTION

Poverty is a difficult concept to define. Traditionally it was considered to be a lack of financial means[1] but today it has taken on a wider social meaning. The Nobel Prize wining economist Amartya Sen added another dimension to it based on deprivation of capability, a notion later elaborated on in the UNDP's Human Development Report of 1997. In a further study that looked at inheritance of poverty between generations, Nishio (1999) defines poverty as the "reduction of a person's capability and opportunities to 'realize oneself', because of prejudices coming from the person's birth or education" (Nishio, 1999:5). Capability deprivation means that people are unable to play a full part in society and their ability to earn a living is inhibited. They are marginalized and become economically inactive. Simply providing them with money will not be sufficient to resolve their deprivation.

Most of the current government's policies for poverty alleviation aim at the self-reliance of the poor as a long-term goal, while financial assistance is used as an immediate and short-term means of relief. In this chapter, I will use the lack of means (of income) as a first indicator of poverty, while capacity deprivation will be my guidepost for reviewing the policy responses to poverty alleviation.

THE QUESTION OF POVERTY IN JAPAN

Over the last century and throughout its successive stages of economic development, Japan has managed to raise the income level of its population dramatically. Spectacular economic growth has lifted the overwhelming majority out of poverty and very few people would consider themselves today as being "poor" in material terms. For this reason poverty is

---

[1] According to the traditional measurement of poverty, i.e. the percentage of the total population whose income is less than 50% of the national average, the "poverty rate" of Japan in 1994 was 8.1% (Nishizaki et al., 1998). This rate is a ratio of total individuals who are poor over the total population.

said to have become "invisible" in Japan. For example, the income level of a household receiving public assistance reached almost 70% of the average household income in 1981, a level that has been maintained to date (Nishio, 1999: 1). This high level of public assistance is criticized as being one of the main weaknesses of the Japanese welfare system, and the main cause of the "poverty trap" into which most households fall once they start receiving it. As there is no time limit to the allocation of public assistance, and for a number of other reasons outlined below, households receiving public assistance tend to do so for exceptionally long periods, about nine years on average (Koyama, 2001).

Can we say, then, that poverty has disappeared completely? Unfortunately, the answer is no. Poverty continues to exist, sometimes in different and completely new forms, which may be more marginalized because of their "invisibility".

On the other hand, one form of highly visible poverty is growing as a consequence of the stagnating Japanese economy: the homeless, or 'shelterless' male day laborers, inhabiting makeshift cardboard constructions, are probably the most conspicuous victims of Japan's economic boosts and backdowns, once flooded with work in the construction booms then suddenly deprived of it in recession. These men depend on daily work contracts on construction sites for their livelihoods. Actually, the homeless and their visibility, discussed in more detail in the following section, may paradoxically be having synergistic impacts on today's recession, where anxiety over the future restrains the consumer's inclination to buy, shrinking internal demand and accentuating stagnation in a kind of vicious circle. The high visibility of the homeless has also pressurized the government to adopt a comprehensive policy to combat their increase, and respond to their immediate needs for shelter and health care.

"Invisible" forms of poverty can only be speculated about from statistical data. For example, data on household income in Japan show that although income distribution is relatively equal by global comparison, there are still about 25% of households with a level of income less than half the national average after redistribution through tax and social security, a percentage that is nowhere near covered by public assistance (according to statistics on households receiving public assistance allowances). This is a far higher estimate that the one made by Nishizaki et al. (1998), whose poverty rate is based on the individual as the unit of analysis. Another invisible form of poverty is rural poverty because of depopulation. Poverty in this case is the consequence of a lack of means coming from exploitable but unexploited capacity, rather than deprivation of capacity. Its direct cause is the depopulation of mountainous/rural areas and migration to urban areas. The government is collecting detailed statistics and actively fighting against this form of impoverishment which has been affecting entire villages since the late 1960s. Poverty is not so visible here because community solidarity and government aid alleviate the lack of income and usually manage to maintain a certain standard of living. This form of poverty is relative, as compared with other rural and urban regions of Japan, rather than absolute. I will now attempt to detail and measure these visible and invisible forms of poverty.

FACTUAL INFORMATION ABOUT THE POOR IN JAPAN

The Homeless

Who They Are

The term homeless refers to people living in makeshift cardboard constructions and tents, usually erected in parks and dry riverbeds, or sleeping rough on the streets in urban centers (definition from the "Law for Special Measures concerning Support for Independence of the homeless", Law No. 105 of August 7, 2002).

Today there are three major homeless districts in Japan, namely San-ya in Tokyo, Kamagasaki in Osaka and Kotobukicho in Yokohama, and about a dozen smaller districts in other cities. The underground of Shinjuku JR Station used to shelter an important community of homeless people in cardboard constructions, which disappeared in 1997 after a hard-line expulsion policy led by the Tokyo Metropolitan Administration, involving violent clashes between the police and the homeless.

In a study of the shrinkage of urban slums in Asia, Shimodaira (1998) relates the history of the San-ya district in Tokyo, currently one of the biggest homeless districts in Japan:

> San-ya was a traditional slum area since pre-war times and by far the largest district where many flophouses were concentrated. These provided accommodation mainly to day labourers … At the time of the [Government's] Survey in 1961, San-ya and Motogi [another important slum area at that time] were conspicuous in their concentration on specific occupations, the former housed day labourers and the second rag collectors (ibid.: 126-7).

The same study indicates the places of birth and origins of inhabitants before the war, showing their routes for entering these districts. About 60-70% were born in other prefectures and one third in Tokyo. Motogi and San-ya had unique characteristics as slums compared with other "deteriorated districts". Because they were highly informal occupations, rag collectors and day laborers were segregated from the formal economic framework and their marginalization was intensified by the enlargement of the formal economy (ibid.). In the mid-1960s, two violent riots provoked by day laborers in San-ya led the Tokyo Metropolitan Government to engage in the construction of a comprehensive welfare center (the Johoku welfare center) in 1965, providing a variety of social services including an employment service, emergency relief, advice and help in applying for public assistance, medical services, a day nursery, library, recreation and amusements. Shimodaira's study further explains the role of the San-ya district as a kind of large pool attracting an increasing number of rural migrants and impoverished people who had been unfavorably affected by high economic growth, in particular people engaged in agriculture or other self-employed fields. While the city was expanding, the demand for unskilled manual laborers in the building, construction and transport industries rapidly increased and San-ya functioned as an abundant supply of day laborers, on which the city economy heavily relied (ibid.: 144). The influx into the district slowed down at the same time as the deceleration in economic growth.

The role played by San-ya and other homeless districts today is more or less the same as thirty years ago. Most of the homeless are day-laborers seeking daily contracts on construction sites. The most direct cause for becoming homeless is unemployment. Other more personal factors, such as maladaptation to social life and bankruptcy, also enmesh with economic factors. The average age of the homeless is high, mainly because there are abundant temporary job opportunities for unskilled youth, principally in the service sector. The authorities, as an immediate measure for providing relief, are aiming to secure free medical care services for the homeless.

Official data on the number of homeless in Japan amount to the sum of surveys by local authorities of people actually identified. In October 1999, this number was 20,451 (rising from 16,247 in March the same year). NGOs and civic associations assisting the homeless estimate their real number to be about three to four times higher. In the last two to three years, they have clearly increased, as a consequence of economic recession and the after-effect of the collapse of the inflated bubble economy.

Having no fixed domicile, most of the homeless are not registered as residents and as such are deprived of social protection. A serious issue is their healthcare. Many of the homeless are in poor health and are elderly.

Policy Response to the Problem of the Homeless

In 1999 the government launched a comprehensive plan to tackle the issues of the homeless. In February of that year, a Homeless Liaison Conference was created at state level to combine the efforts of all ministries concerned and local public authorities to discuss the matter. The conference issued a report in May on "Short-Term Measures against the Issues of the 'Homeless'". These measures consist of five pillars:

1. Establishment of a general structure for providing counseling and self-support assistance to the homeless;
2. Stability of employment;
3. Enhancement of health care for the homeless;
4. Securing housing for the homeless;
5. Installation of a safe and secure regional environment.

Based on this report, the Ministry of Health launched a series of actions in 1999 and 2000, mainly immediate support through the building of shelters, the provision of health checks and job counseling services to encourage self-reliance.

Despite these measures, and because of the stagnating economy, the numbers of homeless have steadily continued to rise, officially reaching 24,000 by September 2001. In view of this the government adopted a new "Law on Special Measures to Assist Self-Support of the Homeless" on August 7, 2002 (Law No. 105). This law expressly announces for the first time the state's obligation to assist the rehabilitation of the homeless.

The law mainly reiterates measures that were already being implemented by the Ministry of Health in 1999 and 2000, but Article 14 asserts that the state shall conduct a national survey on the real current status of the homeless, in collaboration with local public authorities. A survey of that sort has never been conducted before and it will be the occasion, for the first time, to clarify the extent of the homeless problem and to identify the different factors leading to homelessness. This also shows the political importance that the issue is taking now. It is clearly progress that the state is engaging in a specific policy targeted to the homeless and the national survey should provide invaluable information for the future development of policies to combat the phenomenon.

POVERTY DERIVING FROM DISCRIMINATION

Discrimination is universally a factor of poverty. As unemployment is a direct cause of poverty, the exclusion of certain categories of people from having equal access to the labor market or to education exposes them to increased risks of becoming poor.

Discrimination can be based on two types of characteristics: either personal characteristics inherent to the person, like race or national origin, or sex, that do not in principle affect the person's abilities or skills to perform the job; or it can be based on characteristics that may be presumed to affect the person's skills and abilities, like disability or old age. Discrimination in terms of access to employment is widespread in the rigid Japanese labor market, particularly with regard to national origin and sex. With the ageing of the population and the budgetary constraints this is placing on state finances, age discrimination in the labor market is starting to raise attention. Action by the authorities is being directed towards eliminating these practices through sensitization campaigns and legislation specifically prohibiting them, or in the case of people with disabilities, the requirement for a minimum quota (percentage) of employment with the payment of a compensation fee if the quota is not satisfied. Adverse distinctions and exclusions can start at an early stage in life, affecting not only the victim's future but impacting on the life of future generations. It is a direct factor inhibiting a person's capacities to develop, and its elimination should be a basic premise of any attempt by the state to fight unemployment and poverty.

Discrimination Based on Origin

In Japan, discrimination has been traditionally directed against *Buraku (Dowa)* people (with a population of 892,751 according to a survey carried out by the government in 1993), *Ainu, Wiruta, Nibuhi and Kyukyu* peoples, as well as Korean and other foreign residents in Japan. Discrimination adversely affects not only employment, but also education and social life (particularly marriage) in general. Part of the above-mentioned homeless are said to be foreign residents, although there are no statistics providing evidence for that yet. The government is conducting wide anti-discrimination campaigns and a new bill for the protection of human rights containing a specific prohibition of discrimination based on various grounds, including race, origin and sex, is currently being discussed in parliament.

As regards the *Ainu* people, who live on the island of Hokkaido, Government action has been taken to reduce the income and educational gaps between them and the rest of the Japanese population. Although in 1999 the income level of Ainu households (JP Y3.94 million per year) was still about half the national average, and the public assistance rate (3.72%) double the national average (1.94%), these gaps have been decreasing at a steady pace since government action was launched in 1972.[2]

---

[2] See UN treaty body database: Office of the High Commissioner for Human Rights, International Covenant on Economic, Social and Cultural rights, CESCR, Reply to List of Issues, 26/07/2001

Discrimination on the Basis of Sex

Although government efforts strive for the realization of a society where men and women participate equally, wage disparities between men and women in Japan are still very high (close to 40%) and job segregation in the labor market still confines the majority of women to precarious part-time or temporary employment, making them the most vulnerable workers in times of economic recession. Single or divorced women are to an even greater extent exposed to risks of unemployment and poverty. Under the current social security system, the majority of unmarried older women have to rely on public assistance for a living because their old age pension benefits do not meet their needs. Recently, older homeless women have been on the rise in a context where the homeless are overwhelmingly men.

Discrimination Based on Disability or Old Age

The employment rate of disabled people is on average 30% lower than the general employment rate, and households with a disabled person account for 38% of households receiving public assistance (Ministry of Health, Labour and Welfare, 2001).

With Japan's ageing population, the difficulty of gaining access to reemployment encountered by older unemployed people is a very serious issue. Households with an older member account for 46% of households receiving public assistance.

LOW INCOME HOUSEHOLDS

Data on the levels of income and expenditure of households indicate the income distribution in Japan. In the 1998 Survey on National Consumption, households are divided into 16 categories according to annual income levels before and after redistribution through tax and social security (see Tables 6.1 and 6.2).

Over the last twenty years, income inequality before redistribution has widened (the Gini coefficient was 0.3491 in 1981 and 0.4720 in 1999), while the improvement in the redistribution effect (10% in 1981 to 19.2% in 1999) has not been sufficient to compensate for this gap (see the Lorenz curve in Figure 6.1).

Table 6.1. Annual Income Before Tax and Social Security Transfers

Original Income Line Class (Unit: thousand yen)	Number of Households Surveyed	Composition of Households (%)	
		Composition Ratio	Cumulative Ratio
Total	*7,991*	*100.0*	-
Less than 500	1,225	15.3	15.3
500 - 1,000	286	3.6	18.9
1,000 - 1,500	290	3.6	22.5
1,500 - 2,000	319	4.0	26.5
2,000 - 2,500	287	3.6	30.1
2,500 - 3,000	267	3.3	33.5
3,000 - 3,500	296	3.7	37.2
3,500 - 4,000	316	4.0	41.1
4,000 - 4,500	373	4.7	45.8
4,500 - 5,000	389	4.9	50.7
5,000 - 6,000	720	9.0	59.7
6,000 - 7,000	641	8.0	67.7
7,000 - 8,000	545	6.8	74.5
8,000 - 9,000	438	5.5	80.0
9,000 - 10,000	362	4.5	84.5
More than 10,000	1,237	15.5	100.0
Average Original Income	5,831 (thousand yen per year)		

Source: Survey on National Consumption (1998)

Table 6.2. Annual Income After Tax and Social Security Transfers

Income class after Redistribution (Unit: thousand yen)	Number of Households Surveyed	Composition of Households (%)	
		Composition Ratio	Cumulative Ratio
Total	*7,991*	*100.0*	-
Less than 500	145	1.8	1.8
500 - 1,000	227	2.8	4.7
1,000 - 1,500	364	4.6	9.2
1,500 - 2,000	393	4.9	14.1
2,000 - 2,500	409	5.1	19.2
2,500 - 3,000	433	5.4	24.7
3,000 - 3,500	462	5.8	30.4
3,500 - 4,000	519	6.5	36.9
4,000 - 4,500	517	6.5	43.4
4,500 - 5,000	452	5.7	49.1
5,000 - 6,000	865	10.8	59.9
6,000 - 7,000	737	9.2	69.1
7,000 - 8,000	609	7.6	76.7
8,000 - 9,000	48	5.6	82.3
9,000 - 10,000	321	4.0	86.4
More than 10,000	1,090	13.6	100
Average Income After Redistribution	6,129 (thousand yen per year)		

Source: Survey on National Consumption (1998)

Figure 6.1. Lorenz Curve

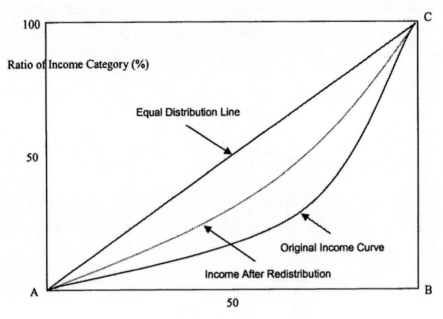

Number of Households: Cumulative Ratio (%)

A comparative study done by Uzuhashi of data on Japan with ten LIS countries analyzed by D. Mitchell in a 1991 study (cited by Uzuhashi), showed that while income inequality before redistribution was relatively small in Japan (Gini coefficient 0.3491), the differences in income between households belonging to the lowest income class and the highest being much smaller than in the United States for example, the redistribution effect through tax and social security was also relatively limited, meaning that in the end income disparities persisted (Gini coefficient 0.3143) (Uzuhashi, 1997).

Despite the recent tendency for income disparities to widen, it is highly improbable that tax reform will go in the direction of a progressive increase in income tax, for example. The need to revitalize the economy, which is also a prerequisite for combating poverty, calls for a revision towards tax reduction and encouragement of private initiative. Facing increased unemployment, the government has, however, adopted special emergency safety net measures to tackle the immediate needs of the newly unemployed.

HOUSEHOLDS RECEIVING PUBLIC ASSISTANCE (SEIKATSU HOGO)

Public assistance is a system aimed at securing a minimum standard of living for people who for whatever reason cannot work, or who cannot find reemployment after having been unemployed, and therefore are in need of income for basic living costs and medical care. It also aims at assisting claimants to regain self-sufficiency once the reason for their inability to work has been resolved.

Concretely, public assistance compensates for income insufficiency according to a minimum living income standard fixed by the state. While there is no official poverty line in Japan, the minimum living income standard (*kijun seikatsuhi*) determined by the Ministry of Health, Labour and Welfare officially serves the same purpose. The minimum living income standard takes into account household composition, number of dependant members, age of the head of household and area of residence (urban/rural areas are classified into six categories according to different levels of living costs). It also takes into consideration a whole list of other factors affecting the household (presence of an elderly, disabled or invalided member of the family, eligibility for housing and education grants, healthcare needs including care for older people and nursing assistance, maternity, expenses incurred in the pursuit of a job or business costs of self-employment, etc.) to calculate the amount corresponding to that particular household. For example, the minimum living income standard for a single elderly household in a Category 6 rural area would be approximately JP Y84,400 (about US $689 at current [December 2002] exchange rates), while for a two-parent household with two children living in a Category 1 urban area that amount would be JP Y225,980 (about US $1,845). The public allowance will correspond to that final amount, minus the household's income (after deduction of the real costs for work, and work income exemption).[3] The minimum living standard for official purposes is thus based on a relative approach and is determined according to an assessment of the average household's lifestyle.

As mentioned earlier, the Japanese public assistance system confronts a serious problem of "poverty trap", and for the majority of recipient households it is extremely difficult to pull out of this situation of dependence. The main reason given for this is a too high level of assistance, combined with a relatively low work incentive (a low level of work income exemption) and the prohibition of any savings. In fact the second purpose of the system, which is to assist recipients to become self-supporting through work, has been somewhat neglected in the design of the system, with the effect of deepening the unemployment trap.

The procedure for the allocation of public assistance is subject to application by the claimant on behalf of a household (individuals are only eligible in exceptional circumstances). Claimants must then comply with a means test implemented by the local welfare office which reviews the household capital (house or land property; electrical appliances whose diffusion exceeds 70% (i.e. they are owned by at least 70% of households in that region); ownership of a car is only considered a basic need if absolutely necessary for work). To be eligible for public assistance, the household income cannot exceed the satisfaction of basic needs. The claimant is also subject to the principle of complementarity which requires the preliminary use of available capital and human resources (the person's ability to work), and assistance by members of the extended family who have a duty of support according to the civil code.

According to the *Report on Social Administration Operation* (by the Ministry of Health, Labour and Welfare), the average monthly number of households receiving public assistance in 2001 was 805,169 (about 1.67% of the total number of households in Japan). Of these, 370,049 (46%) were families comprising an older member, 303,554 (38%) included a disabled or invalided person, and 68,460 (8.5%) were one-parent (mother and child) households.

---

[3] The work income exemption consists in the exemption of a certain percentage of income from work in the calculation of a household's real income, as an incentive for public assistance recipients to earn income through

The social stigma associated with receiving public assistance is very strong in Japan and is the main cause for the very low take-up of public assistance compared with the number of low income households (Tachibanaki, 2000; Koyama, 2001).

The Depopulated Areas

In order to respond to the phenomenon of depopulation of mountainous, agricultural and fishing villages due to migration to the cities during the high economic growth of the 1960s, special measures to address the issue of depopulation have been adopted by law three times since 1970: The Law on Emergency Measures to Fight against Depopulation (1970), The Law on Special Measures for the Revitalization of Underpopulated Areas (1990) and The Law on Special Measures for the Promotion of Self-Support in Underpopulated Areas (2000).

The definition of an underpopulated area according to the law of 1990 is a "Region where as a consequence of significant depopulation, the dynamism of the local community has declined, and the management of production function and the living environment are at an inferior level compared to other regions of the country (Article 1 of the law)". The last survey of underpopulated areas in 1999 counted around 1,230 local communities falling into that category (44 cities; 795 towns and 391 villages), of which 99.3% had a population of less than 30,000. The total population of these areas was 7.97 million (representing 6.3% of the national population), with an average yearly population decline of 4.6%, living in a total area of 184,749 km^2 (48.9% of the national territory) (National Land Agency, 2000). Their financial resources are about 30% of the national average (ibid.). These regions are characterized by a low level of social welfare, high unemployment rates, a very low level of local tax income and heavy reliance on tax allocations from the central government. The special measures were traditionally aimed at raising the level of social welfare, increased job creation, and the reduction of disparities with other regions. The new law of 2000 added to these aims promotion of the region's local industries and original culture to construct unique and independent local communities.

CONCLUSION

As poverty has ceased to constitute an immediate risk affecting the "average" citizen, it no longer constitutes a specific policy issue as such. Instead, as is shown by the fact that the problem of the homeless has become a policy item in itself, it is being treated separately under its various aspects. In the area of employment, for example, policies include prohibiting discrimination in the workplace or promoting the employment of disabled (by means of quotas) or older people.

Meanwhile, Japan is also experiencing a sharp rise in unemployment, a situation that is expected to be further exacerbated by the current structural reforms. This means that the government will have to strengthen the existing safety nets for unemployment. Measures in that direction have, in fact, already been taken: the maximum period for the allocation of unemployment benefits has already been prolonged, and a special budget has been allocated for emergency safety nets aimed at meeting immediate needs. However, in the long term,

work.

addressing the needs of those who are currently poor must lead to preventing its occurrence in the future. In this sense, the current recession and the new social issues that it has given rise to may provide the opportunity to establish, once and for all, strong and sustainable safety nets to counter the problem of unemployment.

REFERENCES

Koyama, Koichi (2001). Reflection on the Reform of Social Security Systems in the US and Europe (Oubei shokoku ni okeru shakai-hoshou seido kaikaku no saikentou). *Financial Review*, No. 55 (Feb. 2001), Ministry of Finance, Policy Research Institute.

Ministry of Health, Labour and Welfare (2001). *Report on Social Administration Operation, 2001.* Tokyo: The Author.

Ministry of Public Management, Home Affairs, Posts and Telecommunications. (1998). *Survey on National Consumption.* Tokyo: The Author.

Mitchell, D. (1991). *Income Transfers in Ten Welfare States.* Aldershot, Brookfield : Avebury.

National Land Agency (currently Ministry of Land, Infrastructure and Transport) (2000). *Outline of the Law on Special Measures for the Promotion of Self-Support of Under-populated Areas.* Tokyo: The Author.

Nishio, Yugo (1999). *Study on the Generational Inheritance of Poverty – Hinkon no sedaikan keishou ni kansuru kenkyu"*, Aikawa Ed.

Nishizaki, B., Yamada, Y. and Ando, E. (1998). *Income Disparities in Japan – Nihon no shotoku kakusa.* Tokyo: Economic Research Institute of the Economic Planning Agency.

Shimodaira, Hiromi (1998). Slums of Tokyo: Their Changing Phases with Economic Development. In Tatsuru Akimoto (Ed.) *Shrinkage of Urban Slums in Asia and Their Employment Aspects*, Bangkok: ILO Regional Office for Asia and the Pacific.

Tachibanaki, T. (2000). *The Economics of Safety Nets-Safety Net No keizai gaku*, Nihon Keizai Shimbun Ed.

Uzuhasi, Takafumi (1997). International Comparison of Contemporary Welfare States – *Gendai fukushi kokka no kokusai hikaku.* Nihon Hyoron Ed., pp. 84-89.

In: *Poverty Monitoring and Alleviation in East Asia*
K. Tang and C. Wong, editors pp. 117-135

ISBN: 1-59033-828-6
© 2003 Nova Science Publishers, Inc.

Chapter 7

POVERTY ALLEVIATION:
A RIGHTS-BASED APPROACH

Glenn Drover

INTRODUCTION

The affirmation of a rights-based approach to poverty alleviation is on the ascendancy at a time when poverty rates in absolute, and in some cases relative, terms are growing throughout the world (World Bank, 2001). Part of the reason for the increased appeal of a rights-based approach results from the violation of human rights and the oppression of the poor which accompanies globalization. It is a way of highlighting the disparity between the promise and the reality of globalization. Another part of the reason is a heightened realization by many national governments and international bodies such as the World Bank that the numbers of people living in poverty has reached a crisis level which if left unattended may lead to political instability and social disorder. Furthermore, an appeal to rights is strengthened by NGOs such as the Fourth World Movement and Oxfam[1] which remind the world community of longstanding legal and institutional commitments which international bodies and national governments have made to eradicate poverty since the Universal Declaration of Human Rights by the United Nations in 1948. Equally, the current resurgence of interest in rights is a reminder that a commitment to rights, as a basis for the alleviation of poverty, has also waxed and waned depending upon economic circumstances and political will. In the developed countries of the north, the economic circumstances have been propitious but the political will has frequently been absent. Among many developing countries, particularly those with a history of socialism, there has been the political will but economies have been insufficiently developed to realize the political commitment.

Fundamentally, there has also been a deep-seated ambiguity about a rights-based approach to poverty alleviation in different parts of the world. In some western countries, the

---

[1] The Fourth World Movement was founded in 1957. It is dedicated to the eradication of extreme poverty. Oxfam was founded in 1942. It is an international development agency which has regularly campaigned on poverty issues (Simmons, Pat, 1995).

ambiguity is expressed as a trade-off between rights that are civil and political nature and those which address social and economic equality. While the former place an emphasis on forbearance, freedom, and choice, the latter imply restraint, deprivation, and sacrifice. As a consequence, some western intellectuals and politicians argue against the notion of social and economic rights on the ground that they limit human creativity, competition and economic growth. Without the latter, they claim that general standards of living will decline and that poverty will be intensified, not alleviated. In some Asian countries, the ambiguity is less about rights (or the norms inherent in rights) than the western justification of rights (Taylor, 1999). According to Asian critics, the very notion of rights is suspect because of its close association with a western commitment to individualism and autonomy. They suggest that Asian values place greater emphasis on roles and responsibilities, relationships and connectedness. It is through the latter, rather than through the protection of rights, that poverty can be best addressed since it is through different roles individuals have in society as parents, spouses, children, and workers that they learn to share and to care. Some Asian critics query whether there can be a universal notion of rights because rights, to the extent that they do exist, are products of governments and particular cultures (Luo, 1999). They are grounded in particularity, not universality.

Still, even if the western tradition of rights contains specific views of human nature and individual autonomy which are not acceptable in all cultures, it is not the only way to understand rights. Nor has a western understanding stopped the growth in national commitments to various institutional expressions of human rights throughout the non-western world. Most societies, whatever their cultural background, generally agree that people should be able to live in dignity, to be protected against undue harm, or to be entitled to basic subsistence. They may provide a different rationale for these "rights" depending upon cultural background but most countries affirm them nevertheless. Perhaps, because of these universal practices, the international covenants and conventions assiduously enunciate rights rather than explain them. Representatives from all parts of the globe have participated in, and contributed to, their enunciation over the years. On the other hand, without some justification of rights, it is difficult to understand their universal appeal. The fact that a rights-based discourse started in western countries is a by-product of history; the potential for its application elsewhere is not necessarily excluded from the realm of possibility if there is a search for universal consensus on norms which are enforceable on governments (Taylor, 1999). For this to happen, and it seems to be happening, two conditions appear to be important: institutional justification and normative justification. The first is increasingly expressed in various declarations or covenants, led by the United Nations and its various agencies, to which more and more governments throughout the globe are committed. The second is an emerging dialogue about the meaning of rights in different cultures.

In this chapter, therefore, I outline the institutional and normative justifications of a rights-based approach to poverty alleviation. Institutional justification indicates how international commitments and government obligations to rights evolved in the latter half of the twentieth century. In the section on normative justification, I attempt to explain how rights, in particular social and economic rights (which are closely related to poverty alleviation), can be justified under different cultural or personal assumptions. Three types of normative justification are considered: Liberalism, Confucianism and Feminism. The Liberal perspective is representative of western notions, the Confucian of eastern, and the Feminist of interpersonal and possibly inter-cultural relevance. In the conclusion to the chapter, I discuss briefly the limitations of a rights-based approach to poverty alleviation.

INSTITUTIONAL JUSTIFICATION

The institutional justification for a rights-based approach to the alleviation of poverty can be divided into two parts: governmental obligations to ensure the right to freedom from poverty, as expressed in international declarations, covenants and conventions; and governmental commitments stipulated in various international conferences and declarations (People's Movement for Human Rights Education, 2001). In both institutional expressions, poverty is increasingly viewed as a violation of human rights and a consensus is emerging, in principle if not in practice, of the importance of human rights as a prerequisite for combating poverty (UN, Office of the High Commission on Human Rights, 2001). The idea behind both is that people throughout the world have a right to be free from want wherever, and under whatever regime, they live. Equally importantly, there is a growing recognition that the right to freedom from poverty is fundamental to the realization of other rights; it is difficult to talk about freedom of speech or freedom of religion if a person does not have enough to eat. Implicit in that logic is a third idea, an idea that has been an inherent part of institutional justification from the beginning, namely that rights are indivisible and interdependent. To understand how these ideas have evolved over time, we explore first governmental obligations, which are specified in provisions of human rights laws which guarantee persons the right to freedom from poverty, and then we look at the governmental commitments which have been made since the Earth Summit in 1992 to ensure the realization of those rights.

Governmental Obligations

Most people would agree that founding of the United Nations, at the end of World War II, put enormous pressure on governments to specify their obligations to protect human rights. At the time, given the horrendous effects of the war in countries around the globe, there was a willingness, and a commitment, to include an international bill of rights in the charter of the UN. Throughout the war, governments of small countries, and non-governmental organizations (NGOs) from many countries pushed the leaders in the global conflict to protect four essential freedoms: freedom of speech, freedom of worship, freedom from want, and freedom from fear (Morsink, 1999: 1). President Franklin Delano Roosevelt initially stipulated the four freedoms in 1941 in defence of domestic initiatives in the United States, but at the time of the founding of the UN in San Francisco in 1945, they were inserted into the preamble of the charter in honour of the deceased president. Furthermore, the charter also required the establishment of a commission to promote human rights, the only commission specifically mandated in the UN system. The first chair of the commission was Eleanor Roosevelt. She set about immediately to assure the drafting of the Universal Declaration of Human Rights and accompanying covenants. She was successful in having the declaration approved in 1948. It would take another two decades of debates before two covenants, one on civil and political rights, the other on economic, social and cultural rights, were approved.

While the universal declaration was a statement of principles without a mechanism of implementation, it was a break-through at the time in building a consensus (or near consensus) among the countries then represented in the United Nations. It was also approved without any specific normative justification of rights, partly because Roosevelt explicitly avoided such a justification due to its potential divisiveness, partly because delegates from different parts of the globe were able to agree about a common list of rights without having to explain their differing reasons for agreement. Within the declaration, four articles specifically related to poverty: twenty-two, twenty-three, twenty-five, and twenty-six (United Nations, Universal Declaration of Human Rights, 1948). Article twenty-two stipulates that each person has a right to social security. Article twenty-three outlines the right to work and equal pay for equal work. Article twenty-five refers to the right to a standard of living adequate for health and well-being including food, clothing, housing, medical care, and necessary social services. Article twenty-six specifies the right to free elementary education. Taken together, they urge governments to assure their citizens the basics necessary for the promotion of human dignity and the free development of personality as well as security in the event of unemployment, sickness, disability, widowhood, old age or any other lack of livelihood in circumstances beyond individual control.

In some ways, the inclusiveness of a wide range of social and economic rights in the declaration is surprising given the reluctance of western governments at the time to view rights beyond civil and political rights. The reason for their inclusion came largely from the countries of Latin American and the socialist countries in Eastern Europe and China. The countries of Western Europe and the United States were primarily concerned about the protection of civil and political liberties. The compromise was an inclusive declaration, which covered both types of rights, but the standoff between the different blocs led to a long process of debate before two corresponding covenants were finally adopted in1966 and implemented ten years later, in 1976. From 1948 to 1976, the link between poverty and human rights was practically absent in the international arena as the two sides became bogged down in "an extensive and deteriorating debates over the prevalence of one or the other category of rights." (Despouy, 2001: 128). In some western countries, only civil and political rights were considered to be human rights. In socialist bloc countries, rights were perceived to be an extension of the state and the first rights to be protected were social and economic rights. The debate, as Despouy (2001) remarks, was sterile and Byzantine. Rather than contributing to the development of human rights, it arrested their further development for almost thirty years. In the end, however, a compromise was reached as both blocs acknowledged that conditions had to be created for persons to enjoy their civil and political rights as well as social and economic rights. The compromise provided an opening for two jointly related documents; the Covenant on Civil and Political Rights and the Covenant on Economic, Social and Cultural Rights.

Of the two, the covenant on economic, social and cultural rights is more relevant to the alleviation of poverty although the covenant on civil and political rights is not without significance since, among other things, it protects the rights of the poor to criticize government. Within the covenant on economic, social and cultural rights, the articles directly addressing poverty are six, seven, nine, eleven, twelve, and thirteen. Articles six and seven affirm the right to work and specify the ways in which states must exercise the right, including education and economic development. They also outline the conditions for fair treatment within the work place. Article nine affirms the right to social security including social insurance. Article eleven specifically recognizes the right of individuals to be free from hunger. Article twelve outlines the conditions for enjoyment of decent standards of physical and mental health including conditions which assure medical services in the event of sickness. Article thirteen affirms the right to a basic education and the liberty of parents to choose that education for children. Like the universal declaration, therefore, the covenant affirms the basic social and economic rights, which if implemented, serve to minimize or alleviate poverty. Unlike a declaration, however, a covenant goes beyond principles to indicate how the states which sign their agreement should fulfil their obligations. To that end, the United Nations has a Committee on Economic, Social and Cultural Rights to oversee the extent of implementation. In recent years, the committee has increasingly examined the extent to which states have alleviated poverty. In 1998, for example, the government of Canada was reprimanded because it allowed poverty and homelessness to exacerbate at a time when economic growth and overall affluence were increasing (National Anti-Poverty Organization, 1999: 9).

The eventual implementation of the international covenant in the mid-seventies was subsequently followed by the implementation of the Convention on the Elimination of All Forms of Discrimination Against Women in 1981 and the Convention on the Rights of the Child in 1990. Each of the conventions served to strengthen the linkage between human rights and poverty. In the convention on women, particular emphasis was placed on equal treatment with men in education, work, and access to health care. In addition, state parties are called upon to eliminate discrimination against women in rural areas so that they can participate fully in rural development. In the convention on children, they are required to recognize the right of every child to a standard of living adequate for the child's physical, mental, spiritual, moral and social development (People's Movement for Human Rights Education, 2001). However, the momentum toward a rights-based approach to poverty alleviation intensified even further in the decade of the nineties as other agencies of the United Nations including the United Nations Development Programme (UNDP) and the World Bank began to address poverty as a denial of human rights. The UNDP claimed that good health, adequate nutrition, literacy, and employment were not favours to be bestowed on the poor. It introduced the concept of a Poverty Index in order to show that poverty was more than lack of income; it also included illiteracy, malnutrition, early death, poor health, and poor access to drinking water (UNDP, 2001). In the 1997 Human Development Report, the agency added more specificity to the universal declaration, the covenant, and the conventions mentioned above by identifying policy measures such as gender equity, pro-poor economic growth, and freedom for the poor to organize. The World Bank followed suit by providing documentation of poverty trends throughout the world and by directing more money into projects specifically designed to reduce poverty.

During the nineties, the Office of the High Commissioner for Human Rights also drew attention to the relationship between human rights and poverty by focussing on extreme poverty. The focus on extreme poverty came about in considerable measure through the efforts of the Fourth World Movement (Wodon, 2001). Extreme poverty, as defined by the founder of the Fourth World Movement, refers to poverty which results from a series of insecurities which persistently affect several areas of existence and jeopardize a person's chances of regaining his or her rights (Wresinski, 2001: 99). The definition reminds us, like the UNDP Poverty Index, that poverty is more than loss of income; it is also about social exclusion. Hence, efforts to bring the very poor back into social discourse are living proof of the indivisibility of human rights, of the need to see all rights - civil and political, social and economic - as interdependent (Courtney, 2001). The Fourth World Movement was influential in encouraging the Human Rights Commission and the Economic and Social Council to request a report on the impact of extreme poverty on human rights. It tried to persuade the Commission and the Council that a refusal to deal with poverty was not just a "denial of a specific right, or of a certain category of rights, but rather of human rights as a whole" (Despouy, 2001: 131). Partly because of the debates which the report created, and also because of growing pressure from social movements for world bodies to address the impact of globalization on the poor, the UN General Assembly proclaimed the year 1995 as the International Year for Poverty Eradication and subsequently, in full recognition of the enormity of the task, proclaimed the first United Nations Decade on Poverty Reduction from 1997 to 2006 (Despouy, 2001: 135).

Governmental Commitments

In addition to the universal declaration, the covenants, the conventions and the proclamations of the United Nations which stipulate governmental obligations to ensure freedom from poverty, governments have made, in recent years, commitments to eradicate poverty in various meetings including the Earth Summit at Rio, the World Summit for Social Development in Copenhagen, the Fourth World Conference on Women in Beijing, and the Habitat II conference in Istanbul (People's Movement for Human Rights Education, 2001). In each of these settings, poverty was clearly identified as being among some of the major obstacles to economic and social development and there was, in principle at least, a renewed commitment to a rights-based approach to poverty alleviation. The Earth Summit at Rio is a case in point. While the main purpose of the summit was to promote a biodiversity treaty and a convention on climate change, the delegations for 178 countries, heads of states from more than 100 countries, and representatives from more than 1000 non-governmental organizations (United Nations Conference on Environment and Development, 2001) realized that environmental commitments could not be met unless the issue of poverty was also addressed. The connection between the two was stated quite firmly in article five of the Rio Declaration (United Nations Environment Programme, 1992) in which it was affirmed that all states and all people must cooperate in the essential task of eradicating poverty as an indispensable requirement for sustainable development. Further in Agenda 21 (United Nations Sustainable Development, 1992), the comprehensive plan of action coming out of the summit, the language that was used to make the case of combating poverty was, in many cases, the language of rights.

The United Nations World Summit for Social Development (1995) said much the same. In the main report, the heads of states who were signatory to the summit vowed, in principle, to support progress and security for people and communities so that every individual in society was able to satisfy his or her basic needs (UN World Summit, 1995, Section B(1). In addition, they committed themselves "to the goal of eradicating poverty in the world, through decisive national actions and international cooperation, as an ethical, social, political and economic imperative of humankind" (UN World Summit, 1995, Section C(2)). In the same year, the Women's Conference in Beijing, highlighted the disproportionate number of women in poverty throughout the world and called upon governments, international agencies, and non-governmental organizations to adopt policies to address the needs of women in poverty, provide adequate safety nets, and to ensure equal rights to economic resources (United Nations Development Programme, 1995, Platform for Action, Section A. Poverty and Women). In specifying these strategic objectives, the conference delegates were emphasizing the need to eradicate the burden of poverty among women by dealing directly with its structural causes and promoting changes in economic structures. Finally, a year later, in 1996, the Habitat II agenda placed a primary focus on the rights of people, including the poor, to adequate housing, acknowledging the violation of human rights as destructive of human settlements, and affirmed the need to promote equitable societies in order to eradicate poverty (United Nations Human Settlements Programme, 1996). On the basis of these various commitments, it seems that heads of states of the major countries of the world, and certainly international non-governmental organizations, have re-affirmed the importance of a rights-based approach to poverty alleviation which was first enunciated in the universal declaration. Taken together, they also have influenced the UN proclamation of a decade for the elimination of poverty in 1997 as well as the enhanced role of the Office of High Commissioner for Human Rights and the agreements with the World Bank to undertake joint projects to deal with poverty. Whether, however, the various obligations and commitments made by governments and international agencies actually will lead to the reduction, and eventual eradication, of poverty remains to be seen.

NORMATIVE JUSTIFICATION

While a rights-based approach to poverty reduction has a long institutional heritage in the United Nations and increasingly in national governments, the normative justification of rights has received far less attention by international or national bodies. In fact, at an international level, a normative justification has been judiciously avoided. Charles Courtney (2001) observes that during the early drafting process of the Universal Declaration of Human Rights, the delegates argued so fiercely about the philosophical and metaphysical bases of rights, the whole project might have been scrapped if the chair (Eleanor Roosevelt) had not determined that they would be silent on such matters. In other words, while it seemed to be possible then, and still is possible today, to create a high degree of international consensus about a list and range of rights, any attempt to find common ground to explain why people have rights is inherently problematic. In a recent seminar on the philosophical divide between eastern (Chinese) and western (Canadian) perspectives on the meaning of human rights (Mendes and Traeholt, 1997), participants raised two fundamental dilemmas about differences of view of the meaning of rights. The first related to cultural difference. The second was about the dialectics of modernity. In consideration of the first dilemma, they came to the conclusion that cultural differences enriched, rather than blocked, an understanding of rights. In terms of the second, they suggested that different stages of economic development influenced the way in which rights were interpreted. The seminar presupposed that Asian values were in fundamental ways different from Western values. Given the differences, which were accepted as a starting rather than an end point, the participants explored the notion of rights within Western culture and differing conceptions within Asian culture or more specifically Confucian culture. In what follows, therefore, the same distinction is explored by contrasting Liberal and Confucian understandings of rights. In addition, a feminist interpretation of rights is considered because it is built on an assumption that women's experiences, while culturally grounded, transcend culture or at least point to interpersonal understandings which transcend culture.

Liberal Justification

The predominant justification of rights within Western culture draws upon a liberal understanding of human autonomy. Within the liberal tradition, there are two schools of thought: egalitarian and libertarian (Jacobs, 1997). Both share a common assumption that the main purpose of rights is to enhance autonomy so that individuals can act freely to maximize their choices and preferences. The most well known and influential egalitarian liberal proponent is John Rawls. He states that the guiding idea for principles of social justice should be determined by free and rational persons to enhance their own interests from an initial position of equality. He calls the resulting distribution 'justice as fairness' because "those who engage in social cooperation choose together, in one joint act, the principles which are used to assign basic rights and duties and to determine the division of social benefits" (Rawls, 1971: 11). In the same way that individuals decide their own goals, groups of individuals decide the basic regulatory principles of social institutions within which personal choices are made. The result, says Rawls, is a social contract. However, such a contract cannot be thought of as an historical state of affairs, merely a hypothetical device through which rational and free people make choices about fair arrangements. An essential feature of the Rawlsian argument is that no one knows in advance his or her position in society including class, intelligence, physical capabilities or social status. Each makes choices about just social arrangements behind a veil of ignorance. Since everyone is similarly located, no one is in a position to propose principles which will favour his or her circumstances.

Rawl's approach to social justice has an important consequence for those who argue for a rights-based approach to poverty alleviation. At the core of his concept of social justice is the idea that, under a veil of ignorance, people agree to a society in which all primary goods-liberty and opportunity, income and wealth, self-respect and power - are to be distributed equally unless an unequal distribution is to the advantage of the poorest. The benefits and burdens of life, therefore, should be distributed on two basic principles: a principle of liberty and a difference principle (Rawls, 1971: 302). The first principle states that "each person is to have an equal right to the most extensive system of equal basic liberties compatible with a similar system of liberty for all." The second is in two parts. It reads that "social and economic equalities are to be arranged so that they are both to the greatest benefit to the least advantaged … and attached to offices and position open to all under conditions of fair equality of opportunity." The importance of the two principles, as Jacobs suggests (1997: 64), is that "Rawls maintains that each individual should have an equal entitlement right to the same liberties, should have an equal right to compete under conditions of fair play for valuable opportunities in society, and that with respect to other advantages the distribution should function to maximize the situation of the worst-off in society." The distinctive feature of primary goods is that they are essential to all individuals in order to enable them to achieve whatever projects or ways of life they think appropriate. Primary goods are rights like those in the Universal Declaration of Human Rights. Rawls treats people as equal, not by removing all inequalities but those which disadvantage someone. Inequalities are allowed if it can be shown that they lead to improvements for the least disadvantaged. In essence, therefore, he is stating the case for a basic minimum to which all people should be entitled.

A limitation of Rawlsian theory is that it makes too many assumptions about human nature (Kymlicka, 1990). One questionable assumption is that people behind a veil of ignorance are naturally sympathetic to the worst off and adjust their expectations of primary goods accordingly. If, instead of playing it safe, the participants have a greater propensity to risk they may be willing to opt for less than an equal distribution of primary goods on the ground that they stand to gain more if they are not among the worst off. Another is that Rawls places too much emphasis on the original distribution of natural endowments, not on the choices which people make with the endowments they have. Therefore, by using a standard of the equal distribution of primary goods to offset the initial distribution of natural endowments, he ignores the arbitrary effects on those who, because of disability, will require more than an equal distribution of primary social goods in order to have same opportunity. Equally, he does not allow for the fact that two people with equal natural endowments might use them in quite different ways, one more productively than the other. Thus while his theory is sensitive to the arbitrary effects of initial endowments, it is less sensitive to the effect of human ambition and disability.

Ronald Dworkin (1978, 1981), another egalitarian liberal, attempts to compensate for the inadequacies of Rawl's justification of support for the least advantaged in society. He suggests that in addition to justifying inequalities on the basis of the advantage to the poorest members of society, it is also important to take into account inequalities, which come about through personal ambition and choice. He makes a distinction between economic inequalities that are a function of circumstances and those, which come about through choice (Jacobs, 1997: 93). Race, sex, ethnicity, or disability, or geography are examples of circumstances which do not result from choice; they are a matter of luck. Therefore, inequalities which result from circumstances cannot be justified on rational grounds. What counts, in Dwokin's view, is the distributional equality of circumstances. People are considered to be equal in their circumstances when resources are distributed in such a way to allow for differentials in unequal talent and capacities. Since, however, people choose to do different things with their circumstances depending upon their personalities, some will come to have control over more resources than others. Thus unlike Rawls, where the income effects of arbitrary endowments are distributed in a manner that is considered advantageous to the worst off, for Dworkin they are distributed in a manner which reflects the opportunity cost to everyone including the least disadvantaged.

In a very real sense, Rawls and Dworkin are associated with a defence of modern liberal society, partly because they highlight the voluntary nature of social union and political obligation, partly because they ground the moral pursuit of rights in a social contract. The idea of contract is basic to the acceptance of majority rule in western democratic institutions. Contract is also implicit in the willingness of the population, either by consent or by acquiescence, to obey the laws of the state and to accept constitutional government. More importantly, though, social obligations reside in an acceptance of the moral ends or objectives of the institutions which are established and the social claims which are made. To the extent that the institutions or the claims rest in social contract, consent, justice, or the general will, they may also be universalizable although ultimately they have to be linked to some notion of human agency if they are to be acceptable across cultures. In the liberal case, rights are important because they protect and nourish individual autonomy, a sine qua non of human agency. Rights serve to protect human autonomy in two ways (Plant, 1991: 267), by constraints upon inappropriate interference in matters of choice and preference (civil and political rights) and by the provision of benefits and services which allow an individual to act as a moral agent (social and economic rights).

Libertarian liberals, however, reject the notion that social and economic rights to a basic minimum identified by Rawls and Dworkin have the same status as civil and political rights. They say that social and economic rights are different from civil and political rights because they are not grounded in the intention of individual agents. According to Hayek (1974), civil and political rights are a genuine expression of justice because they assure the autonomy of the person and are an indispensable link between justice and individual freedom.[2] Central to his thesis is the idea that justice is about universal rules which assure individual autonomy, not about balancing social interests. Hence, injustice arises from the intentional acts of individuals or groups who interfere in the freedom of others. Societies cannot be classified as unjust because individuals, not societies, have intentionality. In a free and open market, those who end up being poor or at risk because of the workings of the market cannot claim that they have been unjustly treated, only that they have been unfortunate in the lottery of life. This may presuppose some moral obligation to assist those at risk but not because they have a right to such assistance.

Because of a sense of moral obligation, Hayek does not reject the necessity for social programs to help the poor provided that the rationale for the intervention is clear. Social programs, he claims, are not provided because of a social right inherent in the individual or to assure human autonomy, but out of a necessity to prevent destitution and social unrest. Beyond a very basic level of support, however, he feels, like Malthus, that any attempt to reduce inequalities through the intervention of the state is a mirage of distributive justice because it will create the deleterious conditions it is intended to ameliorate. A free economy, and a free society, will necessarily have inequalities and the very presence of inequalities will be a benefit to the poor because it is a sign of a growing and dynamic economy. The relative position of the worst off is not a problem of justice provided the standard of living which they enjoy is better than it would be under any other system. In addition, Hayek opposes principles of social justice if they are used to impose overarching standards on society in the name of a collectively defined good. The libertarian view of justice, therefore, is that individual rights and freedoms must prevail and that any attempt to use the state to accomplish some predetermined end, no matter how noble, in the name of distributive justice, will lead to its opposite.

Nozick takes Hayek's view of rights a step further and views all rights, even the right to liberty itself, as a constraint to self-ownership and life itself. According to Nozick (1974, part two), the primary right to self-ownership means that persons have exclusive rights to anything they can and do appropriate, provided that they gain through voluntary exchange, and no person is made worse off by their appropriation. Justice based on entitlement is constrained by three essential conditions: the original acquisition of holdings; the transfer of holdings, and limitations on holdings not obtained under the first two conditions. The basic idea of Nozick is that what each person obtains is obtained by the legitimate acquisition of property in a state of nature or by exchange with others by consent. Any other form of distribution, no matter how well intentioned, is coercive. Thus, whether the holdings are obtained by fraud, by theft,

---

[2]   The next few paragraphs are largely taken from Drover (1992).

or by what he calls patterning, such as distribution by moral worth, they are not legitimate. The best state, therefore, is a minimal state which uses a monopoly on force to protect and defend legitimate distributions voluntarily gained. There is little room for mandatory contribution to social security unless all persons so mandated agree to the provision. And if that were the case, it would be by voluntary provision.

Strangely, Hayek and Nozick are strong defenders of equality even though their notion of equality is more limited than egalitarian liberalism. Many people, for example, would agree with the notion that we own ourselves, that we are own persons, and that we are entitled to the goods and services which we create of our own making. Also, many are likely to agree with the idea that even if resources are evenly divided in a state of nature, they will over time be unevenly divided simply because some people will invest for the future, some will save, and others will consume. Depending upon chance and circumstance, therefore, those who defer current consumption and invest or save for future consumption are likely to reap the benefits and be better off. And if they are better off because they had foresight or patience, why should they be penalized? Similarly, there is likely to be support for the concern which libertarians have about the potential for government, particularly big government, to be tyrannical through regulation, of economic resources. For both these reasons, the self-ownership argument seems, on the surface, intuitively appealing. It does not preclude individuals from helping others out of sense of duty or moral sentiment (in fact, it may encourage it) but it does reinforce the idea that individuals are ends in themselves and cannot be used to achieve other ends without their consent. They are autonomous.

On the other hand, as G.A. Cohen points out (1986), ownership of self has to be distinguished from ownership of resources. "People create nothing ex nihilo, and all external private property either is or was made of something that was once no one's private property, either in fact or morally ..." (Cohen, 1986: 388). To appreciate the limitation of Hayek's defence of civil and political rights and his attack on social and economic rights, it is important to return to the argument about the unintended nature of market allocations. Setting aside the lack of attention to historical determinants of existing market allocations, and even acknowledging that we cannot predict the outcome of market transactions for individuals, it is not true, as Raymond Plant (1991) points out, that one cannot make a judgement about the impact of market allocations on groups. Since opponents of civil and political rights know that as a matter of routine the intended actions of individuals in the market produce a foreseeable but unintended outcome for others, it is inappropriate for them to claim that they cannot assume some responsibility for the consequences of their actions. Furthermore, there appear to be additional doubts about the moral claims of libertarians when one also recognizes that the distribution of resources may not result at all from market allocations but simply because of congenital handicap or even accident. Social justice, therefore, is not only a question of the intention of the action, or the genesis of a particular problem; it is also about the response to a particular outcome. For that reason, social and economic rights, as well as civil and political rights, seem to be a sine qua non of human autonomy.

Confucian Justification

In some respects, it is difficult to talk about a Confucian justification of rights since the language of rights is not a part of classic Confucian discourse. However, as we shall see, some modern day interpretations of Confucianism suggest that the Confucian philosophy may not be incompatible with a notion of rights, even though it would not necessarily base rights on a foundation of human autonomy. In contrast to liberal assumptions of human nature, Confucianism is grounded in a relational ethic.[3] It does not view persons as separate and apart but interdependent and connected. "At the heart of the Confucian moral code is a notion of the agent as 'self-constitutive and 'constituted by others' (Tao, 1990: 125). The basic idea is that individuals have a potentiality that is shaped by the societies into which they are born. They form and are formed by those societies and they achieve their humaneness through self-development and self-reflection in relation with others. "To realize this ideal, Confucianism stresses character formation or personal cultivation of virtues"; "the ultimate goal is to bring human action into harmony" with virtue, not to foster human autonomy (Tao, 1998: 599). Three ways in which the ideal is achieved are through propriety, rightness, and humaneness. To the Confucian, propriety is an acknowledgement of ethical rules and norms that prevent human conflict by delimiting the boundaries of individual pursuits and fashioning an orderly society. It is determined by basic human relationships involving rulers and ruled, men and women, young and old, friends and relations. It is the relational context within which ethical behaviour is formed, the boundaries within which humaneness is cultivated. Rightness, by contrast, is a principle of appropriateness, the obligation to give a person her just due. Hence, it is not possible, in Confucian thinking, to separate rightness and propriety because one's sense of duty or obligation is understood in relation to roles and responsibilities. Social justice, therefore, is oriented to social order and harmony, guided by reason. But it is also about obligations to those who are disadvantaged since without such obligations virtue cannot be sustained. Finally, "what humaneness has to add to a life embedded in the transmitted values of propriety and good manner is love, active sympathy, and respect for the other as a being like oneself" (Tao, 1998: 601). The rule of humaneness is that one does do to others what one does not want done to oneself. While the rule can simply be interpreted as the negative of the golden rule (that one do to others as one would want done to oneself), it highlights the same need for respect.

Confucianism also places considerable emphasis on caring as a basis of understanding the good society. Caring is a natural outcrop of humaneness since it is based on personal relationships more than respect or equal treatment. It is a universal predisposition to benevolence and altruism, a willingness to sacrifice for others who are in need. Even more than that, it stands for goodness and the potential for moral perfection (Tao, 1999: 576); it is naturally grounded in compassion, a sensitivity to the suffering of others. Caring, therefore, is a common good because it is an ideal for individuals and for society. "Weaving through the Confucian care ethic" says Tao, "are the twin principles of 'love by gradation' and 'love by extension'"(1999: 581). The idea of gradation is that one learns the disposition to care for others by those who are closest to you. It also implies a certain ordering of caring in which priority is given to those who are closest. The idea of extension, on the other hand, is that caring reaches beyond one's kin to the whole social order. It involves the active giving of oneself to others in order to fulfill oneself, to be fully human. In a sense, then, caring is the satisfaction of human need both of the caregiver and the person to whom care is given. It

---

[3] The following few paragraphs rely heavily upon the work of Julia Tao who has helped me to understand important concepts within Confucianism and the weaknesses of the liberal tradition from a Confucian perspective. She is not responsible for any misinterpretation on my part.

requires judgment, the weighing of obligations, sensitivity to different moral claims, and a commitment to the general good.

Because of the strong emphasis on a relational ethic and caring, it is sometimes concluded that Confucianism is incompatible with a notion of rights. Indeed, it has even been suggested that any endorsement of a justice-based ethic, with corollary rights, goes against a Confucian view of the world. However, as Joseph Chan suggests, Confucianism is not simply a relation-based morality even though it does place considerable emphasis on social relationships (Chan, 1999: 217). Justice comes into the picture when virtuous relationships break down. Absolute obedience to established roles and responsibilities or the ideal of filial piety under such circumstances seems not only in conflict with the goals of Confucianism but also contradictory. An appeal to justice as fairness also provides a potential antidote to the Confucian ethic of caring where too strong an emphasis on concern and support could lead to paternalism. Because of these potential limitations, Confucianism could incorporate rights as a fallback position "that serves to protect basic human interests in case virtues do not obtain or human relationships clearly break down" (Chan, 1999: 228). Furthermore, social justice, as equitable distribution, may be implicit in Mencius' comment about the necessity for government to divide land in an appropriate manner (the well-field system) so that a correct determination of compensation can be made (Lee, 1996: 132). Fair distribution, Mencius seems to be saying, is critical for the prosperity of a nation. Similarly, justice as equal opportunity is implicit in the discussion of propriety as education in propriety would be open to all in a society where harmonious relations prevail. "Confucius approaches the issue of equality and harmonious human relationships through the principle of what may be characterized as 'reciprocity'" (Swartz, 1985: 70 quoted by Lee, 1996: 135). In this way, he emphasizes social hierarchy and order for practical purposes but for the social order to be morally acceptable, it seems that people must have equal opportunity for moral development, and that implies, at the least, a basic minimum.

Unlike the liberal concept of justice, and derivative rights, a Confucian concept seems to be an attribute of persons in relation. "The entire corpus of Confucian thought, and reason for dominance of Chinese ethical discourse over two millennia, rests on the universal potential for human beings to achieve moral personhood" (Paltiel, 1997: 28). Because of this potential, the state has obligations to people to assure the conditions under which moral behaviour can be realized. The humane rule of the state presumably includes the promotion of public welfare since without such promotion, it is difficult to see how moral personhood can be actualized (Jia, 1999). Perhaps, because of this, modern Chinese society, which invokes elements of Marxism as well as Confucianism, views rights as an extension of the state rather than as an extension of the individual or human autonomy. On the other hand, Liberal and Confucian thought cohere in recognition of the idea that human dignity is a prerequisite for maintaining a civilized society (Mendes and Traeholt, 1997: 9). But as Li Zhaojie (1997: 188) suggests, "the prevailing definition of human dignity places more emphasis on collective welfare and social harmony and order, since both the traditional (i.e., Confucian) notions as well as sinicized Marxist precepts perceive the meaning of the human person from his/her social being in an intricate web of social relationships rather than from ... atomized autonomy." Also, in contrast to liberal rights, based on the human autonomy, recent Chinese leaders and scholars suggest that institutions confer rights and that groups or classes of people are beneficiaries of rights rather than individuals. Further, the same perspective seems to be shared by other Asian leaders as manifest in the Bangkok Human Rights Declaration of 1993 which gives development goals priority over human rights (Potter, 1999). Perhaps the emphasis on groups or class rights also helps to explain why China is a signatory to the Covenant on Economic, Social and Cultural Rights but not the Covenant on Civil and Political Rights. Hence, both east and west share a common commitment to a rights-based approach to poverty alleviation even though the source and beneficiaries of rights are differently conceived.

Feminist Justification

Feminists also have a relational understanding of rights. A starting point in understanding feminist perspectives is a common concern about the lack of attention to private spaces and private relations in liberal theories of social justice. In justice talk, public space has usually been associated with the rights of men while private space or domestic life has been treated as a female responsibility largely outside the domain of rights. Thus, when theories of justice are discussed, rights, and social rights in particular, have tended to be defined with respect to their effect on public rather private life and women's personal autonomy has been subsumed within the family or other institutions. Another concern about the public-private distinction implicit in theories of justice is that it tends to downplay the fact that men and women are likely to reason differently (Gilligan, 1982), with men focusing on competing rights and women on caring and interpersonal relations. While rights and caring need not be incompatible, as a discussion of Confucian justification suggests, there can be little doubt that the implications of caring have received less attention than rights in liberal theories of social justice. An ethic of caring contrasts development of moral dispositions with an understanding of moral principles, the particularity of response with universal applicability, and attendance to relationships with attendance to fairness (Tronto, 1987).

Feminist philosophers have made a similar point with respect to moral agency. Diana Meyers (1998: 381) suggests that autonomy is not simply equated with the transcendence of social relations through free will but also is determined within a context of socialization and a network of interdependencies.[4] Hence, social relationships are not seen as a threat to autonomy but integral to the realization of a self in relation. For that reason, she suggests that education and nurturance are as essential to that realization as much as health and income. The other aspect of moral agency which Meyers stresses is the relationship between self and caring. She suggests that the denial of care as an essential part of self is, in many ways, a denial of moral responsibility (Meyers, 1998: 373). Caring, therefore, is more than self-sacrifice and altruism. It is an affirmation that a moral agent is particularistic, improvisational, and interactive; that moral thought calls upon the cognitive and affective capacities of a human being; and that moral agency requires individuals to satisfy their needs in a relational context.

In feminist thought, therefore, caring and rights have to be considered together. Rights emphasize the application of rules and abstract principles to guide and to prioritize human relations. Caring lays stress on moral sensibilities and social context in the assessment and satisfaction of human rights. Rights imply right ordering. Caring implies compassion and sensitivity to human need regardless of rights. In principle, caring may even require a person

---

[4] The next two paragraphs are drawn from Drover (2000).

to subordinate his or her needs to another because the needs of the other are given priority. At a minimum, caring is recognition of the fragility of human nature as in the case of an infant, the sick, or the disabled. Therefore, it requires minimum support. At maximum, it is a manifestation of mutual trust and affection. Mostly, though, it flows from a sense of duty and responsibility, partly because of the role a person has in a given situation, partly because of the relationships in which a person is engaged. Hence, attention to caring brings to a consideration of social justice a new kind of morality to displace the more narrowly focussed attention to liberal rights (Phillips, 1991).

Kymlicka (1990) suggests that there are three aspects to an ethic of care that are relevant to an understanding of rights: the development of moral dispositions, attendance to particular needs, and attendance to personal relationships. Each helps to clarify the distinction between rights and caring and each provides insight into the way in which caring is important to the concept of active citizenship. Moral dispositions can be contrasted with moral principles. Unlike the latter, which imply that a moral person primarily needs to know and use the correct principles to behave justly, moral dispositions refer to the capacity of people to perceive needs accurately and to respond accordingly. Dispositions are learned by doing, by being aware of the reasons why a certain kind of action comes about and of the reasons for it. Caring is associated with attendance to personal relationships either because the relationships entail responsibilities or respect for individuals. Still, it is not entirely clear whether feminists are arguing for a conception of justice which is inherently different from liberalism or whether they are simply highlighting the need for consistency in the treatment of men and women or proposing an ideal of androgyny (Sterba, 1988). If it is androgyny, it also is not clear whether the intention is to promote an ideal which combines the virtues of both genders or simply recognition of variability and differences in human nature.

The emphasis on caring does not mean that feminists, at least western feminists, are unconcerned about the notion of autonomy as a basis for rights. In terms of the liberal justification of rights, "the starting point of liberal feminist theory is the understanding that women are in fact the same as men, and therefore equal to men. Women are autonomous individuals who should be as free as men to choose their own life plans and have their freedom equally respected by the state" (Mahoney, 1997: 521). The reason why they insist on gender equality is to assure that the state, and state institutions, are not used to subordinate women to men's interests or to block their engagement in the public world as happened under the Taliban regime in Afghanistan. On the other hand, rights have to extend beyond formal equality with men because there are also differences which need to be recognized, including difference resulting from pregnancy and childbirth, work in the home, or sex-based violence. Hence, it is necessary for women to have rights that are based on difference and go beyond formal equality. Other forms of feminism (cultural, radical, postmodern), which have gained force around the world, start with the notion of difference. The value of starting with difference is that it draws attention to the systemic nature of gender discrimination and the absence or exclusion of women's experience from the development of law, including human rights law. Because of difference, the Convention on the Elimination of all Forms of Discrimination Against Women was approved by the United Nations in 1979. Because of difference, feminists are also concerned that the social and economic rights outlined in the United Nations covenant reinforce the public/private distinction by relying too heavily on the state for the implementation and guaranteeing of rights, such as the rights of the work place, which exclude the working reality of a majority of women throughout the world (Mahoney,

1997). In terms of poverty alleviation, therefore, women's private experiences in the family and outside traditional public spaces have to be taken into account for the full realization of rights, including rights related to poverty.

CONCLUSION

It seems that an institutional justification of a rights-based approach to poverty alleviation strengthened in the last half of the twentieth century. Starting with the Universal Declaration of Human Rights, a preliminary and modest commitment to social and economic rights, as a basis or fighting poverty, has grown into a range of international covenants and conventions to which most governments around the world are more or less committed. While there is no equivalent consensus around a normative justification of rights, there is, nevertheless, a growth in rights-talk among intellectuals and non-governmental organizations in different parts of the world. Most Western theories start with a fundamental notion that human autonomy, however defined, is foundational to rights. By contrast, Asian leaders, and to some extent Asian intellectuals, are inclined to disagree with that starting point. Confucian scholars, faithful to the basic core of Confucian thought, caution against rights-talk based on human autonomy and stress instead the need to reconsider the individual in relationship. In addition, some Chinese scholars, influenced by the official position of the Chinese state and the Marxist heritage of the current Chinese regime as well as Confucian principles, attempt to reframe rights as an extension of the state and governance for the protection of groups and classes of people. Feminists, while sharing to some degree a relational ethic and certainly an ethic of caring with Confucianism, and also having similar reservations about the notion of human autonomy as a starting point for the justification of rights, attempt to balance a principle of equality with a principle of difference. The principle of equality pushes them in the direction of an extended liberal interpretation of rights; the principle of difference allows them to recognize the importance of culture as well as class and race in attempting to reframe the justification of rights. Like Liberals and Confucians, there is among Feminists an attempt to come to terms with the notion of rights and to defend the right of people throughout the globe to be free of poverty.

On the other hand, while there is a growing consensus about the value and importance of rights-talk as a means of fighting poverty, there is no equivalent consensus about the meaning and definition of basic minimum as a way of fighting poverty. Both the institutional and normative justifications of a rights-based approach to poverty alleviation substantiate the need for a social minimum but they are relatively silent on what that minimum should be. On the institutional side, the lack of specificity is partly by intention, partly due to uncertainty. By intention, the various declarations, covenants, and conventions have been content to name the kinds of services and programs that are necessary to alleviate poverty rather than the level of benefits which are required. Because of uncertainty about appropriate definitions of poverty, whether in terms of income or more broadly in terms of deprivation, governments throughout the world have been content to develop their own definitions, if they have any at all, in order to accommodate their own developmental priorities. The modest definitions of poverty developed by the United Nations Development Programme and the World Bank represent an international initiative to move in the direction of a common understanding but there is no target which is currently incumbent upon governments or linked to specific rights. To complicate matters further, the growth of poverty in recent years, both in absolute and relative terms among developed and developing countries, suggests that governmental commitments to the reduction of poverty are in the breach as much as in the promise. To make the promise (or the commitments) a reality, some sort of cross-cultural and trans-national consensus about a universal basic minimum will be needed. That, unfortunately, may take another half century.

REFERENCES

Chan, Joseph (1999). A Confucian Perspective on Human Rights for Contemporary China. In Joanne R. Bauer and Daniel A. Bell (Eds.) *The East Asian Challenge for Human Rights*. Cambridge: Cambridge University Press.

Cohen, G.A. (1986). Self-Ownership, World-Ownership, and Equality In F. Lucash (Ed.) *Justice and Equality Here and Now*. Ithaca, Cornell University. Referenced in Will Kellick (Ed.) *Justice in Political Philosophy*, Volume 1, Aldershot, Hants, Edward Elgar Collection, 1992.

Courtney, Charles (2001). Extreme Poverty and Human Rights: Indivisibility Four Times. In Wodon, Quentin (Ed.) *Attacking Extreme Poverty*. World Bank, World Bank Technical Paper No 502.

Despouy, Leandro (1996). *The Realization of Economic, Social and Cultural Rights*, Final Report on Human Rights and Extreme Poverty, Commission on Human Rights, Economic and Social Council, E/CN.4/Sub.2/1996/13.

Despouy, Leandro (2001). Extreme Poverty and Human Rights in the United Nations. In Wodon, Quentin (Ed.) *Attacking Extreme Poverty*. World Bank, World Bank Technical Paper No. 502.

Drover, Glenn (1992). Social Minima and Social Rights: Justifying Social Minima Socially. In Joel Bakan and David Scneiderman, (Eds.) *Social Justice and the Constitution*. Ottawa: Carleton University Press.

_____ . (2000). Rethinking Social Citizenship in a Global Era. *Social Work and Globalization*, Special Issue of Canadian Social Work, 2,1; Canadian Social Work Review 17; and Intervention, Special Edition.

Dworkin, Ronald (1978). *Taking Rights Seriously*. Cambridge: Harvard University Press.

_____ . (1981). What is Equality? Part 2: Equality of Resources. *Philosophy and Public Affairs*, 10.

Gilligan, Carol (1982). *A Different Voice*. Cambridge, Massachusetts: Harvard University Press.

Hayek, F.A. (1976). *The Mirage of Justice, Volume 2, Law, Legislation and Liberty*. London: Routledge and Kegan Paul.

Jacobs, Lesley (1993). *Rights and Deprivation*. Oxford: Clarendon Press.

_____ . (1997). *An Introduction to Modern Political Philosophy*. Toronto: Prentice-Hall.

Jia, Junling (1997). Social Security and Human Rights in China. In Errol Mendes and Anne-Marie Traeholt (Eds.) *Human Rights: Chinese and Canadian Perspectives*. University of Ottawa, Human Rights Research and Education Centre.

Kymlicka, Will (1990). *Contemporary Political Philosophy: An Introduction*. Oxford: Clarendon Press.

Lee, Thomas H.C. (1996). The Idea of Social Justice in Ancient China. In K.D. Irani and Morris Silver (Eds.) *Social Justice in the Ancient World.* Westport, Connecticut: Greenwood Press.

Li, Zhaojie (1997). Cultural Relativity and the Role of Domestic Courts in the Enforcement of International Human Rights. In Errol Mendes and Anne-Marie Traeholt (Eds.), *Human Rights: Chinese and Canadian Perspectives.* University of Ottawa, Human Rights Research and Education Centre.

Luo, Yanhua (1999). Human Rights Research From an East and Southeast Asian Perspective. In Errol Mendes and Anne-Marie Traeholt (Eds.), *Human Rights: Chinese and Canadian Perspectives.* University of Ottawa, Human Rights Research and Education Centre.

Mahoney, Kathleen (1997). Various Theoretical Perspectives on Women's Rights as Human Rights and Strategies for Implementation. In Errol Mendes and Anne-Marie Traeholt (Eds.) *Human Rights: Chinese and Canadian Perspectives.* University of Ottawa, Human Rights Research and Education Centre.

Mendes, Errol and Anne-Marie Traeholt (Eds.) (1997). *Human Rights: Chinese and Canadian Perspectives.* University of Ottawa, Human Rights Research and Education Centre.

Meyers, Diana (1998). Agency. In Alison M. Jaggar and Iris Marion Young (Eds.) *A Companion to Feminist Philosophy.* Oxford: Blackwell.

Morsink, Johannes (1999). *The Universal Declaration of Human Rights.* Philadelphia: University of Pennsylvania Press.

National Anti-Poverty Organization (1999). *It's Time for Justice.* www.napo-onap.ca/publications/index.

Nozick, Robert (1974). *Anarchy, State and Utopia.* New York: Basic Books.

Paltiel, Jeremy (1997). Cultural and Political Determinants of the Chinese Approach to Human Rights. In Errol Mendes and Anne-Marie Traeholt (Eds.), *Human Rights: Chinese and Canadian Perspectives.* University of Ottawa, Human Rights Research and Education Centre.

Peoples Movement for Human Rights Education, The (2001). *Human Rights and Poverty.* www.pdhre.org/rights/poverty.html.

Phillips, Ann (1991). Citizenship and Feminist Politics, In Geoff Andrews (Ed.) *Citizenship.* London: Lawrence and Wishart.

Plant, Raymond (1991*). Modern Political Thought.* Oxford: Basil Blackwell.

Potter, Pitman (1997). The Right to Development: Philosophical Differences and Political Implications. In Errol Mendes and Anne-Marie Traeholt (Eds), *Human Rights: Chinese and Canadian Perspectives.* University of Ottawa, Human Rights Research and Education Centre.

Rawls, John (1971). *A Theory of Justice.* Cambridge, Mass.,: The Belknap Press of Harvard University Press.

Simmons, Pat (1995). *Words into Action: Basic Rights and the Campaign against Poverty.*

Sterba, James P. (1988). *How To Make People Just,* Totowa, Lanham: Rowman and Littlefield.

Schwartz, Benjamin (1985). *The World of Thought in Ancient China.* Boston: Harvard University Press.

Tao, Julia (1990). The Chinese Moral Ethos and the Concept of Individual Rights. *Journal of Applied Philosophy*, 7, 1.

Tao, Julia Po-wah (1998). Confucianism. *Encyclopaedia of Applied Ethics*, Volume 1.

Tao, Julia Lai Po-wah (1999). Does it Really Care? The Harvard Report on Health Care Reform for Hong Kong. *Journal of Medicine and Philosophy*, 24, 6.

Taylor, Charles (1999). Conditions of an Unforced Consensus on Human Rights. In Joanne R. Bauer and Daniel A. Bell (Eds.) *The East Asian Challenge for Human Rights.* Cambridge: Cambridge University Press.

Tronto, J. (1987). Beyond Gender Difference to a Theory of Care. *Signs: Journal of Women in Culture and Society,* 12, 4.

United Nations Conference on Environment and Development Collection (1992). *Abstract/Summary.* www.ciesin.org/datasets/unced/unced.

United Nations Development Programme (1995). *Report of the Fourth World Conference on Women.* gopher.undp.org/00/unconfs/women/off/a--20.en

_____ . (1997). *Human Development to Eradicate Poverty*, Human Development Report Overview. www.undp.org/hdro/e97over.

United Nations Development Programme (2001). *Poverty Overview.* www.undp.org/poverty/overview.

United Nations Environment Programme (1992). *Rio Declaration on Environment and Development*, www.unep.org/unep/rio.

United Nations Human Settlements Programme (1996). *The Habitat Agenda: Istanbul Declaration on Human Settlements.* www.unchs.org/unchs/english/hagenda/ist-dec.

United Nations Office of the High Commissioner for Human Rights (1966). *International Covenant on Civil and Political Rights.* www.unhchr.ch/html/menu3/b/a_ccpr.

_____ . (1966). *International Covenant on Economic, Social and Cultural Rights*, www.unhchr.ch/html/menu3/b/a_cescr.

_____ . (1948). *Universal Declaration of Human Rights*, www.unhchr.ch/udhr/lang/eng.

United Nations Sustainable Development (1992). *Earth Summit Agenda 21.* www.un.org/esa/sustdev/agenda21.

United Nations World Summit for Social Development (1995). *Report of the World Summit for Social Development.* gopher.undp.org/00/unconfs/wssd/summit/off/a--9.en.

Wodon, Quentin (Ed.) (2001). *Attacking Extreme Poverty.* World Bank, World Bank Technical Paper No. 502.

World Bank (2001). *World Development Report 2000/2001: Attacking Poverty.* Oxford University Press: The Author.

Wresinski, Joseph (2001). The Very Poor, Living Proof of the Indivisibility of Human Rights. In Quentin Wodon (Ed.), *Attacking Extreme Poverty.* World Bank, World Bank Technical Paper No. 502.

In: *Poverty Monitoring and Alleviation in East Asia*
K. Tang and C. Wong, editors pp. 137-151

ISBN: 1-59033-828-6
© 2003 Nova Science Publishers, Inc.

Chapter 8

THE ILO'S APPROACH TO POVERTY ALLEVIATION

Kwong-leung Tang

INTRODUCTION

Degrading and poor working conditions are commonplace in many parts of the world. Many workers die or get injured because of hazardous work conditions. Across nations, the incidences of industrial accidents and occupational diseases remain alarming. According to World Health Organization estimates (1997), occupational accidents account for more than 120 million injuries and 220,000 deaths per year. There are some 160 million cases per year of occupational diseases. Studies have shown that the risk of occupational disease and injury is increased by lack of access to sanitation and potable water, malnutrition, illiteracy and poverty (Holtz, 1999). On the other hand, unemployment and its ensuing poverty continue to haunt many developed and developing nations, including the rich economies in East Asia. There is a clear need for international organizations (along with national governments) to act together to tackle these problems. In this regard, the International Labor Organization (ILO) has been the leading specialized international agency that has been set up specifically to promote labor rights.

While the ILO is concerned with the promotion of labor rights through standards and conventions, such action is intricately linked with poverty alleviation. Its early origin has been attributed to the harshness of working conditions after the Industrial Revolution. Such conditions prompted public demands for international regulation to tackle the poverty in which workers lived (De la Cruz et al., 1996). It was felt by those who were concerned about labor conditions that national legislation on labor could not be solidly established in individual countries if not supported by parallel standards adopted internationally. At this time, many also felt that poverty alleviation activities ought to go beyond national boundaries in order to be effective. Gradually, international organizations such as the United Nations and the ILO have become deeply involved one way or another in the alleviation of poverty. And poverty eradication has become a central objective of the United Nations agenda.

The work of international agencies is performed at two levels: the setting up of international normative standards (deemed as human rights) (Strang and Chang, 1993), and the implementation of individual anti-poverty programs (Mishra, 1998). Needless to say, in the present era of globalization the effectiveness of international institutions in promoting and monitoring human rights standards has an added importance. The role of international organizations in rights-based social development is crucial for several reasons. Firstly, they supply a global vision of social justice. Secondly, these organizations provide assistance, resources and technical guidance to member states in their campaigns against poverty. Finally, international monitoring of countries' social rights records puts them under greater scrutiny.

Given the importance of the international organizations, this chapter analyzes the work and achievements of the ILO with respect to poverty alleviation at the global level. We argue that the strength of the ILO lies in the fact that it is one of the oldest and most respected international organizations entrusted with the task of promoting labor rights and eliminating poverty. Almost all nations of the world participate in this international organization. The ILO is not generally thought of as a human rights body. Contrary to common perception, however, we argue here that ILO standards have played a central role in protecting fundamental human rights, including the right from want and hunger. Many ILO standards that define acceptable levels of working conditions and worker protection (such as occupational health and safety, working hours, social security, pensions and health insurance) have an indirect impact on poverty. The enforcement of these international labor standards not only promotes labor rights but also helps to alleviate poverty. While the ILO's role in promoting fundamental labor rights has been well acknowledged, its involvement in poverty alleviation, institutionalized as early as in the Declaration of Philadelphia of 1944, has been important but less conspicuous. This chapter therefore looks at two specific programs for poverty alleviation initiated by the ILO: the basic needs approach and the employment programs. We end our discussion on a cautious note, arguing that economic globalization and the rise of neo-liberalism may put pressure on the ILO to change its social policy orientation. Ultimately this would hamper its poverty alleviation efforts.

SOCIAL JUSTICE MANDATE

At present, the ILO is a specialized, independent agency of the United Nations, based in Geneva, Switzerland, with 175 member countries represented by workers, employers and governments (ILO, 2000). Since its establishment in 1919 under the Treaty of Versailles, the ILO's means of action lie in three areas: standards, technical cooperation (to support countries' social and economic development), and research and dissemination of information (De La Cruz et al., 1996). Specifically, it has developed an extensive body of conventions, standards and recommendations in the field of international labor law pertaining to a safe and healthy work environment, non-discrimination, fair wages, working hours, child labor, convict or forced labor, freedom of association, the right to organize, and the right to collective bargaining. As discussed, these basic labor standards are also considered human rights standards.

Essentially, the ILO adopts a consensual approach when it comes to setting up and enforcing labor conventions and standards. Organizationally, it is the only international agency in which non-governmental sectors of society participate fully with government. This means that tripartism is the cornerstone of the organization. The Governing Body is the executive council of the ILO. It comprises 28 government members, 14 worker and 14 employer members. The International Labor Conference, open to all member states, meets annually to draft, debate and adopt international labor standards in the form of conventions and recommendations. The Conference also monitors the application of existing labor standards and serves as a forum for the discussion of international labor and social issues.

The establishment of the ILO is attributed to the need to promote social justice as an essential precondition of lasting peace (Creighton, 1998). This is evidenced by the 'methods and principles' which were set out in Article 41 of the original Constitution of the ILO and which were incorporated in the preamble to the revised Constitution of 1946. They include:

First.	The guiding principle...that labor should not be regarded merely as a commodity or article of commerce.
Second.	The right of association for all lawful purposes by the employed as well as by the employers.
Third.	The payment to the employed of a wage adequate to maintain a reasonable standard of life as this is understood in their time and country....
Sixth.	The abolition of child labour. ...
Seventh.	The principle that men and women should receive equal remuneration for work of equal value.

The Declaration of Philadelphia of 1944 was formally appended to the ILO Constitution in 1946. This showed not only the ILO's commitment to the protection of fundamental human rights but also its concern with poverty. The Conference reaffirms the fundamental principles on which the organization is based and, in particular, that:

a) labor is not a commodity;

b) freedom of expression and of association are essential to sustained progress;

c) poverty anywhere constitutes a danger to prosperity everywhere;

d) the war against want requires to be carried on with unrelenting vigor within each nation, and by continuous and concerted international effort in which representatives of workers and employers, enjoying equal status with those of governments, join with them in free discussion and democratic decision with a view to the promotion of the common welfare.

CONVENTIONS AND STANDARDS

The traditional function of the ILO has been one of standard setting. The ILO standards were introduced to tackle the "worst of the most basic problems in the labor field" (De La Cruz et al., 1996: 12) and to lay down minimum bases for law to remedy the worst social injustices. There are a number of areas listed in the Preamble to the 1919 Constitution: conditions of work and the working day, the work of women and children, minimum wages, occupational diseases and accidents, migrant workers, unemployment, freedom of association, equal pay, vocational training, and pensions for old age and injury.

In 1944, the Declaration of Philadelphia greatly expanded the scope of the ILO's activities to include the pursuit of broader social policy initiatives. The ILO standards now include human rights, employment, living conditions, development and social welfare. Generally, the ILO conventions and standards offer a model that nations can draw upon to design policy. More importantly, governments occasionally refer to the ILO standards to legitimate their action (Strang and Chang, 1993).

The organization set its Convention obligations at high levels and sometimes in broad terms. It wanted to ensure economic progress in nations is accompanied by social progress. Not surprisingly, for a long time after the Second World War the ILO's approach has been marked by a commitment to a Keynesian economic approach (A Donoso Rubio, 1998). It has continued to endorse a full employment policy.

There was a need to draft the Conventions in detail. The ILO moved policies into the realm of fundamental, universally recognized rights. Compared to some United Nations' human rights treaties (for instance, the International Covenant on Social, Economic and Cultural Rights), the ILO standards would give more protection to workers since these obligations are stipulated in more concrete terms (Meron, 1982).

The ILO Constitution provides that all member states are bound, in all cases, to submit ILO Conventions and Recommendations to their competent authorities within a year or 18 months of their adoption. The Constitution also provides for an enforcement mechanism. It stipulates that states should supply reports not only on Conventions that they have ratified, but also, at the request of the Governing Body of ILO, on non-ratified Conventions and on Recommendations to indicate the position of their law and practice, difficulties encountered, and future prospects. There is a complaints procedure and a system of investigation and reporting. The ILO Conventions can be ratified when a state undertakes to give effect to them. In other words, ratification is voluntary but it is also legally binding. It cannot be accompanied by reservations. Yet, Conventions can be denounced by states, which have ratified them. Britain and other industrial capitalist nations have relied on this provision to denounce some Conventions, which were ratified earlier.

Certain ILO Conventions have positive impacts, both direct and indirect, on poverty alleviation. The various Conventions and Recommendations on Social Security have had a profound influence on the development of national legislation for social security as well as the evolution of schemes in different countries to provide specific protection. In many developed countries, such standards have brought about a realization of the gap between what is necessary and what is in fact available in terms of social security in those countries and have helped to consolidate and improve the coverage and benefits of their social security schemes (Mathew, 1979). The guiding principles contained in the ILO Conventions and Recommendations on Social Security have been instrumental in the development of social insurance that might otherwise have remained selected programs for the benefit of a privileged group of workers. Immediately after the Second World War, the ILO played a decisive role in developing global awareness and acceptance of the new and much broader concept of social security based on the principles of universality of social protection and adequacy of benefit coverage.

Admittedly, empirical validations on the impacts of ILO Conventions have been few and far between. Two recent studies deserve special mention. A research study by Senti (1998), focusing on the effects of ILO-social security conventions on welfare spending in 18 advanced democracies between 1960 and 1989, showed the positive impact of ILO standards.

The statistical results of the pooled cross-sectional and time series analyses supported the proposition that welfare spending development was not only a consequence of national prerequisites, but also of external changes and international cooperation. This study showed that each ratification increased welfare spending by nearly 0.7% of GDP. Certain ILO Conventions establishing minimum standards even increased welfare spending in these countries by 0.9% of GDP.

An earlier study by Strang and Chang (1993) pointed to the same positive impact. The researchers examined the impact of the welfare regime advocated by the ILO. In this study, twenty labor conventions were examined, including worker's compensation, social security, unemployment, invalidity, old-age insurance, and employment injury etc. Both developed (18) and less developed countries (22) were sampled, the latter being defined as countries with per capita GDP of less than US $3,000 in 1975. The researchers found that countries that had recently ratified ILO Conventions related to welfare showed increased growth in spending. The effects of ILO ratification were particularly strong in the industrialized capitalist states (such as Belgium, Denmark, France etc.) where prior welfare spending was low and the working class had a weakly institutionalized role in policymaking.

In their regression study, ILO ratification seemed unimportant when social spending in the 22 less developed countries was considered. Only a few sampled developing countries like Malta, Costa Rica and Cyprus showed substantial growth in welfare spending following their ratification of ILO Conventions. The researchers argued that some developing countries felt that ILO standards on social security were too demanding, given their fiscal and organizational constraints. They cautioned that: "ratification may be connected to slowly evolving programs or to change in programs that do not produce spending increases" (Strang and Chang, 1993: 249). They further concluded that these findings suggested that international norms contributed to policy where they offered compelling models for countries to legitimate policy innovation.

BASIC NEEDS APPROACH

After its standard-setting function, the best known effort initiated by the ILO and the United Nations against poverty is the "basic needs" approach. In the 1970s, both the ILO and the World Bank were at the forefront of championing and articulating this approach, which gives priority to meeting the basic needs of the world's poor (Qizilbash, 1996).

The basic needs approach originated from the final document of the World Labour Conference, organized by the ILO in 1975, which challenged the prevailing trickle-down theory of development that economic growth ultimately leads to the improvement of social conditions and hence will meet the needs of all poor people. By contrast, the strategy of the basic needs approach is for the state to guarantee a minimum income to the poorest groups of the population. Such income must cover the primary needs of a family with regard to food, housing and clothing, but also fundamental services like "the availability of drinking water, public sanitation, transport, medical care, [aside from] an adequately paid job for whoever wished to work" (ILO, 1976). Later, scholars such as Paul Streeten and Francis Steward made further refinements to the theory, arguing for the need to implement public policies to combat poverty based not only on income, but also on the transfer of goods and services in the fields of health and education. Other analysts, such as Sundaram (1996), argued that development means more than the eradication of poverty and that "basic needs" should cover the provision of minimum social needs. Thus, basic-needs development should give priority to human welfare (e.g. education, health and housing). Some academics (Nanda, 1985) further expanded the notion of basic needs, arguing that it includes both material and non-material needs that are vital for self-realization.

The importance of the basic needs initiative must be placed in historical context. There have been several key periods in the post-war history of social policy development in the developing countries. There has been a strategy of economic growth, a concern over equity and redistribution, the basic needs approach, and the revival of economic growth strategy (Hofferbert, 1990; Midgley 1994; Synder and Tadesse, 1995; Tang, 1996). The main thrust of development theory from the end of the Second World War until well into the 1960s focused on the dynamics of national income growth, often measured by change in GNP per capita over some specified period of time. Also known as trickle-down theory, development policy focused on infrastructural development in the expectation that benefits would flow to the population of developing countries. In social welfare, remedial social services sought to tackle pressing social problems (Hardiman and Midgley, 1989). There was a strong conviction that planning would raise incomes through economic growth and that government intervention to meet social needs was unnecessary.

However, improved data and research on income redistribution did not support the predictions of income growth policy (Goulet, 1977; Adelman and Morris, 1984). Evans (1979) pointed out that even the 'Brazilian growth miracle' of the 1960s did not reduce inequality of income. About the same time, the World Bank began to realize that trickle-down economics did not work in the majority of cases. Poverty alleviation became its primary goal in the 1970s and its loans were targeted at poverty groups (Taylor, 1997). Thus, it joined hands with the ILO and promoted the basic needs approach in developing countries.

After its implementation, the basic needs approach has been subjected to critical appraisal. Sen (1984) criticizes this approach for its overemphasis on access to basic goods, thus underemphasizing the ends of development. Some critics feel that the approach is mere political rhetoric. Others argue that it only aims at the amelioration of poverty, rather than its elimination (Gauhar, 1982). Critics further argue that it falls short of providing a new basis for the theory of development (Qizilbash, 1996). Admittedly, sufficient funding is a necessary condition for the success of any basic needs strategy. And this condition is often missing in some countries.

There is no lack of defenders of the basic needs approach. They argue that it has real potential value for improving human capital, strengthening economic development, and developing locally based political institutions (Spalding, 1990). Others believe that the fulfillment of basic needs will lead to improvements in labor productivity. At any rate, the notion of basic needs has become pervasive and it could pose as a policy alternative in both developed and developing countries.

PRODUCTIVE EMPLOYMENT AND POVERTY

The rise of neo-liberalism since the 1980s has partly undermined international action to implement basic needs by putting the policy emphasis back on rapid economic growth as the ultimate solution to poverty. Gradually, the emphasis on poverty reduction on the part of the

ILO has been shifting toward employment. Traditionally, the ILO deals with employment-related matters (Mishra, 1998). This role is all the more germane when lingering unemployment (that is in turn creating poverty) is found in many parts of the world. Most recently, the ILO has been actively involved in an intra-agency collaboration within the United Nations to counter poverty. It played an active role in the World Summit for Social Development (1995). Soon afterwards, as the lead agency of the taskforce that was set up to give operational significance to the Programme of Action adopted by the World Summit, the ILO helped undertake a series of employment policy reviews in seven developing countries. These reviews examined policies related to employment and sustainable livelihoods and those measures that are needed for the achievement of full employment and the eradication of poverty. Since then, the ILO has conducted nine employment reviews in countries like Ireland, Austria, Denmark, Kenya and the Ukraine (ILO, 1999c).

The main emphasis for the ILO is on employment creation. It supports the implementation of an "Employment-Intensive Programme" that is designed to maximize employment generation through public investments. Some US $208 million has been spent on these programs since 1986 in over 35 developing countries (ILO, 1999a; 1999b). Four major guiding themes are upheld by the ILO: the linkages between macro-economic policies and poverty eradication; understanding the mechanisms of poverty generation; the important role of public policy; and rights as a normative framework for poverty eradication (United Nations, 1998).

The ILO now realizes that the implementation of these employment programs must be multi-sectoral and targeted. In its Secretary-General's report presented to the United Nations General Assembly in 1998, the ILO stressed the importance of establishing "an enabling environment for poverty alleviation through employment-intensive growth at the macro and sectoral levels, as well as on specific target groups" (paragraph 106).

The ILO's contribution to poverty alleviation is also encapsulated by its involvement in the follow-up activities to the World Summit. It published two important works, "Successes in Anti-Poverty," which discusses effective policies for poverty eradication in the 1990s and beyond, and "The incidence of poverty in developing countries: An ILO compendium of data," which includes statistics on the incidence of poverty in the developing world (ILO, 1999c).

AN ASSESSMENT

The ILO's work has received some strong endorsements from other international organizations and United Nations agencies. The 1995 World Summit for Social Development in Copenhagen acknowledged that the ILO's core standards were fundamental human rights. Likewise, an OECD study commented that respect for core standards did not undermine the economic competitiveness of developing countries (Frazer and Nyland, 1997).

Overall, the ILO (2000) is positive about its own achievements in the area of labor rights. Needless to say, the tripartite nature of the organization ensures that maximum support from governments, employers and employees is obtained before standards and conventions are put forward. The ILO contends that the existing enforcement mechanism is effective. These standards' enforcement procedures include: systematic checking of national laws and practices against the provisions of ratified conventions; examination of specific complaints filed by other governments or workers' or employers' organizations, and publication of findings. It is estimated that nations have changed 2,230 national laws or practices in response to concerns raised by ILO supervisory bodies.

On the other hand, critics of the ILO argue that its efforts remain fragmented and limited in impact. Some countries are not ready to ratify many of the labor conventions. The average number of ILO ratifications per country in the mid-1990s was 41 (Deacon et al., 1997). When one looks at the number of ratifications in Asian societies, one has to agree with this observation. In Asian countries, compliance with ILO Conventions has not been strong. In mid 1998, Australia ratified 57 of the 178 Conventions that were in place, followed by New Zealand with 52 Conventions ratified. In the same period, Japan ratified 42 Conventions. Singapore had only 21 Conventions ratified, while Indonesia, Malaysia and South Korea had all ratified fewer than 11 Conventions.

Despite the low number of ratifications in Asia, research studies have noted a qualitative change in the acceptance of and receptiveness to ILO standards. A case in point is Communist China. In a study of China's relations with the ILO (1971-89), Kent (1997) found that China changed from a position claiming special exemption and privileges within the ILO to one in which it accepted its reporting obligations and acknowledged the validity of some ILO standards and their applicability to China. Some of these standards were later translated into new Chinese legislation. This change could be explained by China's self-interests within the ILO as well as domestic labor unrest.

The contributions of the ILO can be seen at two levels: global and national. Globally, the ILO standards serve as the benchmark for labor rights. As Weisband (2000) puts it, these standards reduce the risks of state deflection from core labor standards and thereby promote monitoring by learning. A case in point is the convention on child labor. Back in 1973, the ILO issued its Minimum Age Convention (No. 138) to alert world attention to child workers. In 1999, the organization issued the Convention on the Worst Forms of Child Labor (No. 182), calling for the immediate elimination of the worst forms of child labor, including the sale and trafficking of children and child prostitution. Of particular note is the fact that this more recent Convention cited poverty as the main cause of these forms of child labor. Along with other human rights conventions, the ILO standard thus puts the issue of child poverty and labor back on the table.

The ILO is taking a hard stand against violators. Recently, it has taken some strong action against states in violation of its conventions. A case in point concerned Burma where thousands of people were in forced labor. In 1999, it was excluded de facto from the ILO. In an unprecedented resolution submitted to the International Labor Conference, trade unions and employers asked the ILO to refuse Burma all technical assistance and to ban the country's representatives from attending its meetings, because of the systematic use of forced labor by the ruling military junta. The resolution was adopted by a large majority of government, employers' and workers' delegates from the 174 member states of the ILO.

All in all, national welfare programs are affected by supranational initiatives at the global level. Nationally, there are instances where states have to consider whether their social policies comply with ILO standards. Australia's policy initiatives such as the privatizing of prisons and "work-for-the-dole" program have been made to ensure that they comply with the Forced Labor Convention of the ILO (Creighton, 1998).

RECENT CHANGES

Currently, the ILO is facing some critical challenges (Cooney, 1999). As discussed, the ILO's approach was marked by a commitment to a Keynesian economic approach before 1990. This led to an espousal of a statist approach in the promotion of labor rights. Moreover, some critics believe that the organization also set its Convention obligations at high levels, sometimes far ahead of members' economic conditions. Even the ILO acknowledges that it has drafted Convention obligations in excessive detail, discouraging some countries from ratifying certain Conventions. On the other hand, some countries feel that these standards are not precise enough and would be difficult for them to translate them into local laws.

Major policy changes occurred towards the end of twentieth century. Most recently, the ILO has affirmed the relevance of labor conventions and standards in the new world of globalization. But it also decided to pay more attention to core human rights and labor rights, retreating somewhat from its overly broad social goals. Consequently, in its 1998 Declaration on Fundamental Principles and Rights at Work, four fundamental principles for all ILO members were set out: freedom of association and the right to bargain collectively; abolition of forced labor; equal opportunity and treatment in the workplace; and the elimination of child labor. These principles are covered by the ILO's core Conventions. The realization of these principles would be linked to social progress. To some analysts, the Declaration would constitute a binding commitment on the part of the ILO members to advance the core Conventions. They suggest that these four labor principles should be integrated into the World Trade Organization (WTO), holding the community of nations responsible through the threat of a WTO supported trade-based response (Moorman, 2001). Thus, any denial of workers' basic core rights (e.g. the use of forced child labor) by any country would lead to trade sanctions against their products.

As expected, there has been strong support for these fundamental principles from the workers. To promote the importance of fundamental principles and core standards, the workers' representatives in the ILO wanted all countries to recognize these core standards, not through ratification, but by virtue of their membership in the ILO. On the other hand, the government representatives in the ILO sent in a strong dissent, arguing that this would undermine the national sovereignty of states. While it is likely more discussions about the status of these core rights are needed in the near future, some legal experts now argue that these core conventions have already been elevated to the level of customary international law (Frazer and Nyland, 1998). By virtue of this legal precept, these fundamental principles are automatically binding on all the countries that are members of the ILO.

GLOBALIZATION AND THE ILO

A second challenge to the ILO that would carry far more deep-seated ramifications relates to the impact of economic globalization on the ILO's policy orientation (Deacon et al., 1997). It has to be pointed out that some big leaps forward in advancing labor standards were achieved after the two World Wars (periods of social and political catastrophe). Undeniably, fear of Communism prompted many countries to improve labor standards. With the collapse of the Warsaw Bloc, this threat is no longer potent. Intense international competition among countries and increasing global interdependence could easily turn labor standards into a subject of dispute. These forces could trigger a downscaling of labor standards. An ILO study on the social dimension of trade liberalization found that globalization has increased the unwillingness of its member states to ratify ILO standards because they are afraid that these standards will undercut their economic competitiveness (Frazer and Nyland, 1997).

More importantly, in the face of economic globalization there are some signs that the ILO is under more pressure to subscribe to the market-oriented paradigm and abandon Keynesian theory, even though it may still adhere to the principle of some degree of government regulation. Legal scholars such as A. Donoso Rubio (1998) argue that some ILO documents (e.g. the ILO's *World Employment 1996/97*) now endorse the view that employment will be generated through economic growth (rather than government intervention or a basic needs approach). The Director General of the ILO has stated that his organization will not be too "protagonistic" in defining the social policies of member states. The organization is under pressure to drop its preference for specific goals (as defined in its labor conventions) and resort more to the general concepts of "social progress."

This is not an unexpected challenge, since the market-oriented, neo-liberal paradigm has gained such prominence in the world since the 1980s. In a nutshell, neo-liberal proponents argue that social programs harm the economy and global competitiveness requires reductions in social spending. The election of Margaret Thatcher in Britain and Ronald Reagan in the United States led to the ascendancy of neo-liberalism in many parts of the world. Also, the collapse of the USSR reinforced the belief that any statist model was irrelevant in the new world of economic globalization and liberalization.

If this turns out to be the case, it will be a most worrying development since this would ally the ILO more closely to other international organizations like the World Bank and the IMF. These organizations have strongly subscribed to a neo-liberal agenda in the last few decades. Established in 1945, the World Bank and the IMF have been popularly known as "Bretton Woods institutions" that were intended to place the international economy on a sound footing after World War Two. The work of the Bank and the Fund is complementary, though their individual roles are different (IMF, 2002). The World Bank is a lending institution whose aim is to help integrate countries into the wider world economy and promote long-term economic growth that reduces poverty in developing countries. Its work includes the financing of infrastructure projects, such as road-building and improving water supply. On the other hand, the IMF acts as a monitor of the world's currencies by helping to maintain an orderly system of payments between all countries. It lends money to members who face serious balance of payment deficits. The IMF's main focus is on macroeconomic performance, and on macroeconomic and financial sector policies. In short, while the World Bank makes loans for both policy reforms and projects, the IMF concerns itself with policies alone.

The key policy instrument of the IMF is the structural adjustment program. These programs mandate debtor governments to open their economies to foreign corporations, balance budgets through cuts in social programs and privatize publicly owned enterprises. Overall, they aim at achieving economic equilibrium and increasing economic growth in member states. The programs involve both stabilization and liberalization measures that cover reduced government spending and restrictive credit policies. It remains to be seen whether the ILO will give full support to the structural adjustment programs that are championed by the World Bank and the IMF in the developing world. Its proponents contend that they could curb inflation. The adoption of such policies in any country would ultimately reduce the government's scope of activities.

However, these IMF programs have been subject to increasingly vociferous criticism, in terms of their impact on the poor. In their study of Zimbabwe, Kawewe and Dibie (2000) found that these economic programs have inflated poverty, decreased the country's capability to develop a strong diversified domestic economy, and increased the exploitation of workers through economic deregulation (accompanied by environmental degradation). Their devastation of the poor is manifested in recurrences of socioeconomic crises that threaten peace and social justice.

There are other problems. Many critics (Bird, 1996) have pointed to the fact that some programs that were supported by the IMF were not completed, reflecting noncompliance with the components of the program. In some cases, the short-term control over aggregate demand generated political and social unrest. There is also growing empirical literature that throws doubt over the efficacy of these programs. In their study of the socioeconomic impacts of structural adjustment programs in sixteen Latin American countries, Crisp and Kelly (1999) found that these programs seemed to reduce inflation but adjustment was weakly associated with economic growth.

Many people have criticized the IMF and the World Bank for imposing these inappropriate policies on some Asian states after the economic crisis in 1997. In retrospect, the Asian financial crisis drove home the point that structural adjustment programs (imposed by the IMF and the World Bank on selected Asian countries) were faulty and should not be followed uncritically. Even these international organizations were urged to rethink their stabilization programs after they found that they had not brought about the desired impact. Earlier, the 1995 World Summit for Social Development, in its Copenhagen Declaration and Program of Action, made some proposals designed to reorient structural adjustment programs into a human-centered strategy for promoting productive employment, poverty eradication, and the enhancement of social integration (Adedeji, 1999).

Nevertheless, there are instances that show the ILO is still committed to a statist approach that emphasizes statutory social protection. In the early 1990s, it fought against the World Bank's thinking on pension reform, arguing that the European pension system was sustainable and there was no population pressure for the privatization of pensions (Deacon et al., 1997). Moreover, the current position of the ILO on labor standards could be seen as an attempt to counter and moderate the impact of the structural adjustment programs advocated by the IMF and the World Bank. In its contribution to the World Summit on Social Development (1995), for instance, the ILO contended that its standard-setting activities were not incompatible with policy to eradicate poverty in developing countries.

Two other examples are relevant to this discussion. The first instance concerns the ILO's response to the Asian financial crisis and its fallouts, while the second occasion captures the latest official stand of the ILO. It is common knowledge that the Asian financial crisis hit hard at some countries. The official response of the IMF (1999a; 1999b) was to implement structural adjustment programs in the countries affected. The long-term goal was economic revitalization. But it also acknowledged the importance of social protection "to shelter the poor from the adverse effects of the economic crisis" (IMF, 1999a). And it quickly pointed out that "the challenge has been to establish cost-effective, sustainable social programs that do not create large labor market disincentives or discourage job creation" (ibid.). Immediately after the Asian financial crisis, the ILO, taking a stand that differed significantly from that of the IMF and the World Bank, urged all East Asian states to expend more resources on social programs as there were massive social needs (i.e. rising poverty and unemployment). Emphasizing the necessity to alleviate the plight of the needy, it urged countries to introduce or strengthen their social security systems. While the governments in Hong Kong, Singapore and Taiwan brushed aside this suggestion, South Korea followed its advice and considerably strengthened its unemployment insurance program to assist the retrenched workers (ILO, 1999a, 1999b; Tang, 2000).

Interestingly, the ILO recently adopted the UN's Administrative Committee on Coordination statement pertaining to action to eradicate poverty in its report to the General Assembly in 2000 (ILO, 1999c). The ACC's stand is clearly not a neo-liberal one. In discussing the role of economic growth and its impact on poverty, it has this to say:

> 13. ACC recognizes that growth, though necessary, is not sufficient for rapid poverty reduction. Growth should be equitable-employment-intensive and pro-poor. Policies should aim to create productive and freely chosen employment as the most effective way of reducing poverty. Growth must be underpinned by sound policies to promote social justice and redress social inequities. The character and pattern of growth ultimately determine its impact on the lives of the poor. Pro-poor growth calls for rural development, employment creation and access to science and technology (United Nations, 1998).

Another interesting development involves the collaboration of the ILO with the World Bank and IMF. Recently, the ILO has participated with other international organizations such as the World Bank and the International Monetary Fund in their poverty reduction efforts. The most notable activity involves the ILO's participation in the preparation of a country's Poverty Reduction Strategy Paper (PRSP). Since 1999 all financing decisions at the country level by these international organizations are subject to the preparation of an acceptable PRSP. As the basis for their debt relief decisions and their lending to low-income countries, countries prepare a Strategy Paper in consultation with the ILO, the World Bank and the IMF that deals with economic and social policies and programs designed to stimulate economic growth and eradicate poverty.

Admittedly, there are other constraints on the pursuit of a global neo-liberal agenda. To some extent, the current global grassroots movement against capitalism and globalizing capital (since the "Battle in Seattle" in 1999) serves to put a curb on the overarching influences of neo-liberal economic policies. Above all, the tripartite structure of the ILO should guarantee that workers' points of view in the organization can be heard. The stronger this voice becomes, the less chance that the neo-liberal agenda will prevail within the ILO in the long run.

REFERENCES

Adedeji, A. (1999). Structural Adjustment Policies in Africa. *International Social Science Journal*, 51, 4(162), December, pp. 521-528.

Adelman, I. and Morris, C.T. (1984). *Economic Growth and Social Equity in Developing Countries*. Stanford, CA: Stanford University Press.

A. Donoso Rubio, Ignacio (1998). Economic Limits on International Regulation: A Case Study of ILO Standard Setting. *Queen's Law Journal*, 24, pp. 189-236.

Bird, G. (1996). Borrowing from the IMF: The Policy Implications of Recent Empirical Research. *World Development*, 24(11): 1753-1760.

Cooney, Sean (1999). Testing Times for the ILO: Institutional Reform for the New International Political Economy. *Comparative Labor Law and Policy Journal*, 20(3): 365-400.

Creighton, B. (1998). The ILO and the Protection of Fundamental Human Rights in Australia. *Melbourne University Law Review*, 22 (2): 239-80.

Crisp, B. F. and Kelly, M. J. (1999). The Socioeconomic Impacts of Structural Adjustment. *International Studies Quarterly*, 43, 533-552.

Deacon, Bob (with M. Hulse and P. Stubbs) (1997). *Global Social Policy*. Thousand Oaks, California: Sage Publications.

De la Cruz, H B., Potobsky, G. V. and Swepston, L. (1996). *The International Labor Organization: The International Standards System and Basic Human Rights*. Boulder, Colorado: Westview Press.

Evans, Peter (1979). *Dependent Development*. New Jersey: Princeton University Press.

Frazer, A. and Nyland, C. (1998). In Search of the Middle Way: The ILO, Standard Setting and Globalization. *Australian Journal of Labor Law*, 10:280-286.

Gauhar (1982). What is Wrong with Basic Needs? *Third World Quarterly*, 11.

Goulet, D. (1977). *The Cruel Choice: A New Concept in the Theory of Development*. New York: Atheneum.

Hardiman, M. and Midgley, J. (1989). *The Social Dimensions of Development*. London: Wiley.

Hofferbert, R.I. (1990). *The Reach and Grasp of Policy Analysis*. Tuscaloosa: University of Alabama.

Holtz, T. H. (1999). Labour Rights are Human Rights. *Lancet*, Vol. 353, Issue 9156, p.923.

International Labour Organization (1976). *Programme of Action*. UN Doc E/5857(1976).

_____ . (1999a). The ILO Governing Board to Examine Response to Asian Crisis. Press Statement, March 16. See http://www.ilo.org/public/english/bureau/inf/pr/1999/6.htm.

_____ . (1999b). The ILO's Response to the Financial Crisis in East and South-East Asia. Evolution of the Asian Financial Crisis and Determination of Policy Needs and Response. Governing Body, 274th Session (GB.274/4/2). Geneva, March.

_____ . (1999c). ILO's Activities in the Context of the UN System. See www.ilo.org/public/english/comp/poverty/context.htm.

_____ . (2000). *International Labour Organization*. http://us.ilo.org/aboutilo/facts.html#what.

International Monetary Fund (1999a). *Economic and Financial Situation in Asia: Latest Developments*. Background Paper for presentation by Michel Camdessus, Managing Director of the IMF Asia-Europe Finance Ministers Meeting, Frankfurt, Germany, 16 January. See www.imf.org/external/np/speeches/1999/011699.HTM.

International Monetary Fund (1999b). *The IMF's Response to the Asian Crisis*, 17 January. See www.imf.org/External/np/exr/facts/asia.HTM.

_____ . (2002). IMF. http://www.worldbank.org/

Kawewe, S. M. and Dibie, R. (2000). The Impact of Economic Structural Adjustment Programs on Women and Children: Implications for Social Welfare in Zimbabwe. *Journal of Sociology and Social Welfare*, 27, 4, December, 79-107

Kent, Ann (1997). China, International Organizations and Regimes: The ILO as A Case Study in Organizational Learning. *Pacific Affairs*, 70(4): 517-532.

Landy, G. A. (1996). *The Effectiveness of International Supervision: Thirty Years of ILO Experience*. London: Stevens and Sons.

Mathew, T.I. (1979). Concepts, Methods and Programmes of Social Security with particular reference to ILO's Role and Activities in Promotion of Social Security in Developing Countries in Asia. In *Role of Trade Unions in Social Security in Asia and the Pacific: Report of a Regional Seminar* (pp. 71-107). Geneva: ILO.

Meron, T. (1982). Norm Making and Supervision in International Human Rights: Reflection on International Law. *American Journal of International Law*, 76(4): 754-778.

Midgley, J. (1994). Defining Social Development: Historical Trends and Conceptual Formulations. *Social Development Issues*, 16, 3-19.

Mishra, R. (1998). Beyond the Nation State: Social Policy in an Age of Globalization. *Social Policy and Administration*, 32(5): 481-500.

Moorman, Y. (2001). Integration of ILO Core Rights Labor Standards into the WTO. *Columbia Journal of Transnational Law*, 39: 555-583.

Nanda, Ved P. (1985). Development as an Emerging Human Right under International Law. *Denver Journal of International Law and Policy*, 13(2/3): 161-180.

Qizilbash, M. (1996). Ethical Considerations. *World Development*, 24(7), July, 1209-1221.

Sen, A. K. (1984). Goods and People. In A. K. Sen (Ed.) *Resources, Values and Development*. Oxford: Blackwell.

Senti, M. (1998). The Impact of International Organization on National Social Security Expenditure: The Case of ILO 1960-1989. *Politische Viertejahreschrift*, 39(3), September.

Synder, M.C. and Tadesse, M. (1995). African Women and Development. London: Zed Books.

Spalding, N. (1990). The Relevance of Basic Needs for Political and Economic Development. *Studies in Comparative International Development*, 25(3): 90-115.

Strang, David and Chang, Patricia M.Y. (1993). The International Labour Organization and the Welfare State: Institutional Effects on National Welfare Spending, 1960-80. *International Organization,* 47: 235- 62.

Sundaram, I. S. (1996). Basic Needs Approach to Development. *Social Action*, 46(3), July-Sept, 225-239.

Tang, K. L. (1996). The Marginalization of Social Welfare in Developing Countries: The Relevance of Theories of Social Policy Development. *Journal of Sociology and Social Welfare*, 23(2): 41-58.

_____ . (2000). Asian Crisis, Social Welfare, and Policy Responses: Hong Kong and Korea Compared. *International Journal of Sociology and Social Policy*, 20(5-6): 49-91, December.

Taylor, L. (1997). The Revival of the Liberal Creed – The IMF and the World Bank in a Globalized Economy. *World Development*, 25(2): 145-152.

United Nations (1998). Statement of Commitment of the Administrative Committee on the Coordination for Action to Eradicate Poverty. See www.ilo.org/public/english/comp/poverty/accstate.htm.

Waugh, D. (1997). The ILO and Human Rights. *Comparative Labor Law*, 5(2): 186-196, Spring.

Weisband, E. (2000). Discursive Multilateralism: Global Benchmarks, Shame, and Learning in the ILO Labor Standards. *International Studies Quarterly*, 44(4): 643-666.

World Health Organization (1997). *Fact Sheet No 84*. Geneva: WHO, December.

In: *Poverty Monitoring and Alleviation in East Asia*   ISBN: 1-59033-828-6
K. Tang and C. Wong, editors pp. 153-176   © 2003 Nova Science Publishers, Inc.

Chapter 9

POVERTY AND THE SOCIAL DEVELOPMENT APPROACH

James Midgley

INTRODUCTION

'Social development' emerged in the years following the Second World War as a distinctive approach for addressing the problem of poverty. This was a time when many previously colonized societies in the Global South secured independence from European imperial rule and when many sought to modernize their economies through pursuing industrialization policies. It was believed that industrialization would draw the mass of the population who lived in rural subsistence poverty into regular wage employment. As incomes and standards of living rose, the incidence of poverty would decline.

However, the narrow emphasis on industrialization as a solution to the poverty problem was challenged for being too limited in scope and for complacently assuming that economic growth would, of itself, eradicate poverty. While critics accepted the need for economic development, they argued that poverty can only be eradicated if economic development is directly linked to social policies and programs. By the 1960s, the term 'social development' was being used in development circles to connote a variety of social interventions that sought to achieve this goal. These interventions transcended the narrow preoccupation with economic growth in development circles. They also transcended the welfarist approaches, which were then being adopted in the Western industrial nations. Unlike these approaches, social development policies and programs were linked to economic development effort and were designed to contribute positively to development.

Of course, social development is not only concerned with poverty alleviation. Although the problem of poverty has long been a primary concern, social development should be viewed more broadly as an approach for promoting social welfare that can be contrasted with other institutionalized approaches such as social work, philanthropy and social administration (Midgley, 1995). Similarly, while social development has historically been associated with 'Third World' economic development, its proponents argue that it is also relevant to the industrial nations of the Global North (Midgley, 1996). Nevertheless, it is with reference to the problem of mass poverty in the Global South that social development has historically been linked and with which it is still most frequently identified.

This chapter describes the social development approach by examining its key conceptual features and discussing the interventions that have been adopted over the years to address the poverty problem. While these interventions reflect different normative and ideological preferences, all are linked to economic development effort and all share a common commitment to raising the standards of living of all the 'world's people.' After reviewing these interventions, the chapter concludes with a brief discussion of social development's contribution and future role in poverty alleviation.

KEY CONCEPTUAL PREMISES

Although social development is a distinctive approach for addressing the problem of poverty, it has absorbed a variety of conceptual and normative ideas with the result that it now comprises an eclectic and pragmatic approach to poverty alleviation. For this reason, it lacks the coherence and clarity of other poverty alleviation approaches. In addition, social development has been defined differently by different writers and quite different programmatic interventions for poverty alleviation have been formulated and implemented. Although social development has been accused of being vague and nebulous, efforts have recently been made to formulate a more coherent and theoretically refined conceptualization with clear programmatic prescriptions (Midgley, 1994, 1995; Midgley and Sherraden, 2000; Midgley and Tang, 2001). Accordingly, there is greater clarity about what social development's anti-poverty interventions entail. Similarly, various writers have sought to articulate the conceptual and normative ideas on which social development interventions are based, and they have identified a number of conceptual notions that have informed the field. These are concerned with issues of change, intervention, inclusivity and the harmonization of economic and social policies.

Social Development and Social Change

Social development is based on a dynamic conception of poverty alleviation in which the idea of social change plays a key role. The proponents of social development argue that effective poverty alleviation strategies must address the causes of poverty. They do not accept the view that poverty is historically inevitable and they reject the argument that the poor are responsible for their condition. They are also critical of policies and programs that seek to ameliorate poverty by merely transferring resources to the poor. They believe that the 'charity' approach which is widely practiced by religious and secular philanthropic organizations as well as many governments through conventional income maintenance programs does not address the basic causes of poverty. A static approach of this kind tends to maintain the poor at unacceptably low income levels.

In the years following the Second World War, it was believed that economic modernization through industrialization would draw the bulk of the poor of the developing nations out of subsistence poverty into wage employment and that incomes and standards of living would dramatically rise. After all, industrialization had transformed the economies of Europe, North America and other nations during the 19th and 20th centuries practically eradicating mass poverty. While the proponents of social development agree that economic development is the propellant of change, they insist that economic development can only successfully alleviate poverty if it is accompanied by social policies and programs designed specifically to raise standards of living. They argue that poverty in the industrial nations was effectively reduced by a combination of economic and social measures. It is only when economic and social policies are harmonized within a dynamic process of change that the problem of poverty can be solved.

Social development writers argue that a balanced process of economic and social development is needed to address the problem of lopsided or distorted development which had characterized much development effort in the past. Despite its impressive results, economic development had differentially benefited urban dwellers, those in wage employment, professional groups, and business and political elite's. Without social development policies and programs, economic development will fail to eradicate poverty and to address the problems of urban squaller and deprivation that continue to characterize many developing nations. Although much more needs to be done to promote social development, many governments in the Global South as well as international and local non-governmental organizations have long accepted the need for economic and social change. Indeed, it was in the years following the Second World War that social development first emerged as a distinctive approach to social welfare. This was a time when the nationalist leaders of the newly independent countries embraced economic development. Most also approved of the incremental expansion of the education, health and social service programs that had been introduced by the colonial administrations and missionaries. As James Midgley (1994) reported, social development ideas first began to take shape when welfare administrators in West Africa introduced 'developmental' welfare programs in the rural areas which linked local productive economic projects with social welfare interventions. These events facilitated the adoption of the term *social* development as a counterpart to the idea of *economic* development. Like contemporary proponents of social development, they urged the use of interventions that combined economic and social policies within a dynamic process of planned change designed to benefit the population as a whole.

Social Development and Social Intervention

As a poverty alleviation approach, social development stresses the need for purposeful interventions that direct the process of change and bring about significant improvements in standards of living. Human agency is, therefore, a key feature of the social development approach. Social development advocates believe that poverty can be solved through human effort. Acting collectively, human being can find effective solutions to the poverty problem that has historically plagued human societies.

As noted earlier, social development writers reject the idea that poverty is a regrettable but unavoidable characteristic of social life. They also reject the view that economic modernization will, of itself, eradicate poverty. They contend that specific social interventions that address the basic needs of the population, reduce inequalities, enhance human capabilities through social investments, and enhance economic participation are needed if the problem of poverty is to be effectively addressed.

The idea that poverty will somehow resolve itself was popularized during the latter half of the 20th century. It found expression in the years after the Second World War in the belief that industrialization held the key to prosperity. More recently, the view that poverty can be solved spontaneously through economic processes, has been resurrected in the neo-liberal belief that free markets foster a dynamic process of economic growth that automatically reduces the incidence of poverty. Proponents of this approach insist that governments refrain from interfering in the natural process of dynamic growth that accompanies the marketization of the economy. They argue that state's proclivity to engage in planning and regulation and to provide extensive social services must be resisted if the market is to work its magic, produce rapid growth and solve the poverty problem.

A number of social development interventions that specifically address the problem of poverty have been identified over the years. These will be discussed in more depth in the following section. They are implemented at different levels focusing simultaneously on individuals, groups, communities and nation states. Efforts have also been made to promote these interventions at the international level. Different groups and organizations have been engaged in social development over the years. They include cooperatives, community groups, non-governmental organizations, public agencies and international donors. While their contribution is recognized, some social development scholars believe that national governments have a key role to play in promoting, directing and implementing social development. Although state interventionism has been severely curtailed in many developing countries as a result of debt and the imposition of structural adjustment programs, they continue to argue forcefully that governments give leadership in formulating and implementing policies and programs that address the poverty problem.

Universalism and Inclusivity in Social Development

Social development advocates emphasize the need for universality and inclusivity noting that social development interventions transcend a concern with the most needy and vulnerable and instead benefit groups, communities and societies as a whole. Unlike philanthropy, social work and means tested public programs, social development interventions are demographically universalistic seeking to enhance the well-being of the entire population.

In addition to addressing the problem of distorted development which was mentioned earlier, social development writers urge the adoption of policies that tackle the marked inequalities that characterize many countries today. Although development discourse now accords little importance to egalitarianism, most social development advocates continue to believe that efforts to promote the welfare of all are unlikely to succeed in the absence of redistributive policies that address the tendency of economic growth to favor a minority of the population. The problem can be solved through universalistic policies and programs that enhance the well-being of all.

However, a commitment to universalism does not preclude social development programs from focusing on the most needy, exploited and vulnerable groups. Social development practitioners have always given high priority to their needs and this has involved a particularistic concern with rural communities and with urban slum and squatter settlements where poor people are concentrated. Social development has also emphasized programs directed at poor women and their children and at other groups such as ethnic and tribal minorities, nomadic and immigrant communities who are disadvantaged and often discriminated against. But priority interventions designed to address the needs of these groups are implemented within a universalistic set of policies and programs that seek to promote the welfare of all. Social development has long practiced what Theda Skocpol (1995) describes as 'targeting within universalism.'

Harmonizing Social and Economic Policies and Programs

A commitment to inclusivity in social development thinking reflects a wider methodological approach that stresses the need to integrate and harmonize apparently disparate elements in social welfare. It has already been shown that social development is not narrowly concerned with remedial or maintenance oriented interventions but, by harmonizing the social and economic components of the development process, it offers a holistic, inclusive set of policy prescriptions for addressing the poverty problem and enhancing human well-being.

Social development writers contend that social and economic policies can only be effectively integrated if economic and social welfare interventions are given equal weight. They argue that economic policies and programs should produce tangible social benefits and that social policies and programs should contribute positively to economic development. They point out that economic development is meaningless if it is not accompanied by significant improvements in people's welfare. Economic policies and programs that promote a 'people-centered' development process are needed. Economic policies that create employment, ensure adequate earnings, invest in human capital, adopt progressive taxation, facilitate access to credit and ensure the maximum participation of people in the productive economy are emphasized. These measures must be accompanied by programs that suppress economic corruption, safeguard democratic institutions and ensure that property rights are protected. Policies that prevent economic exploitation and discrimination are also needed. Since the 1980s, social development advocates have also placed great stress on economic policies that do not damage the environment. Social development and sustainable development have become closely linked in the literature.

Social development writers also stress the need for social welfare policies and programs that contribute positively to economic development. This emphasis on *productivism* is a unique and defining feature of the social development approach. By emphasizing the role of productive social policies and programs that promote social investments and enhance what Amartya Sen (1985, 1999) calls 'human capabilities,' social development advocates seek to transcend the historic role of resource transfers in social welfare thinking. By stressing social investment, poor people are helped to participate in the productive economy and to contribute and benefit meaningfully from economic development.

KEY DEVELOPMENTAL POVERTY ALLEVIATION INTERVENTIONS

Drawing on these key conceptual premises, a variety of social development interventions that address the problem of poverty have emerged over the years. They include national planning, food for work, asset development, community action, employment placement, micro-enterprise and micro-credit programs to name only a few. However, as was noted earlier, social development has been criticized for being vague and nebulous. Social development has also been criticized for being little more than a crude amalgamation of disparate anti-poverty interventions. Although there is some validity in this argument, it has been shown that social development scholars have clarified the conceptual bases of social development practice. They have also drawn these interventions together within a normative framework that offers a distinctive, pragmatic and eclectic set of proposals for poverty alleviation (Midgley and Tang, 2001).

Social development's normative framework is based on the conceptual premises described earlier. It has also been shaped by different ideological influences. Midgley (1993) has shown that different programmatic interventions reflect different normative preferences about the best way of alleviating poverty. Communitarian, populist, collectivist and even individualist ideologies have inspired different interventions at different times. Social development's historic association with community projects and its commitment to mobilizing *the people* to engage in social development activities reflects the influence of populist and communitarian beliefs. The involvement of governments and the promotion of social development goals through national planning, the adoption of redistributive social policies and the provision of social programs through bureaucratic service delivery systems all reveal a preference for state collectivism. In more recent times, social development discourse has been infused with the rhetoric of individual responsibility. Interventions such as micro-credit and micro-enterprise projects that promote individual functioning have become increasingly prominent in social development thinking. The growing emphasis on individualism has also been accompanied by the advocacy of what the World Bank (1991) calls 'market friendly' social development strategies.

Although these divergent normative perspectives are usually regarded as incompatible and even antagonistic, it has been argued that they can, in fact, be synthesized to offer a comprehensive practice framework that recognizes their strengths and mutuality (Midgley, 1995; Dean, 2001). It is within this framework that the role of the market, community and state can be recognized and mobilized to address the problem of poverty and to promote the well being of all. This normative synthesis is facilitated by the harmonization of economic and social policies at different levels of social development effort.

Similarly, the fact that social development interventions are implemented at different levels, by different agents does not mean that they are incompatible. Individuals, small groups of people, non-governmental organizations, communities and governments all implement social development policies and programs. As was noted earlier, efforts have even been made to promote social development at the international level. The United Nations and its affiliated agencies such as the United Nations Children's Fund (UNICEF), and the International Labour Office (ILO) have been major advocates of the social development approach. The United Nations World Summit which was held in Copenhagen in 1995 was particularly important for seeking to boost social development's relevance at a time that neo-liberal thinking dominates economic and social policy at the global level (United Nations, 1996).

The promotion of social development poverty alleviation policies and programs at these different levels involves complex organizational arrangements, systems of service delivery, personnel resources and budgetary allocations. Obviously, community based interventions require quite different organizational arrangements than those implemented at the national level. Similarly, different types of personnel will be required at different levels. A fair amount has been written about the role of community level para-professionals, social workers, administrators, anthropologists, social planners, economists and others in implementing promoting social development policies and programs. While some of these groups have claimed a monopoly on social development practice, it is clear that they can all contribute to the attainment of social development goals.

Individual and Group Level Interventions

It was noted earlier that social development advocates are critical of interventions that seek to address the problem of poverty through conventional charitable or income maintenance programs and instead, they have stressed the need for macro-level interventions particularly at the community level. Indeed, it is at the community level that social development initiatives are usually implemented. But this does not mean that social development advocates are disdainful of interventions that enhance individual capabilities or facilitate the integration of individuals into the productive economy. But, as was noted earlier, this concern with individuals is situated within the wider context of macro-policies and programs that have a clear developmental commitment. In addition, these policies and programs seek to link individual functioning to cooperative endeavor within group and community settings.

Whether directed at individuals or groups of individuals acting cooperatively, a variety of interventions that increase the ability of individuals to participate effectively in the productive economy have been identified and implemented. These include human capital programs, employment placement programs, asset development and micro enterprise programs. However, it should be stressed that while they operate at the individual level, they are linked to national policies and function most effectively within the framework of these policies.

Human Capital Programs
Social development places great stress on policies and programs that inculcate the knowledge and skills that individuals need to participate effectively and meaningfully in the productive economy. Although human capital programs, as these interventions are known, also encompass investments in health and nutrition (Abel-Smith, 1976; Schultz, 1981), they have traditionally focused on educational and skill development. They are designed to alleviate poverty by inculcating the knowledge and skills people need to participate in the productive economy. Although they are particularly concerned with the educational development of children, they are not limited to children. In addition to adult literacy, a great variety of vocational training programs for adults have been established. The rapid pace of knowledge innovation also suggests that human capital development will be a life-long preoccupation.

Nevertheless, it is with reference to children that human capital programs have been emphasized by social development advocates. Special emphasis has been given to ensuring that children from poor families have access to adequate schooling and increasingly, the importance of interventions targeted at preschool children living in slum and squatter settlements and in low income rural communities is stressed. UNICEF has played a major role in promoting programs of this kind and many developing countries today operate networks of day care centers where young children come to acquire basic educational skills, engage in sociable play, receive nutritional supplements and health checks. One example is India's Integrated Child Development Services Scheme, which now operates throughout the country to enhance human capital among literally millions of poor children. Indeed, as Young (2002) observes, it is the largest early childhood development program in the world serving some 32 million children.

Social development advocates also place great stress on literacy education as another important form of human capital development. Indeed, Midgley (1994) reports that the first nationally organized social development programs, which were introduced in West Africa in the 1940s, were concerned with literacy training. These programs continue throughout the world today and play a vital role in social development's poverty alleviation approach.

Employment and Employment Placement Programs

It is widely accepted that steady wage employment in modern industrial, commercial and service occupations is the best means of raising incomes and reducing the incidence of poverty. It is for this reason that policies designed to create and sustain employment have been given high priority in social development circles. Social development advocates believe strongly that governments need to intervene at the national level to create a positive climate for employment creation and for the development of skills and opportunities that enhance the participation of people in the productive economy. These wider employment creation policies will be discussed later in this chapter.

A variety of social development programs designed to increase employment among the poor and those with special needs have been introduced over the years. Among the earliest were sheltered employment programs for people with disabilities. These were among the first to introduce a developmental perspective into social welfare. Instead of assigning those with special needs to residential institutions where they were often warehoused in unsatisfactory conditions, the idea that they could engage in productive employment gradually emerged. Although sheltered workshops and similar facilities continue to provide employment for those with special needs, far greater emphasis is now placed on 'mainstreaming' so that they are increasingly placed in regular jobs. This trend has been accompanied by anti-discriminatory policies that facilitate their employment in the open labor market. A good example is the Americans with Disabilities Act, which requires employers to make reasonable accommodations for those with disabilities. For those requiring special assistance to function in regular jobs, social workers now have access to a variety of supported employment programs which provide access to transport, technologies and other supports that assist them to function effectively in regular jobs.

There has been a growing emphasis in the industrial nations on welfare to work programs in recent years. These programs seek to transcend the payment of cash assistance to poor people by facilitating employment or part-time employment. In the United States, programs of this kind were first introduced during the 1960s to provide for education, job training and employment placement. However, since 1996, a more coercive approach has been adopted which makes the continued payment of benefits contingent on employment. Welfare recipients have also been required to work in public sector jobs. Because the number of people claiming welfare benefits in the United States has fallen substantially since 1996, it is widely accepted that the coercive approach has been effective. Social development writers disagree and reject the use of this approach arguing instead for a social investment approach that makes far more use of education, skills development and other supports that facilitate employment. Generally, welfare to work programs in Europe have been less coercive than those adopted in the United States.

In the developing world, food for work and similar programs have been in existence for many years. During the colonial period, programs of this kind were widely used to mobilize labor for infrastructural development projects and workers were often paid in kind for contributing their labor. These programs have also been used during periods of climatic adversity when droughts and other disasters have placed large numbers of poor people at risk of being malnourished. In these cases, famine relief has often taken the form of providing food for work. However, food for work and similar programs are also used during normal times in an attempt to increase the well being of the poor by raising their incomes. Of course, these programs also help to construct roads, water supplies and other amenities, particularly in the rural areas of the developing world. The World Bank (1990) has shown that public works programs have made a significant contribution to poverty alleviation in many low-income countries.

Employment generating policies and programs are often accompanied by employment referral and placement services targeted at young people and others who are seeking work. This is particularly true in the Western industrial countries. Many of these countries have extensive networks of employment centers that obtain and disseminate information about job vacancies and assist job seekers secure regular work. They have also assumed greater responsibility for promoting human capital and for referring job seekers to educational institutions to upgrade or refocus their educational qualifications. In recent years, as welfare to work programs have become more popular in these nations, job referral and placement services have become an important resource to those seeking work.

Asset Accounts

Social development's poverty alleviation interventions are also concerned with the accumulation of assets. Many social development writers now recognize those policies and programs designed to promote asset accumulation are as important as those that increase disposable income and foster consumption are. Based on an idea formulated by Michael Sherraden (1991), matched individual development accounts (or IDAs) are becoming an increasingly popular social development intervention. They are designed to encourage poor people to save by matching their savings with deposits from government or non-governmental sources. Programs of this kind have been established in many parts of the United States by non-profit organizations and government agencies. Savings are matched by varying factors - usually between 100% and 400% of the saver's deposit. Accumulations may be withdrawn for socially approved purposes such as education or housing.

A recent evaluation of 13 asset savings account projects (Sherraden, 2001) with approximately 1,300 participants in various parts of the United States, revealed that participants were, on average, saving about $33 per month. Two thirds of participants were saving regularly and more than 70% were meeting the savings goals they had set for themselves. Although the amounts saved are not substantial, the evaluation project found that poor people do respond to incentives to save and that their savings have a positive impact on their lives. Asset accounts also help to address some of the challenges facing the poor. Among these is the creation of a credit record, which permits participants to obtain subsidized credit for housing or for education. Advocates of the asset savings approach also believe that asset development programs promote self-sufficiency and that they change attitudes, values and work habits.

Micro-Credit and Micro-Enterprise Policies and Programs

Although social development proponents have emphasized the importance of using employment-generating policies to alleviate poverty, they recognize that the challenge of creating wage employment on a large scale is formidable and that a significant period of time may be needed before this goal is achieved. The optimism that attended development thinking in the 1950s and 1960s has been dampened by the divergent industrialization experiences of the developing countries. While some countries in East Asia and Central and South America have indeed been able to increase modern wage employment, others have not, and this has often resulted in the growth of a large informal sector economy in which individuals and families engage in a great variety of labor intensive economic activities ranging from backyard repair work to street vending and even scavenging (Bromley and Gerry, 1979; Portes, Castells and Bentol 1989; Thomas, 1992).

In the 1970s, the International Labour Office recommended that those engaged in informal sector self-employment be recognized and supported by government economic development policies and programs. Governments were urged to relax the regulations governing micro-enterprise and to provide credit and technical assistance to informal sector businessmen. While some countries such as the Philippines actively adopted policies of this kind, micro enterprise development has been uneven. However, some writers such as Hernan de Soto (1989) continued to advocate for small scale entrepreneurship and since the 1980s, when neo-liberal ideas became more influential in development circles, micro-enterprises and micro credit programs have become much more prominent. Although few social development writers believe that micro-enterprise programs are a panacea to the poverty problems, they agree that these programs form an effective part of wider poverty alleviating strategies.

Micro-enterprise programs have now become very popular. Many governments have promoted these programs and a large number of non-governmental organizations have also become involved. Through technical assistance, subsidies and preferential access to credit, these programs have proliferated. The need for credit has been particularly acute. Few informal sector businesses are able to secure credit on commercial markets and for this reason, many governments have created loan programs for low-income entrepreneurs, which offer credit at preferential rates. However, as the ability of governments to maintain micro-credit programs have been diminished through fiscal adversity and structural adjustment, non-governmental organizations have become more active. The Grameen Bank in Bangladesh is undoubtedly the best known of these initiatives (Yunus, 1991). Its peer-lending model is well regarded and many non-profit agencies have now adopted this approach. In terms of the Grameen model, micro-enterprises are not created by individuals but by small cooperatives whose members assume joint responsibility for obtaining credit and ensuring that their enterprises are successful.

Community Level Interventions

Social welfare programs designed to link economic and social programs within a wider context of development effort were originally implemented at the community level. These programs sought to mobilize the community to participate in activities that would enhance their collective well being. Known as 'community development', they focused primarily on the needs of the rural poor in developing countries. As noted earlier in this chapter, these programs were introduced by social welfare administrators in West Africa in the 1940s who were concerned that conventional, urban based social welfare interventions focused narrowly on the most conspicuously needy groups, neglecting the rural majority who lived in subsistence poverty. Although they initially promoted adult literacy, the scope of these activities was subsequently extended to cover a variety of community level interventions that enhanced standards of living for the whole community. Known as community development, these efforts to introduce developmental forms of social welfare were compatible with wider, national efforts to promote economic development (Midgley, 1994).

Community Development Programs and Projects

Although community development emerged in the 1940s, it has much older roots (Brokensha and Hodge, 1969). Traditional societies around the world have historic traditions of cooperative endeavor and communal ownership that reflect and support reciprocal social and economic relationships. The role of these collective institutions was extolled by many nationalist leaders who argued that the cooperative institutions of village life could be harnessed for development purposes. Their contribution was also recognized by colonial officials who advocated the allocation of resources to strengthen indigenous cooperativism as well as the mobilization of local people for local infrastructural development. At a conference in Cambridge in 1948, the neologism 'community development' was formally adopted to connote a variety of projects that would improve traditional forms of economic activities, strengthen local social networks, enhance people's participation, develop community infrastructure and alleviate poverty.

It was also at this conference that some of the basic normative tenets attending community development were articulated. The idea that community development depended on local participation and self-help, that it comprised a partnership between government and local communities, and that local self-determination should govern community development practice were all accepted. These premises subsequently attained canonical status within the field (Brokensha and Hodge, 1969).

Community development programs are typically managed by government agencies which work with local community leaders to establish a variety of projects and programs that foster developmental goals. Local paraprofessional workers play a key role in the process which begins when they work with local leaders and village people to decide which types of projects should be given priority. Resources, usually in the form of materials and technical expertise are then secured from the government, and these are combined with local voluntary labor. Infrastructural investments such as the construction of community centers, schools, clinics, roads, bridges and water supply and sanitary projects are probably the most common form of community development but productive projects such as poultry raising, crafts, vegetable gardening, communal forestry management are also popular. These activities have historically been linked to cooperative programs. The cooperative storage, marketing and distribution of agricultural produce has formed an integral part of community development. Community development projects have also been accompanied by educational programs designed not only to foster literacy but to teach parenting skills, family planning and hygiene. In addition, community development advocates have stressed the need to link material, anti-poverty interventions to those that focus on the non-material goals of enhancing democratic decision making and encouraging self-help and local responsibility.

In addition to operating as an organized, bureaucratically managed national program in many countries, community development also emerged as a method or approach for enhancing people's welfare. The idea of local self-help and self-determination became an important aspect of health, nutrition and housing programs in developing countries. The World Bank's support for self-help housing projects designed to upgrade squatter settlements in the urban areas of poor countries (United Nations, 1971) and the World Health Organization's 'health by the people' approach (Newell, 1975) all drew on community development ideas (Hollnsteiner, 1982). In time, community development methods were widely adopted by non-governmental organizations around the world.

Although the British played a key role in promoting community development, the United Nations also supported its adoption among its member states, providing technical assistance and aid for community development programs. Several countries such as India, the Philippines and Tanzania linked community development with local government assigning key community development functions as well as resources to local village authorities. Urban-based community development programs also became more common. By the 1960s, many developing countries had established training centers for paraprofessional community development workers and academic programs for social workers and others wishing to administer these programs had also proliferated. In addition, numerous journals and books on the subject were available. Community development was regarded by many as an effective developmental intervention for poverty alleviation.

Community Action

Although many political leaders in the Global South claimed that community development gave expression to indigenous mutual aid traditions and reinforced traditional democratic decision-making, critics took a very different view. By the 1970s, these programs were often condemned for being excessively bureaucratic, inefficient, wasteful and even corrupt (Mayo, 1975; Marsen and Oakley, 1982). It was argued that community development officials were insensitive to the wishes of local people. Instead of meeting local needs, they cajoled local people to work on government road, water supply, sanitation and irrigation projects. Community development projects were also accused of being poorly conceived, badly funded and poorly implemented. Equally serious was the claim that these projects were being used for political and electoral purposes. Communities that supported the ruling political party were more likely to receive funds for community development and in many cases, these projects favored local leaders, landlords and wealthy farmers. The needs of the poorest and most vulnerable groups such as women and tribal minorities were often ignored.

These criticisms reflected a growing disenchantment with state directed development. This was a time when radical writers of the Neo-Marxist Dependency School claimed that the developing countries were part of a global system of capitalist exploitation in which the Western industrial countries expropriated the wealth of the developing world and ensured that they maintained hegemonic control over local resources (Cardoso and Faletto, 1979; Frank,

1974; Rodney, 1972). The governments of the developing nations were comprised of a *comprador* elite who were willing collaborators in this process of exploitation. For this reason, it was ludicrous to suggest that the state would act in the interests of its citizens and seek to eradicate poverty.

This critique was reinforced by radical populists who claimed that government sponsored community development programs would not solve the poverty problem. They argued instead that poverty could be best dealt with when local communities rejected government involvement, challenged corrupt local leaders and took responsibility for their own development. Although local self-determination had been a key element of community development, advocates of the new community action or community participation approach, as it was also known were highly critical of conventional community development which they regarded as an instrument of the oppressive state. Many were particularly incensed by the use of community development as a counter insurgency device by the United States and other Western powers which promoted community development specifically to mollify local discontent and suppress support for radical movements.

These critics favored an activist style of intervention that required the full participation of the poor in social development projects. In addition to drawing inspiration from the neo-Marxist dependency writers, advocates of community action were influenced by the writings of populist radicals such as Saul Alinky (1946, 1971) in the United States, who provided practical guidelines for social action, and by the writings of Paulo Freire (1972) in Brazil whose theory of popular education stressed the need for conscientization as a technique for raising the political awareness of the poor and oppressed. By engaging them in a dialogue about power, inequality and oppression, they would appreciate their position in the social structure, and be empowered to engage in radical collective action that would find local solutions to the poverty problem. This approach stresses the importance of an activist style of intervention that relies less on the provision of material resources than on the active involvement of the poor in these projects (Midgley, Hall, Hardiman and Narine, 1986).

As criticisms of conventional community development programmes intensified, international donors began to allocate more resources to non-profit organizations working with local community groups. Governments in the industrial nations also began to divert a larger share of their social development aid from public agencies to international non-governmental organizations. In turn, these organizations expanded their local operations and began to collaborate more closely with local grass roots organizations that were viewed as more authentically representative of the poor and oppressed. International agencies such as UNICEF and WHO also supported the non-governmental sector recognizing that community interventions would be more effective if local people participated fully in program design and implementation. As a result of these developments, social development writers such as Maia Green (1992) now situate social development within the non-governmental sector and see little role for state involvement.

Social Capital and Community Economic Development

The anti-statist sentiments of radical populists were accompanied by the growing popularity of neo-liberal economics in development circles. Neo-liberals also criticized government waste and inefficiency and the apparent deleterious effect of government programs on economic development. It is in this climate that community based poverty alleviation strategies have been linked to the more recent idea of social capital. Social capital theorists such as James Coleman (1988) and Robert Putnam (1993, 2000) suggest that civic engagement creates relationships and networks that are not only desirable in terms of their social and political impact but in terms of their economic effects. Although social capital theory gives expression to communitarian beliefs and stresses the moral virtues of people's engagement in civil society, it also has a materialist connotation which suggests that enhanced civic involvement promotes economic activities with positive outcomes for all who participate in community life.

While social capital makes a distinctive contribution that explicitly links the notion of capital to income generation, much of the recent literature on social capital has paid little attention to this aspect of social capital programs. Instead, it has focused on the nature of social ties and the apparent decline in civic engagement. It has also been concerned with the ways sociability can be enhanced. On the other hand, social capital's economic aspects have direct implications for poverty alleviation. If mutuality and sociability can enhance economic activities and generate increased income and wealth for the community as a whole, it will have a pivotal role in poverty alleviation.

In his formative conception of social capital, Coleman (1988) argues that social capital, like physical capital, is productive in that economic development is more likely to occur in communities and societies with strong social networks and a high degree of civic trust. Coleman also made a link between human and social capital pointing out that children attending schools with a high commitment to associational activities have higher levels of educational attainment than those attending schools where these activities as well as wider ties and networks are weak or underdeveloped. Putnam's (1993) research with a group of colleagues in Italy reached a similar conclusion showing that the country's regions with a high degree of civic engagement had higher levels of economic development than those with poorly developed civic traditions.

Although strong social networks and associational activities contribute indirectly to economic development by spontaneously creating networks that people can use for economic purposes, it is desirable that specific steps be taken to enhance and strengthen social capital. Midgley and Michelle Livermore (1998) suggest that it is possible to transcend an indirect approach of this kind by implementing policies and programs that direct social capital towards economic activities at the local level. For example, community social workers can promote social capital through community organization and community building activities that mobilize local people encourage participation and build coalitions. In addition to generating social capital, they can also work more closely with urban planners and local economic development specialists to create new enterprises particularly among poor women and other needy groups whose access to social capital as well as credit, and other investments is limited. They can foster micro-enterprises and create business cooperatives. They can also establish local associations to represent the interests of small businesses. Networks for employment referral purposes can also be fostered and measures that encourage the community to support local enterprise should be introduced. These examples suggest that a more active engagement with local economic development can contribute positively to poverty alleviation.

National Level Interventions

Social development advocates also urge the adoption of policies and programs at the national level that promote the effective participation of all in the productive economy, ensure that economic development has positive social welfare implications and that social programs contribute to economic development. Although the current climate of anti-statism is not conducive to government involvement in social development, they believe that effective poverty alleviation requires government intervention. Individual, group and community level interventions are most effective when implemented within a comprehensive set of national policies and programs that support and complement different poverty alleviation efforts.

While social development proponents recognize that markets play a vital role in promoting development, they vigorously oppose policies that subjugate the state to commercial interests. Social development writers point out that, despite their free market rhetoric, many business leaders and pro-business politicians regularly call on government to act in ways that promote their sectional interests. Trade protection, massive commercial and industrial subsidies, tax exemptions and other incentives that increase profits and executive incomes are widely advocated by the business community and the supporters of 'free' market development. If government is willing to support these interest groups, social development writers argue that it should also be willing to intervene to alleviate poverty. Although they do not argue for a return to centralized planning, nationalization and the stultifying regulations and bureaucratic management that typified development effort in many countries, they urge the adoption of national policies that regulate market economies and ensure that they function to promote the well-being of all. Judicious state involvement and direction of national economic and social development will, they contend, be needed if the poverty problem is to be addressed.

Planning and State Intervention

Governments have historically played a major role in promoting social development. Although formative social development efforts were directed at communities, it has already been shown that community development relied on government support for local effort. Government involvement increased in the 1960s when leading development economists, such as Gunnar Myrdal, Dudley Seers, Benjamin Higgins and Hans Singer, whose views were shaped by Keynesian and interventionist ideas, urged the adoption of policies that contributed directly to poverty alleviation and the attainment of social welfare goals (Myrdal, 1968, 1970; Seers, 1972; United Nations, 1971b).

These developments paved the way for the emergence of an interventionist approach to economic development that transcended Keynesian demand management and employed planning, egalitarian redistributive and employment creation policies. This approach also involves the expansion of social programs to improve health, education, nutrition and housing. Myrdal (1971b) urged the national planning agencies of developing countries to transcend their commitment to increasing investments in industrial enterprises, promoting trade and securing international aid and instead place greater emphasis on what he described as 'unified' socio-economic planning. He argued that social policies should be integral to economic development planning. These ideas were adopted by the United Nations. Through a series of resolutions and through technical assistance, the organization encouraged the governments of the developing countries to redefine economic growth to include a concern with standards of living, inequality and poverty alleviation. Urging that social indicators be developed and widely used to assess social progress, the organization sponsored the creation of the United Nations Research Institute for Social Development (UNRISD) in Geneva in the early 1960s. UNRISD was specifically charged with this task.

Other international agencies such as the World Bank and the International Labor Office also endorsed the need for government policies and programs to address the poverty problem. In a widely reported speech to the Governors of the World Bank in 1972, Robert McNamara surprised his audience by arguing that the Bank's activities should be redirected towards poverty alleviation. He proposed that the Bank's lending policies should be focused on the needs of the poorest 40% of the population of developing countries. In the aftermath of his speech, the Bank produced numerous policy documents and publications focusing specifically on poverty alleviation (World Bank, 1974).

The Bank also collaborated in a major study of the relationship between poverty, inequality and economic development. Although conventional wisdom dictated that redistributive policies would harm economic development, a group of economists led by Hollis Chenery, the World Bank's chief economist (Chenery, Ahluwalia, Bell, Duloy and Jolly, 1974), refuted this claim arguing instead that redistributive policies, in fact, promote economic growth. These ideas were consonant with Myrdal's (1968) earlier insistence that the problem of poverty could not be solved unless the problem of inequality was addressed. Social development now becomes associated with egalitarian development and the adoption of a range of policies and programs that reduced inequality.

However, by the 1970s, the interventionist and egalitarian approaches advocates by social development writers were being challenged by neo-liberals who argued that planning and state directed development was bound to fail. Urging the adoption of policies that would liberalize the economies of the developing countries, they rejected planning and advocated measures to promote entrepreneurship, encourage trade and attract international investment (Bauer, 1976; Lal, 1983). These ideas were actively promoted by the Reagan administration in the United States, the Thatcher government in Britain, and by the governments of some developing countries such as Chile during General Pinochet's military dictatorship.

In the 1980s, neo-liberalism also became the development orthodoxy of the International Monetary Fund (IMF) and the World Bank. Both organizations claimed that national planning and economic regulation had harmed economic development efforts. They also promoted the diffusion of neo-liberalism to the developing world through the imposition of structural adjustment programs. Facing serious problems of economic stagnation and debt, many developing countries were compelled to seek assistance from the IMF and the World Bank. The structural adjustment programmes imposed by these agencies required that state owned enterprises be privatized, and that government regulations be eased. In addition, public expenditures were slashed, and taxers and tariffs were reduced. Social welfare and community development programs were particularly affected as budgets and staff were retrenched.

Neo-liberals claim that these national policy measures were a more effective means than directive economic planning and the other forms of state intervention that had characterized development effort between the 1950s and 1980s. By reducing state intervention, cutting taxes and easing regulations, economic growth would accelerate and the incidence of poverty would dramatically decline. More recently, they have placed great stress on the need to integrate local economies with the global capitalist economic system. By ensuring greater integration into the global economy, growth rates, employment opportunities and other changes that reduce poverty will be achieved. The adoption of these national policies in many countries has dramatically altered the nature of state intervention and, many would claim, has not produced the desired effect.

Developmental Social Service Provision

Social development advocates also urge the creation of social service programs that are compatible with development effort and target resources at the poor. Social service programs have historically been linked to social development. As was shown earlier, the importation of Western approaches was regarded by early social development advocates as highly inappropriate to the development context and it was for this reason that they sought to promote community based interventions that would reach larger numbers of people and address the poverty problem within the context of national development effort.

The United Nations played a major role in promoting appropriate social service programs. It urged its member states to formulate social sectoral plans for the expansion of health, education, housing and social welfare and to incorporate them into national plans. It also promoted the idea that conventional social work and human services programs become more developmental in character. This required a greater degree of appropriateness and cost effectiveness in social service provision. The replication of high cost social service programs in the developing countries should be ended and replaced with approaches that were compatible with the economic, social and cultural realities of these countries.

The United Nations also emphasized the need for social programs that promoted economic participation among welfare clients. Because of resource constraints and the pervasiveness of deprivation, social assistance and other social service programs could not hope to meet the needs of the poor. For this reason, policies and programs that integrated people into the development process so that they contributed positively to economic development goals were urgently needed. At an important international meeting of Ministers of Social Welfare in New York in 1968, the United Nations urged its member states to make greater efforts to identify and implement developmental forms of social welfare (United Nations, 1969).

These ideas were reinforced by popularization of the Basic Needs approach. Basic Needs was promoted by the International Labour Office and formally adopted at the World Employment Conference in 1976 (International Labour Office, 1976). Basic needs placed high priority on policies and programmes that would ensure that the poorest people of the Global South had access to clean drinking water, nutrition, adequate shelter, heath care, education and income security. Rather than waiting for economic growth to solve the problems of poverty and social deprivation, Basic Needs advocates urged governments to seek to address these problems immediately (Stewart, 1985; Streeten and Burki, 1978; Streeten, Burki, Ul Haq, Hicks and Stewart, 1981). Unfortunately, budgetary reductions and the other changes resulting from the imposition of structural adjustment programs impeded the far-reaching implementation of Basic Needs with the result that poverty and social deprivation became more acute in many parts of the Global South in the 1980s and 1990s.

Employment Creation Policies

National policies designed to promote employment have featured prominently on social development's agenda. Employment creation has been recognized as the primary purpose of economic development since the 1950s, and a range of policy proposals to promote this goal have emerged. Initially, these policy proposals were compatible with the modernization school's focus on industrialization as a way of drawing labor out of the subsistence sector into wage employment. Some of the greatest development economists of the Post War years, including Paul Rosenstein Rodan, Arthur Lewis, Ragnar Nurkse and Walt Rostow all stressed the need for investments in modern industry as a means of achieving this goal.

Historically, there is no doubt that the creation of mass wage employment through economic modernization has substantially reduced poverty. However, the extent to which poverty is responsive to modernization depends on the extent of wage employment, its permanence and the level of income it provides. Many developing countries have experienced economic growth but failed to create wage employment for a sizable proportion of the population. This has resulted in some parts of the developing world in the emergence of a small elite of workers in regular wage employment, and in the persistence of subsistence poverty not only in the rural areas but in the cities which attract large numbers of people in search of work. Here, many eke out a living in the informal sector of the economy.

Social development advocates stress the need for economic development policies that create jobs on a scale sufficient to absorb labor from the subsistence sectors. This challenge is the very essence of economic and social development effort. Many believe that economic development policies that fail to create mass employment and to substantially reduce the incidence of poverty can hardly be described as development (Seers, 1972; Myrdal, 1968). Of course, there are wide differences of opinion on how employment-generating growth can be achieved and no shortage of policy proposals for achieving this goal. Neo-liberals, Keynesians, socialists and others have all offered prescriptions for promoting mass employment. While these groups have very different ideas on the subject, all recognize that the state has a vital role to play in employment creation. Despite claiming to espouse a *laissez faire* approach to development, the Neo-liberal's advocacy of free markets, entrepreneurship, low taxation, subsidies and other measures requires government intervention and the implementation of policies and programs that enhance market activities. Of course, development economists of a Keynesian persuasion are not reticent about the need for national policies that stimulate demand in order to foster economic growth and create jobs. They also favor the use of public works programs in time of high unemployment. These and other approach all require state intervention. However, the debate about which of these policy approaches are the most effective has been raging for more than a century, and has not been resolved.

Income Guarantees and Subsidies

The government of many industrial countries have adopted policies that seek to prevent the exploitation of workers. Minimum wage policies to ensure that workers are adequately remunerated for their labor are widely used in the industrial nations for this purpose. However, the minimum wage level is usually very low and, in some countries such as the United States, it has been supplemented by the living wage policies introduced by progressive municipalities. Living wage policies have been implemented in several American cities. These policies typically require firms with contracts or those receiving incentives and subsidies from the municipality to pay minimum wages well above the national level. David Neumark (2002) reported that many cities with living wage policies require payment levels in excess of 30 % than the national minimum wage. In some cities, such as Hartford,

Connecticut and San Jose, California, the living wage requirement is about 80% higher than the national minimum wage.

These income guarantees are compatible with regulations that protect workers from arbitrary dismissal, unhealthy and unsafe working conditions and other adverse conditions. Legislation to reform the grim working conditions which characterized industrial employment in the 19th century has been extended by the introduction of extensive work safety regulations that ensure that workers are not exposed to harmful risks at their places of work and that the work environment is conducive to their health and safety. Although these regulations were initially directed at industrial occupations they now extend to the commercial and service fields as well.

Many governments have also used the tax system to increase the incomes of low-income workers. Traditionally, the tax system has been used to subsidize the costs of raising children but, in recent years, the governments of countries such as the Britain and the United States have provided direct tax credits to subsidize the incomes of low paid workers. The Earned Income Tax Credit (EITC) in the United States is a prime example of this approach (Hoffman and Seidman, 2003; Meyer and Hotz-Eakin, 2001). Provided low-income workers pay taxes and claim the credit, they can significantly increase their take home pay. This approach is viewed by some experts as a preferable alternative to the universal child benefits which are paid to all families in many industrial countries.

Affirmative and Anti-discriminatory Employment Policies

Policies and programs designed to foster employment have often been accompanied by policies that facilitate the employment of women, minority ethnic groups, people with disabilities and others who have historically faced discrimination on the job market. Although the contribution of these programs to promoting fair employment practices are well documented in the Western industrial nations, less is known about their role in the developing countries. Nevertheless, countries such as India and more recently South Africa have adopted policies of this kind to promote the employment of disadvantaged groups and to foster their participation in the productive economy.

These policies are needed to remove the many barriers which impede economic participation among women, minorities and others who have long experienced difficulties in accessing jobs, credit and the other resources needed to facilitate their effective engagement in economic activities. But barriers of this kind do not only involve discrimination against particular groups. The absence of affordable transportation in many countries is a major barrier which prevents poor people from securing employment. For example, as service jobs have increasingly moved to suburban areas in industrial countries such as the United States, poor people who live in the inner city have experienced difficulty in traveling to work in these areas. In many developing countries, shantytown dwellers who live on the outskirts of cities have difficulty in coming into the city center to work. It is for this reason that many simply sleep on the streets during weekdays. The lack of day care programs for preschool children also impedes the employment of mothers in the productive economy. The community based day care programs which were mentioned earlier in this chapter not only enhance human capital but help to remove a major barrier to securing productive employment or self-employment.

Social development proponents also favor the adoption of policies that facilitate a climate that is conducive to economic and social development. They point out that political instability, widespread corruption, institutionalized racism and discrimination, endemic violence and similar conditions are major barriers to economic and social development. Similarly, they argue that an attitude of benign indifference on the parts of political, business and professional elite's to poverty, unemployment, discrimination, crime, violence and other social ills, incur huge costs which impede economic development and the well-being of all. Policies and programs that address these problems are not only required on moral but on economic grounds. By permitting these problems to fester, governments harm national development effort with deleterious results for all citizens, including the wealthy, and powerful.

THE FUTURE OF SOCIAL DEVELOPMENT

Since the 1970s, when social development ideas were highly influential in development circles, problems of debt, the imposition of structural adjustment, frequent economic recessions and adverse global capital flows have impeded their implementation. Efforts to promote developmental poverty alleviation policies and programs have not only been hindered by the retrenchment of government programs, but by the ascendancy of neo-liberal thinking. Over the last two decades, neo-liberal theory has debilitated Keynesian and other interventionist approaches. Social development's key normative premises have also been effectively challenged by neo-liberalism. The neo-liberal argument that poverty will automatically decline as a result of economic growth engendered by vigorous free market economic policies is now widely accepted. While the need for policies and programs that seek specifically to address the poverty problem are still advocated, resources to fund these programs have become increasingly scarce. Few governments in the Global South are now able to implement comprehensive developmental poverty alleviation programs and instead, social development interventions are increasingly managed by non-governmental organizations funded by international donors. In the absence of national policy frameworks, social development effort has become fragmented and haphazard. The problem is exacerbated by widespread political instability, increased ethnic and religious conflict, the weakening of national governments, the disintegration of nation states and other adverse developments.

Despite these negative trends, social development writers point out that there have been enormous improvements in standards of living for hundreds of millions people around the world over the last fifty years. These gains have come about because governments have not only pursued economic development but have to varying degrees adopted and implemented social development ideas. The results are most evident in the gains that have been recorded in health, education and nutrition. It is not only that per capita incomes have increased, but that life expectancy, literacy, nutritional and other social indicators have improved. These improvements have been most dramatic in nations that have successfully combined economic growth with social development strategies. They include countries such as Botswana, Costa Rica, Cyprus, Kuwait, Malaysia, Mauritius, Singapore, Sri Lanka, Tunisia and Taiwan. On the other hand, many countries have experienced rapid economic growth without concomitant improvements in standards of living. For example, while many Latin American nations have recorded high rates of economic growth, the incidence of poverty and deprivation remains high. On the other hand, many countries, particularly in Sub-Saharan Africa, have experienced relatively little economic development and social conditions for the bulk of the population remain appalling.

These national experiences reveal very divergent development trends in the Global South with a varying impact on the poverty problem. While poverty has declined, particularly in China which has a large proportion of the world's population, it remains a huge problem in many other regions. In addition, high fertility rates among the poor impede significant reductions in the incidence of absolute poverty which is now estimated, in terms of the one dollar per day line, to characterize the lives of 1.2 billion people around the world. The incidence of absolute poverty has also increased in some parts of the world. In Sub-Saharan Africa, the numbers of poor people increased by about 50 million during the 1990s (World Bank, 2001).

In an attempt to reinvigorate the social development approach, the United Nations convened the World Summit on Social Development in Copenhagen in 1995. Attended by official delegations from the vast majority of the world's nations, including 117 heads of state, the 'Social Summit' as it was also known, reaffirmed a commitment, made almost half a century earlier, to harness the power of economic development for poverty eradication and the enhancement of people's welfare. As a result of the adoption of the Copenhagen Declaration and the Plan of Action, the world's governments committed themselves to transcend the goal of poverty alleviation and instead to adopt policies and programs that will totally *eradicate* absolute poverty. They also agreed to promote full employment, enhance social integration, achieve gender equity, attain universal access to education and health care and mitigate the negative effects of structural adjustment programs through social measures. The specific goal of reducing the numbers of people living in absolute poverty (as defined by the one dollar per day line) by the year 2015 has since been widely advocated by international development agencies.

Although the United Nations General Assembly met in 2001 in Geneva to review progress on the implementation of the Copenhagen Declaration and the Plan of Action, Copenhagen +5. as the event was known, was not accompanied by the same enthusiasm that characterized the 1995 Summit. Nor was it widely reported in the press and in the development literature. Similarly, it appears that support for a global social agenda has waned not only among the international agencies but among world governments. The commitment to eradicate poverty through implementing social development policies and programs, seems to have dissipated The governments of the world's industrial nations seem to have lost interest in social development issues and without the support of the government of the United States, it not clear that much can be achieved. The current Bush administration's social policies are hardly conducive to fostering an international social development agenda. Indeed, with the resurgence of American imperialism, it is likely that global capitalism and American neo-liberalism will be more actively promoted in the future. Although this climate is not conducive to the successful implementation of social development's anti-poverty strategies, the proponents of social development remain optimistic that the poverty problem can best be solved through the adoption of economic and social policies that foster growth, enhance economic participation and enhance the well-being of all.

REFERENCES

Abel-Smith, B. (1976). *Value for Money in Health Services*. London: Heinemann.

Alinsky, Saul (1946). *Reveille for Radicals*. Chicago: University of Chicago Press.

Alinsky, Saul (1971). *Rules for Radicals*. New York: Random House.

Bauer, P. T. (1976). *Dissent on Development*. London: Weidenfeld and Nicolson.

Brokensha, D. and Hodge, P. (1969). *Community Development: An Interpretation*. San Francisco, CA: Chandler.

Bromley, R. and Gerry, C. (Eds.) (1979). *Casual Work and Poverty in Third World Cities*. Chichester: Wiley.

Cardoso, F. H. and Faletto, E. (1979). *Dependency and Development in Latin America*. Berkeley: University of California Press.

Chenery, H., Ahluwalia M., Bell, C., Duloy, J. H. and Jolly, R. (1974). *Redistribution with Growth*. Oxford: Oxford University Press.

Coleman, J. (1988). Social Capital in the Creation of Human Capital. *American Journal of Sociology*, 94, S95-S120.

Dean, H. (2001). Poverty and Citizenship: Moral Repertoire and Welfare Regimes. In F. Wilson, N. Kanji and E. Braathen (Eds.), *Poverty Reduction: What Role of the State in Today's Globalized Economy?* (pp.54-73). London: Zed Books.

de Soto, Hernando (1989). *The Other Path: The Invisible Revolution in the Third World*. New York: Harper and Row.

Frank, A. G. (1974). *On Capitalist Underdevelopment*. New York: Oxford University Press.

Freire, P. (1972). *Pedagogy of the Oppressed*. Harmondsworth: Penguin Books.

Green, M. (2002). Social Development: Issues and Approaches. In U. Kothari and M. Minogue (Eds.), *Development Theory and Practice* (pp.55-72). New York: Palgrave.

Hoffman, S. D. and Seidman, L. S. (2003). *Helping Working Families: The Earned Income Tax Credit*. Kalamazoo, MI: W.E. Upjohn Institute for Employment Research.

International Labour Office (1976). *Employment, Growth and Basic Needs: A One World Problem*. Geneva: The Author.

Lal, D. (1983). *The Poverty of Development Economics*. London: Institute of Economic Affairs.

Marsden, D. and Oakley, P. (1982). Radical Community Development in the Third World. In G. Craig, N. Derricourt and M. Loney (Eds.), *Community Work and the State* (pp. 153-163). London: Routledge and Kegan Paul.

Mayo, M. (1975). Community Development: A Radical Alternative? In. R. Bailey and M. Brake (Eds.), *Radical Social Work* (pp. 129-143). London: Edward Arnold.

Meyer, B. D. and Hotz-Eakin, D. (Eds.) (2001). *Making Work Pay: The Earned Income Tax Credit and its Impact on America's Families*. New York: Russell Sage Foundation.

Midgley, J. (1993). Ideological Roots of Social Development Strategies. *Social Development Issues*, 15 (1): 1-13.

_____ . (1994). Defining Social Development: Historical Trends and Conceptual Formulations. *Social Development Issues*, 16 (3), 3-19.

_____ . (1995). *Social Development: The Developmental Perspective in Social Welfare*. Thousand Oaks, CA. and London: Sage Publications.

_____ . (1996). Toward a Developmental Model of Social Policy: Relevance of the Third World Experience. *Journal of Sociology and Social Welfare*, 23 (1): 59-74.

_____ . (1999). Growth, Redistribution and Welfare: Towards Social Investment. *Social Service Review*, 73 (1): 1-12.

Midgley, J. with Hall, A., Hardiman, M. and Narine, D. (1986). *Community Participation, Social Development and the State*. New York: Methuen.

Midgley, J. and Livermore, M. (1998). Social Capital and Local Economic Development: Implications for Community Social Work Practice. *Journal of Community Practice*, 5 (1/2): 29-40.

Midgley, J. and Sherraden, M. (2000). The Social Development Perspective in Social Policy. In J. Midgley, M. B. Tracy and M. Livermore (Eds.), *The Handbook of Social Policy* (pp. 435-446). Thousand Oaks, CA: Sage Publications.

Midgley, J. and Tang, K. L. (2001). Introduction: Social Policy, Economic Growth and Developmental Welfare. *International Journal of Social Welfare*. 10 (4): 244-252.

Myrdal, G. (1968). *Asian Drama: An Inquiry into the Poverty of Nations*. Harmondsworth: Penguin.

Myrdal, G. (1970). *The Challenge of World Poverty*. Harmondsworth, England: Penguin Books.

Neumark, D. (2002). *How Living Wage Laws Affect Low-wage Workers and Low Income Families*. San Francisco, CA: Public Policy Institute of California.

Newell, K. (Ed.) (1975). *Health by the People*. Geneva: World Health Organization.

Portes, A., Castells, M. and Bentol, L. A. (1989). *The Informal Economy: Studies in Advanced and less Developed Countries*. Baltimore, MD: Johns Hopkins University Press.

Putnam, R. D. with Leonardi, R. and Nanetti, R. Y. (1993). *Making Democracy Work: Civic Traditions in Modern Italy*. Princeton: Princeton University Press.

Putnam, R. D. (2000). *Bowling Alone: The Collapse and Revival of American Community*. New York: Simon and Schuster.

Rodney, W. (1972). *How Europe Underdeveloped Africa*. Dar-es-Salaam: Tanzania Publishing House.

Schultz, T. W. (1981). *Investing in People*. Berkeley, CA: University of California Press.

Seers, Dudley (1972). The Meaning of Development. In N. T. Uphoff and W. F. Ilchman (Eds.), *The Political Economy of Development* (pp. 123-129). Berkeley, CA: University of California Press.

Sen, A. (1985). *Commodities and Capabilities*. Amsterdam: North-Holland.

_____ . (1999). *Development as Freedom*. New York: Knopf.

Sherraden, M. (1991) *Assets and the Poor: A New American Welfare Policy*. Armonk, NY: M. E. Sharpe.

_____ . (2001). Asset Building Policy and Programs for the Poor. In T. M. Shapiro and E. N. Wolff, (Eds.), *Assets for the Poor* (pp. 302-323). New York: Russell Sage Foundation.

Skocpol, T. (1995). Targeting Within Universalism: Politically Viable Policies to Combat Poverty in the United States. In T. Skocpol (Ed.), *Social Policy in the United States: Future Possibilities in Historical Perspective* (pp.250-274). Princeton, NJ: Princeton University Press.

Stewart, F. (1985). *Basic Needs in Developing Countries*. Baltimore, MD: Johns Hopkins University Press.

Streeten, P. and Burki, S. J. (1978). Basic Needs: Some Issues. *World Development*, 6 (3): 411-421.

Thomas, J. J. (1992). *Informal Sector Activity*. Ann Arbor: University of Michigan Press.

United Nations (1969). *Proceedings of the International Conference of Ministers Responsible for Social Welfare*. New York: The Author.

_____ . (1971a). *Popular Participation in Development*. New York: The Author.

_____ . (1971b). Social Policy and Planning in National Development. *International Social Development Review*, 3, 4-15.

_____ . (1996). *Report of the World Summit for Social Development: Copenhagen, 6-12 March 1995*. New York: The Author.

World Bank (1990). *World Development Report, 1990: Poverty*. Washington, DC: The Author

_____ . (1991). *World Development Report, 1991: The Challenge of Development*. Washington, DC: The Author

Young, M. E. (2002). *From Early Child Development to Human Development*. Washington, DC: World Bank.

Yunus, M. (1991). *Grameen Bank: Experiences and Reflections*. Dhaka: Grameen Bank.

In: *Poverty Monitoring and Alleviation in East Asia*   ISBN: 1-59033-828-6
K. Tang and C. Wong, editors pp. 177-189   © 2003 Nova Science Publishers, Inc.

Chapter 10

AN INSTITUTIONAL ANALYSIS OF POVERTY

Chack-kie Wong

INTRODUCTION

Institutions are socially created. They are active structures that determine people's behaviour and influence their values (Islam, 1995:46; North, 1990:.3). Hence it is reasonable to assume that an institutional approach should be meaningful in the analysis of poverty. In the study of poverty, the nature, extent and causes of poverty are frequently examined. The development of institutions for poverty alleviation also catches the attention of academic and policy analysts. However, only a few analysts treat institutions as an independent or intervening factor in the study of poverty. Even though they study the development or the contribution of institutions to poverty alleviation, the special meanings attached to the institutional approach are not fully appreciated.

Indeed, the institutional setting of various state institutions for poverty alleviation takes on special meanings. The decision–making process of state institutions on policy about poverty and how that policy affects people's choices are areas of great interest and importance to the understanding of policy for poverty. Underlying the idea that state institutions can influence people's behaviour is the assumption that institutions may act autonomously in terms of their own interests or they can moderate the impact of structural changes on human behaviour.

A review of literature on poverty identifies only a few analyses that approach poverty in relation to institutions, but these do not take on the special meanings outlined above. Two dominant approaches in the study of poverty have been identified. The first is an individualistic perspective in which poverty is regarded as a factor of individual faults: the poor lack will-power, they are morally deficit. In other words, they belong to a different group. This is an individualistic perspective to poverty. Secondly, poverty is perceived as being caused by structural factors such as economy, class, education, family etc. In this approach, the poor can do nothing about their fate as their destiny lies in structural factors beyond their control. This is a structural approach in which the environment is the key factor.

In this chapter, we introduce a third approach, that is, to examine poverty from an institutional perspective. This assumes that institutions matter.

The beginning of this chapter explores the special meanings of an institutional analysis of poverty. It starts by introducing a few poverty studies that explicitly adopts the concept of institutions in the analyses of poverty and policy for poverty alleviation. Two concepts of institutions are noted in the analysis of institutions in relation to poverty. Firstly, institutions are viewed as organizations in a micro-level analysis and how conditions of poverty are affected by these organizations is examined. Secondly, institutions are seen as macro-institutional structures such as capitalism and welfare state in a macro-level conceptualisation. The focus is on the need of these macro-institutional structures to tackle poverty to meet their own systemic requirement. We then look at institutions at the meso or intermediate level. We clarify the meanings of institutions in the context of an institutional approach. References to scholarly writings in other social science disciplines will also be made. This is followed by an outline of the key features of this institutional analysis of poverty and what that analysis implies for our understanding of poverty and poverty alleviation.

THE EXTERNAL ANALYSES OF INSTITUTIONS IN POVERTY STUDY

Our point of departure is Peter Townsend's analysis of poverty. As far as we know from the review of literature on poverty, Townsend is the first poverty analyst who mentions a structural' or 'institutional' approach of poverty (1983, 1993).

In his view, institutions affect the allocation of resources, nationally or internationally. In the case of national institutions such as state institutions and big corporations, they shape wage and social security systems within a country. For instance, the legislature of a country "enacts laws, produces regulations and encourages conformist behaviour" (Townsend, 1983: 73-76). It is clear that laws and regulations passed by the legislature have coercive power over people within its jurisdiction. In the case of multi-national corporations, they also influence the rise of unemployment across national borders when they reallocate their industrial production base elsewhere. In Townsend's institutional analysis of poverty, the activities of international institutions such as the World Bank also explain poverty in both rich and poor countries (1993: 102). In Townsend's view, institutions take the form of organizations; they can be government or non-government organizations, in the economic, social or political sector.

Townsend approaches the relation between institutions and poverty from a distributional perspective. He places strong emphasis on the responsibility of international organizations in his 'institutional' or 'structural' analysis of poverty. However international organizations such as the World Bank, contrary to Townsend's analysis, look to state institutions for explaining poverty because they regard the latter as having power to redistribute resources for the benefit of the poor (2001: 16). Hence from the distributional perspective, similar controversies are inevitable once resources and power are involved.

In essence, the above impact analysis of institutions on poverty in the form of organizations, primarily looks at poverty as due to the lack of resources available to the poor. Hence, the resource distributors - state, social, economic, or international institutions - have a role to play in poverty alleviation. This line of analysis can be traced to the 'radical' social administration tradition in social policy in which Townsend is its principal proponent.

Another authority on social policy, Jordan (1996), following Polanyi's analysis of the 'Great Transformation', takes an inter-institutional perspective in analysing poverty. He refers to the need of poverty alleviation and regulatory institutions to tame the destructive market forces, which are also economic institutions (Jordan, 1996: 223-224). More specifically, Jordan affirms the utility of welfare states, which "provide the advanced industrialized countries with institutional ways of restraining both costly internal conflicts and their international spillovers" (1996: 226). The institutions referred by Jordan are the macro-institutional structures of capitalism and welfare states. Jordan's theory of poverty is, indeed, based on a political economy perspective. It can also be re-conceptualised as a supply-based theory of poverty because poverty alleviation is considered as a result of the *enforced need* of the state to restrain the "costly internal conflicts and their international spillovers" (Jordan, 1996: 226).

Essentially, Townsend's and Jordan's institutional analyses of poverty are external rather than internal analyses of institutions on poverty. Both analyses do not inform us about how institutions, as an independent or intervening factor, affect the conditions of poverty and behaviour of the poor. Henceforth, we need to look to an internal analysis of institutions on poverty other than the perspectives of either the distributive power of organizations or the need of the state to institutionalise poverty alleviation.

WHAT DOES AN INSTITUTIONAL ANALYSIS OF POVERTY MEAN?

In our review of the literature on poverty, we have identified a few publications that analyse poverty from an institutional perspective, as we tentatively suggested. As a result we have to refer to writings by scholars not only in the field of social welfare and social policy in order to construct an institutional analysis of poverty other than the two foregoing analyses that regard institutions as micro-level organizations and macro-level structures respectively.

In an article on rural poverty, Islam (1995: 46) defines institutions as encompassing "arrangements, rules, and norms upon which economic or social behaviour is constructed". Iatridis (1994: 12), a social policy analyst, refers to institutions as social practices built around a distinct set of values, sanctioned and maintained by norms. North (1990: 3), an economic historian, defines institutions as either "the rules of the game in a society" or more formally, "the humanly devised constraints that shape human interaction". Ashford (1986: 6), another social policy analyst, adopts a similar line in understanding the constraining function of institutions, and refers to it as "the manifested expressions of how a people limit the use of collective authority".

The above few selected definitions seem to indicate that institutions define individual behaviour by their 'rules of the game' such as rules, norms, habits, and routines. However, it is fruitful to stress that an institutional perspective also sees individuals as capable of purposeful action. For instance as suggested by North (1990), despite constraints placed by institutions on decision-making, individuals can alter those constraints. Nielsen (2001: 5) shares similar views about the capacity of individuals. They are human agencies: purposeful, rational, with some freedom to deliberate or choose in accordance with their individual psychology.

Here in this chapter, we do not intend to pursue a review of the various institutionalist or neo-institutionalist schools of thoughts. What we endeavour is to apply their basic ideas into poverty studies. In general, our concern is why and how institutions affect social practices and poverty conditions. On the basis of the foregoing analysis, we have identified two essential variables underlying an institutional analysis for the limited purpose of this study. Firstly, an institutional analysis looks at the constraints imposed upon the exercise of collective authority that is about how those who have the authority are constrained by rules and norms. By all means, values play a significant part. Secondly, an institutional analysis also looks at how rules and norms around poverty alleviation affect the poor. It is necessary to clarify that we do not intend to focus on the idea of whether individuals can deliberate choices and alter the constraints imposed upon them. Our reason is simple, that the primary aim of this chapter is to relate an institutional analysis to the study of poverty.

If our institutional approach is used to analyse poverty, there will be a particular need to make a distinction between institutions as organizations and institutions as a form of social practice. North (1990) cites an example to illustrate the distinction between the two different conceptions of institutions. According to him, the players and the rules of the game can be clearly differentiated in competitive team sport. The purpose of the rules is to define or limit the ways in which a competitive team sport is played. But the objective of participating teams within that "set of rules is to win the game by a combination of skills, strategy, and coordination; by fair means and sometimes by foul means" (North, 1990: 4-5). In other words, the organizations (i.e. the participating teams in this case) are groups of individuals bound by some common purpose to achieve the objective of winning the game. The rules of the game, or institutions in our conceptualisation, are human creation; but organizations have to develop within the institutional framework that defines their behaviour.

The competitive team sport example differentiates between institutions as organizations and institutions as a form of social practice. Because the meaning of institutions according to the latter definition is more conducive to our understanding of poverty, we adopt it here. Hereafter in our discussion, institutions are not taken as organizations. They are social practices built around a set of values, sanctioned by rules and norms. There are legal institutions of the rule of law; democratic institutions of free press and free associations; social institutions of family, religion, community, and school; and state institutions for poverty alleviation, for instance.

In the case of poverty alleviation institutions, Islam (1995) cites some examples which have significant impact on rural poverty. Institutions such as the structure of ownership and control of productive assets, arrangements for credit and irrigation and even methods of wage payments have great impact on rural poverty and its alleviation. These institutions can influence economic growth as well as the distribution of benefits through growth. Hence the level of earnings of the poor, who are usually low-paid workers and peasants in rural areas, are closely related to the operations and functions of institutions.

Another similar conception of institutions in poverty analysis is also documented in a World Bank (2001) report on poverty alleviation. The report conceptualises institutions as rules and norms such as rules of inheritance and norms for gender roles, which are cited as barriers between the socially disadvantaged women and the opportunity and resources they need to advance their interest (The World Bank, 2001: 18). According to this analysis, women are stricken by poverty because social institutions in the form of rules and norms, rather than specific organizations, moderate their life chances.

We come close to outlining an institutional analysis, which regards institutions as an explanation, hence an independent or intervening variable, of poverty and poverty alleviation.

Firstly, in this analytical perspective, institutions do not simply take on an organizational form, albeit which has a great impact on poverty. Secondly, they are not the dependent arrangements, stemming from the political economy analysis, for the state to supply the resources for the need of poverty alleviation. This perspective looks promising as it treats institutions on their own right in the analysis of poverty.

On the basis of the above discussion on the meanings of institution and from the perspective of an institutional approach just stated, we are led to ask a different set of questions or reference points on poverty and poverty alleviation. It first focuses on the internal analysis of poverty alleviation institutions. Secondly, it looks at the ways that poverty alleviation institutions moderate the behaviour and values of the poor. However before we go into these two aspects, we need to establish why institutions explain poverty. This is the prerequisite for treating poverty alleviation institutions as an independent or intervening variable. These three aspects and their implications for policy are elaborated below.

INSTITUTIONS AS AN EXPLANATION OF POVERTY

A meso-institutional analysis of poverty assumes that human beings are essentially social creatures, which have and need a social milieu to develop their human qualities (Twine, 1994: 9). One of the human qualities is the building of institutions which also defines the opportunities and constraints confronting people. Poverty alleviation institutions are such social milieu, which define opportunities and constraints confronting people especially those who are at the lower strata in urban, industrial settings. Hence, it is reasonable to assume that poverty alleviation institutions, or their absence, would be perceived as an explanation of poverty, apart from the individualist and structural explanations (Townsend, 1983, 1993).

The reasons for arguing institutions as an independent or intervening variable are simple. Firstly, life chances in complex urban and industrial societies are characterized by numerous risks that are beyond individual control. Character weakness or fate is no longer a satisfactory explanation. Ample evidences suggest that poverty conditions in urban, industrial setting can happen to people even though they possess work skills, are industrious, and even after a lifelong working career. They can still be poor especially in this global era.

Secondly, structural explanations have proved inadequate. Capitalism and class structure, for example, are powerful explanations of human behaviour. However their effects tend to be broad and general. Hence they are inadequate in explaining the variations of behaviour among the same capitalist countries or among the same class of people. For example, class difference seems to be more obvious in Britain than in the United States, but the reverse is the case with regard to race relations although both are capitalist countries. Apparently, there can be meso-institutions that mediate the effect of macro-institutions. In poverty alleviation, state institutions as meso-institutions have a significant role to play. One reason is that people expect their governments to have a particular responsibility in their society. This perception is not only shaped by what they experience in their own society, but is also affected by their knowledge about poverty alleviation practices in other countries as our world has become increasingly globalized.

The third is the belief that poverty conditions are essentially remediable. The key to this change is the disassociation of poverty from the victims' character or walk of life. Poverty is often reduced to a non-moral issue – a single, bare fact – the lack of money (de Swaan, 1989:

161). Coupled with the belief that state institutions have the power to levy taxes and impose membership, e.g., collectivised transfer and saving, it is not surprising to notice that institutional failures have become an explanation on poverty conditions in the urban, industrial setting.

Readers may notice that we have followed the arguments advanced by Townsend in his 'structural' or 'institutional' analysis of poverty, but we have extended it to include the autonomous role of institutions as the explanatory factor. We elaborate this point in the following circumstances where poverty conditions are primarily perceived as the result of lack of or inadequate, improper institutional arrangements.

The 1997 Asian Financial Crisis is a first case in point. Incidences of poverty and unemployment drastically rose in some East and South-East Asian countries as a result of this economic event which is primarily perceived as an external factor beyond individual control. For instance, the newly industrializing economies in East Asia had enormous growth before the Crisis. Hence, their poverty alleviation institutions were built on the assumption that those who wanted to work could find jobs. The structural and international nature of the Crisis has shaken this assumption. Poverty alleviation institutions there did not sufficiently cover their employed population who were suddenly fallen into this unexpected social risk in a massive scale. Some countries took action to remedy this poverty condition in the aftermath of the Crisis. South Korea is a case in point. In 1998, it extended the unemployment insurance to cover full-time workers in companies with five or more employees. In 2000, it further extended its poverty alleviation benefits to working adults. The initiative was nevertheless related to the strong labour mobilization in South Korea. In response to massive unemployment and poverty, the unemployed and trade unions in South Korea did not only blame structural factors, but also directed their grievances at the state on the inadequate provision for poverty alleviation.

It is clear that not only individuals but also countries are exposed to risks beyond their control. However, their responses are different. The difference in institutional responses among countries conveys the message that government efforts can make a difference to poverty conditions. For instance, because of the lack of unemployment insurance, low-income workers in Hong Kong have to rely on social assistance and be counted as poor. Henceforth, being poor as a result of the Crisis can easily be perceived as unrelated to character weakness and fate as job opportunities or contributory unemployment benefits were not available.

The second circumstance concerns the transitional economies of the former Soviet bloc countries where the dismantling of the Centrally Planned Economy went hand in hand with the collapse of poverty alleviation institutions. The sudden increase of people falling into poverty is another clear evidence of circumstances beyond individual control. For instance, between 1989 and 1991, real incomes in Poland were down 60% in farmer households and 71% in worker households. During the same period, the proportion of persons below the minimum income standards rose from 15% to 37% in employee households and from 24% to 34% in pensioner households (Danecki, 1994). In Russia, 30.7% of the population had an income below the minimum subsistence level at the beginning of 1994 (Tchernina, 1994). The institutional transformations in many of these countries have until now continued to deprive many of a stable income and led many others into poverty. In essence, the sudden deterioration of life opportunities and the rise in constraints inflicted upon many people in these countries could hardly be explained by individual faults. State institutions, the essential part in the rules of the game for poverty alleviation, are to blame as they had healthy track records in those good old days.

The third circumstance applies to countries of considerable wealth – the OECD countries. In these countries, given that economic systems and wealth levels are similar, differences in poverty incidence and extent can only be explained by the outcome of different institutional arrangements in poverty alleviation. For instance, a recent report finds that the Netherlands, in comparison with two other OECD countries, Germany and the United States, had the lowest levels of poverty because of its universal benefits system (Goodin, Heady, Muffels and Dirven, 1999). Universal poverty alleviation benefits are the ascribed explanation. In this regard, poverty status is more likely to be perceived as a factor of the institutional arrangement for poverty alleviation.

All these circumstances illustrate that institutions have become either an independent or intervening variable in explaining poverty. It does not mean that individualist and structural explanations have lost their appeal. But the institutional explanation should have its share for the blame of this social misery. With this view in mind, it is appropriate to suggest that poverty alleviation institutions explain the variations in the incidence and extent of poverty. If personal, cultural and structural factors are held constant, institutions will become the determining factor. We have already illustrated this in the above OECD example. Indeed, an institutional analysis is not new in poverty studies; the point is that it has not received the attention it deserves.

FROM EXTERNAL TO INTERNAL ANALYSIS OF INSTITUTIONS FOR POVERTY ALLEVIATION

Now we come to an internal analysis of institutions for poverty alleviation. March and Olsen (1989), in their study of institutions of politics, offer an explanation that helps our analysis of poverty from an internal analysis of institutions.

In their view, institutions of politics provide order and influence in politics because they are the fundamental features of politics. Institutions of politics, such as bureaucratic agencies, legislative committees, and appellate courts are organizations themselves and arenas for contending social forces (March and Olsen, 1989: 16-17). The essence of their idea is that institutions, in their organization forms, cannot attend to everything at once. They have their own logic – i.e., to follow the collections of standard operating procedures and structures that define values, norms, interests, identities and beliefs. Most important of all, they simplify the problems before them to manageable magnitude. Hence certainties can be ensured. In other words, some potential participants, issues, viewpoints, values, and beliefs are ignored or suppressed if they are not in line with the underlying rules and norms of institutions.

Henceforth, it is necessary to look at poverty alleviation institutions as if they have full autonomy over decisions on poverty alleviation. This is not to disregard the functions of external, contextual factors, but to take the position that poverty alleviation institutions can legitimately decide on matters within their jurisdiction. This stance is similar to the relative autonomy thesis of state in neo-Marxist theory. Here, we need to reiterate that poverty alleviation institutions are not equal to the sum of organizations involved in poverty alleviation. Institutions, as we have mentioned in the foregoing paragraphs, are about the rules of the game. Thus, poverty alleviation institutions can be taken as the rules of the game in poverty alleviation. In other words, organizations in poverty alleviation institutions such as bureaucracies, benefits system and related organizations such as health services and public housing together with the people involved at different organizational levels, have to act according to the values underpinning poverty alleviation institutions. Needless to say, their social practices are sanctioned by institutional rules and norms.

Now, we place poverty alleviation institutions in the centre ground of our internal analysis of institutions for poverty alleviation. Ashford provides us with some hints in his analysis of how the state operates according to the ground rules for exercising authority (1986: 6). In his words, the ground rules are found "in the basic practices attached to the work of political executive, the organization and powers of bureaucracy and the accepted methods of formulating, implementing and evaluating policies" (*ibid.*). In the same vein, poverty alleviation institutions also operate according to the ground rules that define the powers of those who formulate, implement and evaluate policies about poverty alleviation. For instance, if a ground rule in poverty alleviation in a country is to delegate relief work to local governments on the condition of limited financial support, we can imagine great regional disparities in poverty conditions in that country. The establishment of an open-ended minimum poverty assistance scheme in urban China is a case in point. It was necessitated by the need to provide a safety net of the last resort to those who could not fend for themselves under the new social and economic reality of economic reform. The previous poverty assistance scheme was inadequate in providing relief to new comers in poverty – those unemployed and the retired who do not have adequate means – because the discharge of poverty relief was primarily based on the financial capacity of each municipal authority. The new poverty relief scheme has changed this basic ground rule in poverty alleviation in urban China. Local municipal governments now have new basic practices about poverty alleviation. In essence, they have to organize it according to the new ground rule based on the principle of need.

In view of our broad definition of poverty alleviation institutions, the ground rules are interpreted in accordance with underlying institutional values. Then, we need to ask: What are the underlying values of poverty alleviation institutions? The dominant values underlying poverty alleviation institutions are about the legitimacy in the use of institutionalised or collective authority. In this sense, institutional values do not only refer to normative values as we understand them, such as social needs and social stability. In institutional terms, they are also about the legitimacy of the institution over the concerned issue. In other words, decisions-makers have to consider whether their decisions over the issue are in accordance with rules and norms set for their use of the institutionalised or collective authority. We go back to the ground rule example in reform China for the establishment of an open-ended poverty assistance scheme for further elaboration. In that case, if the 'new poor' (i.e., the unemployed and the retired who have genuine needs) are not being taken good care of, the legitimacy of the government as a whole would be weakened. As a result, the institutional value of serving the needy is in question.

Hence, there might be a gap between the ground rules attached to the powers of those who are directly responsible for decision-making and implementation of poverty alleviation policies and the institutional values of poverty alleviation. Perhaps controversies over the interpretation of the ground rules may arise among those who have power over resources and those who have stakes in poverty alleviation. This is exactly likened to what we mentioned about the competitive team sport illustration in which some players may manipulate or break the rules for their advantage. Again, the Chinese case of adopting an open-ended poverty assistance scheme offers good reference. The old ground rule of basing poverty relief on financial capacity could not meet the changing needs arising from economic reform and posed a legitimacy problem to the authorities. At that time, the institutional value of poverty alleviation had been questioned. The open-ended poverty assistance scheme with its new ground rule, came in. However, not all municipal governments in China have the financial capacity to make ends meet in accordance with the new ground rule of basing need in poverty alleviation. Hence, unmet needs of the new poor are still reported from time to time in urban China despite the claim that the new open-ended poverty assistance scheme has been fully implemented. Evidently, some municipal governments may have broken the ground rule.

We come to illustrate how decisions are made in accordance with an institutional perspective. The institutional policy choice to advance workfare requirements into the benefits system is a case in point. In accordance with class or pluralist analyses, the decision to advance this policy may follow the need for perceived contextual changes or the need to be responsive to organized pressures. However, an institutional perspective has a dynamics of its own because the legitimacy to make decisions in this particular case lies in the institution itself: the institution has the jurisdiction to make its own decisions. External pressures are to be processed through the mediation on the institutional arena if they have any impact on decisions that are to be made. In this case, decision-makers have to ensure that external pressures such as the incidence and the extent of welfare dependency do not translate into doubts about institutional efficacy. Decision makers also needed to ensure that political and administrative support are available, and that a redirection of institutional capacity is possible.

In the end, decision-making in the above case is primarily about the legitimacy of the institution as affected by the issue. By taking action, poverty alleviation institutions reduce uncertainties about their legitimacy if the behaviour of the perceived welfare dependants is moderated by the new rules and norms around workfare. Nevertheless, decision-makers as human agencies are also able to exploit controversies in society and the institutional rules and norms to their advantage.

In the case of workfare, the institutional autonomy in the response to contextual changes or political pressures illustrates that poverty alleviation institutions may not be in touch with the reality. This is because the bases of decision-making are rules and norms of institutions and their prescribed processes. Therefore, for the sake of securing certainties, institutional practices tend to be conservative. In the case of poverty measure, the state's minimum income standards are usually not based on the scientific study of poverty (Veit-Wilson, 1998); they are always a compromise between the ideal solution and the capacity of government.

THE CHANGES IN THE RULES OF THE GAME AND THEIR EFFECTS ON THE POOR

In the coming paragraphs, we move to look at how the rules of the game in poverty alleviation affect the poor. Understanding the causation of poverty is important, but the ways poverty alleviation institutions work and how they affect the behaviour and values of beneficiaries are equally important. This suggests that beneficiaries are influenced by institutional structure despite of their different reasons for falling into the safety net. For instance, high replacement ratio may induce unemployed beneficiaries to stay in the benefits system despite improvements in the availability of job opportunities in the labour market (George and Wilding, 1984: 174-178). Hence, people's behaviour as well as their values can be changed as a factor of institutional arrangements.

China's economic restructuring offers a case in point. In a comparative study of public attitudes towards welfare provisions of two Chinese cities in 1996, Lee and Wong (2001) identified a more positive and receptive view towards the reduction of state welfare provisions as well as reform initiatives in housing, medical, and retirement benefits in the city where economic reform was initiated earlier. For example, in the city with more exposure to economic reform, only four-tenths of respondents disagreed, in different extent, to the statement that "one should seek help from relatives when one's own financial resources are inadequate". Whereas in the city with less exposure to economic reform, seven-tenths of their compatriots were in disagreement to the above statement, a difference of nearly thirty percentage points (Lee and Wong, 2001, Table 4.4). They suggest that such attitudinal difference is rooted in an institutional context despite the fact that both cities were exposed to the same Chinese culture which is assumed to have placed a high value on the help of family members and relatives.

The institutional context, the ground rule referred to in our analysis, is the changing policy package in urban China, from one which is about 'permanent employment, low wage and extensive state welfare' to one about 'insecure employment, high wage and social welfare'. In the latter case, workers in urban China are less dependent on state welfare because they have a different incentive structure under the new ground rule. They could secure more personal resources than before. In this respect, it is assumed that respondents would be more accepting of help from relatives, instead of from the state, as we have just illustrated. Therefore, the attitudinal shift reflects a different rule of the game in which people have less expectations of their state. Hence, norms, e.g., statism and familism in our above illustration, which are to sanction behavior are in fact affected by a change in the rules of the game.

Back to poverty studies, it is clear that a change in the rules of the game should have independent impact on people's behaviour on poverty. The fact that people are moving out of poverty all the time (i.e., the dynamic analysis of poverty, see for example Walker, 1995) should enable us to draw lessons from the ways they are affected by different institutional structures of incentive and constraint. The recent experience in Hong Kong is a good case in point.

A recent inclusion of workfare measures in 1999 of those employable beneficiaries had resulted in a substantial drop in total number of unemployed cases on social assistance in this East Asian 'tiger' economy. Under the new rule, the employable beneficiaries are required to apply for jobs and to take up community services in exchange for benefits. These changes in institutional arrangements in poverty alleviation, as mentioned in above, illustrate that a change in rules was assumed to moderate people's behaviour in relation to their poverty status. Part of the reason for introducing these workfare measures was in response to the public outcry that the benefits received by some beneficiary households with employable adults enabled them to enjoy a better standard of living than those low-income households who worked hard for their living. The application of more stringent means, indeed, was to ensure that the underlying institutional value of self-reliance was perceived as intact. It is worthwhile to note that the change of rules had resulted in a significant drop of cases in the category of unemployment, from 30,922 in July 1999, the second month when the rule was implemented, to 23,364, two years' later in July 2001.[1] Whether this is desirable is definitely a normative judgment.

In the following paragraphs, we could postulate a more systematic analysis of the effects of a change in the rules of the game on the poor on the basis of our understanding from poverty studies. We shall look at the benefits system, a poverty alleviation institution itself, from a systems perspective. First of all, we need to know why the poor 'enter' or 'do not enter' into a benefits system. Stigma plays a significant part in constituting the phenomenon of what is called the 'non-take-up' rate in means-tested social assistance benefits. In essence, norms work. Secondly, once the poor are in the benefits system, why do they stay or leave? Thirdly, when they leave the system, what are the factors contributing to their 're-entry' or their remaining outside the system? In general, an institutional perspective is to ask whether a change in the rules of the benefits system is the key variable in the issue in question.

In responding to these questions, an internal analysis of institutions for poverty alleviation looks at factors about rules such as replacement ratios, childcare arrangements, training and employment counselling, incentives to reemployment, etc. These factors, with their underlying rules, can moderate the behaviour of the poor even if the labour market were held constant. In essence, an internal analysis of institutions for poverty alleviation is about the restructuring of incentives or constraints that may induce a change in the behaviour of the poor in regards to work, family obligations, benefits entitlement and the like.

CONCLUSION

In this chapter, we started out with the review of literature on poverty and found that very few analyses approached the study in relation to institutions. Even if they did, the special meanings of an institutional analysis were not fully appreciated. We pieced together ideas in the institutionalist thinking by scholars, not only in the field of social welfare and social policy, to postulate a different set of questions on poverty and poverty conditions. On this account, we identified that some prevalent institutional analyses of poverty were indeed external analyses of institutions on poverty. Then we moved to extend Peter Townsend's argument to include institutions themselves as an independent or intervening explanation of poverty, followed by the reasoning of an internal analysis of institutions for poverty alleviation. At the end, we presented postulates of circumstances on how a change of rules affected the behaviour of the poor.

In sum, this chapter is a preliminary attempt to outline an institutional analysis of poverty on the basis of institutions as an independent or intervening variable. This perspective is seemingly an area where very few social policy analysts have worked on. In contrast, a review of literature on institutions in the category of institutionalism or neo-institutionalism can easily identify a substantial pool of publications in the fields of economics, politics, and public administration over the past two decades. We ponder whether the insufficient attention, if not reflecting a neglect on the relation between institutions and poverty, is a factor of the

---

[1] Source: Social Welfare Department, The Hong Kong Government of the Special Administration Region, *An Update on CSSA*, 23 October 2002.

overwhelming concern of social policy analysts on 'desirability' rather than 'feasibility' issues. It seems clear that, an institutional analysis might not lead us to normative, desirable alternatives. In the case of poverty, an institutional analysis *could* stop at the 'official' poverty line, i.e., minimum income standards, as it may be the 'feasible' compromise between the ideal solution and the capacity of government. Despite its conservative nature, an institutional analysis of poverty helps step into the shoes of those who make the choice within constraints. On that basis, it is possible to postulate practical solutions for reform.

Before we end, it is helpful to point out that poverty alleviation institutions, according to our analysis, are variable to conceptions. The reason is simple. Poverty alleviation institutions are more than organizations; they are the rules of the game that define social practices. For instance, benefits system is part of the rules of the game. Whether the addition of retraining program for the unemployed expands the institutional boundary or it just adds an organization has no straightforward answer. Henceforth, we need to be specific about what we mean by poverty alleviation institutions in an institutional analysis of poverty.

Despite our above reservations on an institutional analysis of poverty, it provides the meso-foundations for the macro-analyses of social policy and poverty. Apparently, institutions are an independent or intervening factor in any controversy or debate about macro-themes such as social justice, social values, and contextual changes in society, because they are where decisions are made about where and how state capacities should be directed or redirected, about how social practices for managing problems or satisfying needs are institutionalised, and most important of all, about how people's behaviours are constrained by the rules of the game.

REFERENCES

Ashford, D.E. (1986). *The Emergence of the Welfare States*. Oxford: Basil Blackwell.

Danecki, J. (1994). Social Costs of System Transformation in Poland, In S. Ringen and C. Wallace (Eds.) *Societies in Transition: East-Central Europe Today* (47-60). Aldershot, Avebury : Ashgate.

George, V. and Wilding, P. (1984). *The Impact of Social Policy*. London: Routledge and Kegan Paul.

Goodin, R.E. Heady, B. Muffels, R. and Dirven, H. (1999). *The Real Worlds of Welfare Capitalism*. Cambridge: Cambridge University Press.

Iatridis, D. (1994). *Social Policy Institutional Context of Social Development and Human Services*. Pacific Grove: Brooks/Cole.

Islam, R. (1995). Rural Institutions and Poverty in Asia, In Rodger, van der Hoeven, R. (Eds.) *New Approaches in Poverty Analysis and Policy – III* (pp. 38-58). Geneva: International Institute for Labour Studies, ILO.

Jordan, B. (1996). *A Theory of Poverty and Social Exclusion*. Cambridge: Polity Press.

Lee, N.S. and Wong, C.K. (2001). The Tale of Two Chinese Cities: Rolling Back the Boundary of the Welfare State During the Reform Era. In Lee, N.P. and Lo, C. W. (Eds.) *Remaking China's Public Management* (pp.67-96). Westport: Quorum.

March, J.G. and Olsen, J.P. (1989). *Rediscovering Institutions, The Organizational Basis of Politics*. New York and London: The Free Press.

Nielsen, K. (2001). Institutionalist Approaches in the Social Sciences: Typology, Dialogue, and Future Challenges. *Journal of Economic Issues*; Vol. 35(2) (Electronic version).

North, D.C. (1990). *Institutions, Institutional Change and Economic Performance*. Cambridge: Cambridge University Press.

de Swaan, A. (1988). *In Care of State*. Oxford: Basil Blackwell.

Townsend, P. (1983). A Theory of Poverty and the Role of Social Policy. Loney, M., Boswell, D. and Clarke, J. (Eds.) *Social Policy and Social Welfare* (pp.59-82) Milton Keynes: Open University Press.

_____ . (1993). *The International Analysis of Poverty*. New York: Harvester Wheatsheaf.

Tchernina, N.V. (1994). Unemployment and the Emergence of Poverty During Economic Reform in Russia. *International Labour Review*, 133(5 & 6): 599-611

Twine, F. (1994). *Citizenship and Social Rights*. London: Sage.

Veit-Wilson, J. (1998). *Setting Adequacy Standards*. Bristol: The Policy Press.

Walker, R. (1995). The Dynamic of Poverty and Social Exclusion. In G. Room (Ed.) *Beyond the Threshold* (pp.102-128). Bristol: Policy Press.

World Bank (2001). *World Development Report 2000/2001: Attacking Poverty*. Oxford: Oxford University Press.

In: *Poverty Monitoring and Alleviation in East Asia*   ISBN: 1-59033-828-6
K. Tang and C. Wong, editors pp. 191-205   © 2003 Nova Science Publishers, Inc.

Chapter 11

GLOBAL SOCIAL PROTESTS:
AN ANSWER TO WORLD POVERTY?

Arlene Herman and Kwong-leung Tang

> What we saw in Seattle across these tumultuous days stretching from November 28 through December 3, 1999 … was the flowering of a new radical movement in America and across the world, rambunctious, anarchic, internationalist, well informed and in some ways more imaginative and supple than kindred popular eruptions in recent decades (Alexander Cockburn and Jeffrey St. Clair, 2001:5).

INTRODUCTION

Global social activism against the ills of globalization captured much world attention as the twentieth century drew to a close. Of particular note was "the Battle in Seattle" in 1999 where demonstrators against the World Trade Organization (WTO) caused a four-day closure of the retail core of Seattle (Levi and Olson, 2000). Thousands of protestors violently clashed with the police in Seattle. Their action finally made the WTO cut short its meeting, without adopting any resolution. It highlighted the potency of global social activism against neo-liberal globalization. As one observer puts it, "the broader message coming from the streets of Seattle is unmistakable: A corporate-dominated WTO that puts profits before people and property rights before human rights can no longer sustain its current course" (Cooper, 1999:21).

Over 700 organizations were involved in "the Battle in Seattle," including some prominent ones such as the Ruckus Society, Global Exchange, Direct Action Network, People's Global Action and Third World Network. While these organizations have different social concerns, an important question in the eyes of many of these organizations is whether free trade across the nations has benefited the poor.

Global social protests are renowned for the diffuse character of their concerns. A wide variety of concerns have indeed been raised: labor rights, the growth of poverty and inequity, loss of democratic sovereignty, global cultural homogeneity and environmental degradation (McMurtry, 2002). The goals are diverse – eradication of poverty and promotion of equity between groups, advancing humanitarian principles, and championing human and labor rights and social standards – but all are directed against the adverse impacts of crude market liberalism.

Following the "Battle in Seattle", some analysts predicted heightened public awareness and media coverage of anti-globalization protests would fuel the increasing "globalization of social movements" (Ericson and Doyle, 1999). History has proven them right. Importantly, two recent events demonstrate the resilience of global social activism: the World Social Forum in Brazil and the protests in the French city of Evian.

In early 2002, thousands of anti-globalization activists converged on the Brazilian city of Porto Alegre for the World Social Summit (*New York Times,* January 23, 2002). This summit was created as a counterpoint to the World Economic Forum held in Davos, Switzerland. The World Social Forum's first meeting brought some 16,000 activists together from 120 countries and 1,000 organizations to Porto Alegre to explore alternative visions for more positive economic and social policies throughout the world. The theme of this meeting was illuminating and suggestive: "another world was possible." Some topics were raised and discussed among the participants: the cancellation of debt for Third World countries, taxation of capital flows and alternative trade pacts with more environmental and child labor considerations. Participants of the forum were diverse: farmers, union workers, environmentalists, anarchists, and left-wing activists.

More recently, as the Group of Eight (G-8) met in France, their leaders encountered another round of anti-globalization protest. Some 75,000 anti-globalization activists from around the world marched to the French-Swiss border in defiance to the G8 leaders meeting in the French resort of Evian (*The Guardian, June 1, 2003*, *G8 Protestors Riots in Lausanne*). The morning protests kicked off a day of protests coinciding with the arrival in Evian of most of the leaders of the world's seven industrial powers and Russia. Two marches, one from the French town Annemasse and one from Geneva, converged near the Swiss side of the border before heading back to France. Soon afterwards, thousands of protesters blocked highways and bridges, set fire to barricades and drew volleys of tear gas and rubber pellets from the police. The most violent protests were in the Swiss city Lausanne, which was not too far from the G-8 summit. Demonstrators wearing masks hurled rocks at police. The clashes bore some similarities to those occurring in Genoa two years ago where one protester was shot dead during three days of pitched battles between protestors and police. Protests against the G8 meeting quickly disintegrated into the worst riots Europe had seen for a generation.

Such protest against corporate globalization is not unprecedented. In the past few years, there have been constant protests in different parts of the world against G-8, WTO and IMF/World Bank meetings. Various efforts have been made to illuminate on the nature of such global social activism. To some observers, these protests represent "a mishmash of causes", from anti-globalization to relief of Third World debt and environmental protection. They accuse the G-8 of profiting by exploiting the world's poor nations. Clearly, many protestors believe that social action and social change is indispensable to counter the hegemony of capitalism. Also, these protests are good for media exposure and morale-building. On the other hand, proponents of globalization and free world trade have quickly written off these protests as reckless or irrelevant.

In this chapter we look into the question of what significance is of such popular resistance to the international organizations championing neo-liberal globalization. In this paper, after reviewing some of the leading analyses on global social protests, we maintain that Karl Polanyi's notion of double movement can be used to understand the nature and significance of these protests. The implications of using a Polanyian analysis of global social protests are discussed at the end of this contribution.

A String of Global Protests

After the Seattle protests, hundreds of protestors clashed with police at the annual meeting of the World Economic Forum in Davos, Switzerland in January 2000. These demonstrators contended that globalization and free trade only benefit the rich. Similar demonstrations that turned violent were seen in Washington DC in April 2000 when the protestors denounced global capitalism. Soon afterward, demonstrators (students, anti-poverty groups and labor organizations) penetrated the globalization summit held by the Organization of American States (OAS) in Windsor in June 2000, protesting against global free trade. Not long after the OAS meeting, thousands of demonstrators showed up at the meeting of the IMF and the World Bank in Prague. Violent struggles with the police ensued. Accusing these international organizations of accelerating poverty, the demonstrators justified their action on the grounds that public awareness of the problems caused by globalization needs to be raised.

Global protests do not spring from anywhere. As some observers (Borosage, 1999; Lorna, 2000; Smith; 2001;) note, the protests against the WTO in Seattle were preceded by various social protests that erupted and gained in strength as a result of the fight against and victory over the Multilateral Agreement on Investment (MAI) talks at the Organization for Economic Cooperation and Development (OECD) in 1998. The stalling of the MAI boosted their confidence and gave new meaning to global grassroots activism. Regionally, years of protests against the North American Free Trade Agreement (NAFTA) had strengthened the linkages between protestors. In the developing world, opposition to the IMF's structural adjustment policies was widespread. In short, global (and regional) economic negotiations and corporate-dominated trading arrangements have shaped transnational dissent (Ayres, 2001). Neo-liberal ideas and accords, as an important fuel for economic globalization, serve as lightning rods for these protests. The link between international political processes and the rise of transnational social organizations and coalitions could mean significant transnational mobilizations in the future.

GLOBALIZATION AND NEO-LIBERALISM

Global protests target globalization, which is itself a complex and poorly defined concept. Globalization could, for example, mean a breakdown of international borders (Ericson and Doyle, 1999) yielding enhanced human interaction within a one-world system (Giddens, 1999). It is the realm of international economic arrangements and activities that generates so much controversy (Midgley, 2000). Specifically, economic globalization refers to the notion of a rapid acceleration of flows of goods, services and capital across national borders over the last 50 years. As Foster (2003) observes, economic globalization involves the expansion of capitalist economies that ultimately would supplant local control. Under the influence of neo-liberalism, countries are encouraged to exploit all their resources and public goods are to be opened up to complete privatization. In the process, environmental regulations are to be geared to the lowest common denominator so that free trade will not be hampered.

An elaborate discussion of the linkage between globalization, world governance structures and neo-liberalism is offered by Teeple (1995). He argues that the "global economy" rests on the freedom of international capital to move within state economies without restraint. Globalization in this sense reflects a redesigning of the world's political and economic arrangements. It also suggests that economic, technological and ecological developments have moved beyond the control of nation states in order to conform to the corporate agenda of the global economy. Nation states have adopted policies that support deregulation, privatization, transformation of the tax structure, reduction of the national debt, downsizing of government, dismantling the welfare state, circumscription of trade union powers and general restrictions to democracy. These policies are designed to provide a favorable climate for corporations and to harmonize the business environment across countries. Massive reductions in social spending across, health, education and welfare sectors occur. Global economic organizations such as the World Bank, the WTO and the IMF are working hard to enforce these agendas throughout the world.

Empirically, recent studies have not found major and systematic welfare retrenchment taking place in the advanced industrialized countries. Castles (2002) examines the Social Expenditure Database of the OECD to devise measures of the extent, structure and character of trajectories of welfare state change and reform in 21 OECD countries over the period 1984 to 1997. On the basis of these measures, he finds that there has been little sign of systematic welfare retrenchment in recent years and only limited evidence of major structural change.

Despite this, the main limitation of economic development with an emphasis on unlimited growth is that it is pursued without sufficient consideration of its impact on social development. According to the United Nations Development Project (UNDP, 1999), growing poverty and inequality are the world's main problems. As we begin the millennium, the absolute number of poor people in the world is alarmingly high. Stiglitz (2001), using the international poverty line of US$1 and US$2, estimates some 1.2 billion and 2.8 billion people (respectively) are living in poverty. Likewise, the UNDP (2003) estimates that more than a billion people live on less than US$1 a day. They come from sub-Saharan Africa, Latin America and the Caribbean, and parts of Europe and Central Asia. Specific groups, like women, are becoming poorer and more marginalized.

Parallel to this, there is increasing inequality in the worldwide distribution of income. According to Thorbecke and Charumilind (2002), the level of world income inequality is high and has been steadily increasing. Between 1988 and 1993, the Gini index (calculated from household surveys of 91 countries) worsened from 62.8 to 66.0 – Gini coefficients range from 0 (perfect equality) to 1 (perfect inequality). They further determine that in the same period, the advanced industrialized countries of the United States, Japan and Western Europe received 49.55% of the world's income with only 12.81% of the world's population.

Countering such worldwide social problems, the UNDP put much of the blame on globalization and market expansion. Thus its annual report in 1999 contended that: "When the market goes too far in dominating social and political outcomes, the opportunities and rewards of globalization spread unequally and inequitably. The past decade has shown increasing concentration of income, resources, and wealth." (p.2) Along the same line of thinking, Oxfam (1999) urges the WTO to pay greater attention to the impact of trade liberalization on poverty across nations. It argues that the poor countries have been marginalized, lacking the opportunity to shift world attention towards pro-poor issues.

Nationally, academics like Jane Wills (2002: 90) highlight the harmful impact of neo-liberal social policy in the context of Britain:

> From a British perspective, neoliberal capitalism has come to a new political conjuncture. While corporations are larger, make greater returns and are more politically powerful than ever before, the crumbling social infrastructure of the country is often unable to provide the stable environment that capitalism requires to function ... Years of neglect, under-funding and poor management in the public sector have been compounded by the madness of privatization.

She further contends that the excesses of neo-liberalism have been much discredited:

> After 20 years of proselytizing the need to "roll back the State," even the Confederation of British Industry has recently urged the government to invest in improved public transport, education and training. Neoliberalism has been at least partly discredited in the UK, just as it has in the wake of economic crisis of Asia and Eastern Europe (ibid.: 90).

The Asian economic crisis is illustrative of the deleterious impact of "neo-liberal globalism." After decades of rapid economic growth, the situation in many Asian countries changed dramatically with the economic crisis of 1997. The crisis was precipitated by the withdrawal of deposits by international investors who were concerned that banks in Thailand and other countries in the region had engaged in excessively risky loans. To a certain extent, these events were linked to 'globalization' and the free transfer of capital, which is often cited as the prime cause of the crisis. Along this line of inquiry, Godement (1999: 29) argues that:

> Culture, communities, bureaucracies and authoritarian states do not engineer financial meltdowns, markets do. The basic cause of the Crash [the Asian crisis] must be identified in the confrontation between global market forces and local institutions which have not adapted well to new realities.

There was a sudden fall in currency values, stock market declines and capital flight. In the process, panic and psychological contagion served as intervening factors for the crisis. Many Asian countries were seriously affected. These included some of the most successful East Asian economies such as South Korea, as well as newer industrializing economies such as Indonesia and Thailand. Faced with the crisis, several governments in the region turned to international organizations like the IMF for assistance. They have been encouraged by these organizations, as well as the government of the United States, to abandon their statist policies and to embrace neo-liberal reforms (Tang and Midgley, 2002). Ironically, in the context of Asia, the cause of the crisis (i.e. economic liberalism at international level) is employed by the international organizations as the solution to the problem.

THE MEANING OF GLOBAL SOCIAL PROTESTS

Responses to the Seattle protests by proponents of neo-liberalism range from dismissive and indignant to troubled. A variety of derisory portrayals have been made of the protestors, including: "flat-earth advocates" (*New York Times, December 1, 1999*), "cranks, bullies and hypocrites" (*Financial Times, December 8, 1999*) "a mere rabble of exuberant irrationalists" (*The Economist, September 23, 2000, Editorial*) and "a representative collection of people who can't stand prosperity" (*Wall Street Journal, November 30, 1999*). Others argue that those who oppose free trade are misled, uninformed and do not really know what they are protesting against (McMurtry, 2002). Their negative assessments of anti-globalization protesters are rather consistent.

Most academics disagree with such reactive and dismissive responses from neo-liberal supporters. They ask key questions about the meaning and significance of the anti-globalization protests. Many on the left of the political spectrum argue that global social protests show the promise of a nascent international labor movement which offers a critique of capitalist exploitation on a worldwide level. Specifically, some argue that the protests in Seattle show the potency of an international labor movement over the issue of international labor standards and their enforcement. Thus, Lambert and Webster (2001) pin their hope on the search for a new form of labor unionism – global social movement unionism – that may offer greater scope for a more effective resistance to the logic of globalization.

On the other hand, Gill (2000) argues that the Seattle protests in 1999 and the Washington Protest in spring 2000 are part of a larger worldwide movement that reflects a new form of global political agency that is both plural and differentiated. This movement contains some key features of Gramsci's *The Modern Prince* (1959) and Machiavelli's *The Prince* (1944). Gill (2000: 138) states that this 'Postmodern Prince' (i.e. The Battle in Seattle) is "well beyond the politics of identity and difference; it has gender, race and class aspects and is also connected to issues of ecological and social reproduction." He argues that because the protestors are a diverse group of human rights activists, labor activists, environmental activists, students, teachers etc., the protest itself has become what Gramsci (1971: 129) called an "organism with the beginning qualities of a 'collective will'." Within this context, the protest is seen as a set of interconnections between problems and movements worldwide that is inclusive of political, educational and cultural forms. Gill (2000) further argues that the global aspects of social movements cannot be studied in isolation from their local and personal dimension and that it is within this context that optimism about a new form of globalism lies.

Academics from a critical tradition also attempt to understand the significance of these protests. Some see them as "a systemic and alarming crisis of legitimacy" (Bleiker, 2002). It is a development that opens up new possibilities for popular participation in the struggle over global governance. It fosters a new international democratic ethos. Evaluating the Seattle protest, Grundy and Howell (2001) focus on issues of access and equity. They argue that the protest movement is part of a hierarchy of radicalism that is white-centric, masculine and militaristic in nature. They argue for a de-privileging of protest-based politics that is mediated by race, class and gender and recommend decentralized and localized equity struggles as a more sustainable and effective form of the anti-globalization movement.

To those analysts advocating for social development, accelerating globalization through narrow trade and liberalization investment strategies only means the neglect of social dimensions of development (Howard, 1999). In their eyes, the Seattle protests illustrate popular dissatisfaction with the environmental, social and democratic deficits of globalization and mark the beginning of the end of "irresponsible globalization." Many analysts contend that these recent protests against corporate globalization suggest the emergence of an anti-globalization movement. Specifically, they represent "international struggle against neoliberal policies" (Seoane and Taddei, 2002).

SOCIAL MOVEMENT THEORY AND GLOBAL PROTESTS

Some of these explanations are plausible and enlightening on the nature and meaning of the protests. As many academics (O'Connor, 2001; Smith, 2001; Yuen at al., 2001; Seoane and Taddei, 2002, for example) equate global social protests with an anti-globalization social movement, this raises the question of whether contemporary social movement theory is able to shed light on this worldwide movement.

In the past few decades, social movement theory has evolved rapidly. Overall, it emphasizes the importance of resource mobilization as well as the politics of identity and culture within a society. Two theories of social movement are often discussed in the literature: resource mobilization and New Social Movement (NSM). Associated with the work of Zald and McCarthy, and Tilly, resource mobilization theory focuses upon the goals, organization and leadership of movements, the resources and opportunities available to them and the strategies they employ. In essence, the theory contends that the availability of resources is the most important determinant in the emergence and likely success of collective action (Orsini, 2002; Williams, 1999).

NSM theory, another leading perspective, is represented by the work of Touraine, Offe, Melucci and Castells. This theory attempts to understand the development of "new" types of social movements (other than labor movements) in developed societies using the concepts of quality of life and lifestyle (as opposed to material issues). New social movements are viewed as movements of the post-industrial era (Melucci, 1989). People in these movements are drawn predominantly from the "new middle-class." They are bound by common values rather than by ethnic, religious or class-based affiliations.

NSM theory has been used extensively to explain the development of peace, women's and environmental movements in advanced industrialized countries. Melucci (1989), who first coins the term "new social movement," contends that issues of collective identity are central to the creation of social movement organizations. Essentially, NSM theory tries to understand how collective actors strive to create the identities and solidarities that they defend. The movement's collective identity is centered on several narratives that help establish boundaries, identify antagonists and create a collective consciousness. Together these narratives form a web of beliefs that adheres members to the movement (Melucci, 1989; Steward et al., 2002). Additionally, the theory attempts to understand how structural and cultural developments within society (such as social relations of power and domination and cultural orientations) contribute to the development of a social movement, the principal concern of which is the self-defense of civil society against the state. Accordingly, the role of the state (its capacity and propensity for repression) needs to be vigorously examined.

Principally, NSM theory is concerned with a movements' resistance to state control of cultural matters, while reclaiming matters of identity and autonomy.

Academics (Morris and Mueller, 1992; Williams, 1999; Orsini, 2002) maintain that both theories have contributed toward a richer understanding of social movements at local, regional and national levels. Thus, researchers continue to look at the presence of resources or the forging of collective consciousness as important determinants of social action. These determinants are particularly relevant to the question of "how" a social movement evolves and gains momentum.

Although it yields useful insights into the dynamics involved in social action, social movement theory is ultimately too narrow to grapple with all social struggles (Clark, 2002). Thus, Shakespeare (1993: 49) contends that "new social movement theory, while useful in the analysis of environmentalism, post-materialism, and some varieties of nationalism, cannot fully grasp the essence of liberation politics." Other critics maintain that contemporary social movement perspectives could better attend to the question of "how" a movement evolves than "why."

Importantly, the locus of social movement theory is often confined to the national boundary since most social movements operate within state boundaries. Specifically, some critics see NSM theory as limited in focus: it treats all new social movements as a form of cultural defense while ignoring ongoing struggles with the state and capital (Adam, 1993). Such theorizing ignores and underestimates the enduring effects of the political economy of advanced capitalism in shaping the trajectory of new social movements.

Invariably, social movement theory cannot fully explain each and every aspect of community action that takes place. Its efficacy must be put in specific context. Without modifications or conceptual extension, it would not be easy to apply theories like resource mobilization or NSM to global social protests (Vahabzadeh, 2001). Clearly, the boundary of global social protests transcends those of national social movements. Notably, few studies have tried to theorize the linkages between social movements and world politics (Mittelman, 1998). In this respect, the emergence of global social action against international corporate power and globalization, conceived as a global phenomenon targeting international organizations and the world capitalist economic order, calls for a re-examination of social theories to account for the multi-dimensionality and multi-layering of worldwide struggles.

There is a second reason to move beyond conventional social movement theory for the study of global social protests. As Seoane and Taddei (2002) convincingly argue, "the Battle in Seattle" has allied the US labor movement to a multitude of movements (such as women's, environmental and student movements and the movement calling for the eradication of Third World debt). It is a convergence of social movements at the international level. In other words, anti-WTO social protest in Seattle is deemed as "an aggregate of numerous movements into a counter-hegemonic front" (Vahabzadeh, 2001: 629). Indeed, global social protests are marked by the breadth and heterogeneity of movements they represent. The essence and origin of this convergence (i.e. a "globalization of social movements") cannot fully be captured by any one variant of social movement theory. Instead, a macro social theory is needed to analyze transnational social movements. Needless to say, the use of such a macro social theory to account for global social protests should be complemented by analysis of individual movements (using contemporary social movement theory) if one is to examine the development of disparate movements at national, regional or local levels. To do so is clearly beyond the purview of this contribution.

GLOBAL SOCIAL PROTESTS: A POLANYIAN INTERPRETATION

In light of the above discussion, we ground our analysis of global social protests in the work of Karl Polanyi's *The Great Transformation* (1944). Polanyi, one of the most influential economic historians of the twentieth century, delineates and explains the economic and social transformations of capitalist societies and presents a critique of the market economy. In the last two decades, his analysis of the market economy has been extensively applied in various academic disciplines: economics, sociology, development studies, environmental science and anthropology. The level of analysis of the capitalist economy in his theory is both macro and structural. He is considered one of the few master thinkers who offer "traces of a finely grained analysis of the emergence of social movements within the global political economy of their times" (Mittelman, 1998: 851).

In *The Great Transformation*, Polanyi argues that market practices have existed throughout history but they were never more than subsidiary to economic life (Levitt, 1995). The idea of a self-regulating market whereby people have their needs met through treating land, labor and money as commodities only took root in the modern era. Proponents of market economy contend that the liberalization of economies fosters economic growth and serves the best interests of the world's poor.

To Polanyi, capitalism, along with the expansion of the market economy, is historically unique. While acknowledging that there are alternative and viable forms of economic system, Polanyi is particularly attentive to the disruptive nature of a self-adjusting market and the ideology of economic liberalism. A market economy is neither sustainable nor problem-free. Individualism and excessive market intervention could fiercely intrude into social relations, thus fostering inequalities and weakening social bonds (Sandbrook, 2000). The market economy has brought about great social dislocations. To Polanyi, such a self-regulating market ultimately implies "a stark utopia." He warns that: "such an institution could not exist for any length of time without annihilating the human and natural substance of society" (1944: 3).

Polanyi (1944: 106-7) is highly critical of the doctrine of economic liberalism that had gained so much support:

> Scholars proclaimed in unison that a science had been discovered which put the laws governing man's world beyond any doubt. It was at the behest of these laws that compassion was removed from the hearts, and a stoic determination to renounce human solidarity in the name of the greatest happiness of the greatest number gained the dignity of secular religion.

To analyze the way in which capitalist society functions, he put forward the theory of embedding, arguing that the contemporary capitalist economy has become disembedded from social relations and social institutions. This is conceived as a unique development since historically other economic systems have been embedded in social institutions and social relationships. Importantly, Polanyi maintains that as market forces attempt to dissembled the economy from society, there is a protective countermovement that emerges to resist such disembedding of the economy (Block, 2001). Thus, Polanyi (1944: 151) maintains that: "the liberal movement, intent on the spreading of the market system, was met by a protective countermovement tending toward its restriction."

In short, Polanyi argues that the development of capitalist economies is driven by two countervailing forces: the expansion of the market and the development of social protection. In contrast to the Marxists, Polanyi believes that such resistance does not only come from the working classes but from all groups that are adversely affected by the disembedding process.

In sum, Polanyi posits a dual movement of market expansion (fuelled by economic liberalism) on the one hand, matched by an increasingly protective response (i.e. social protection) on the other. Barham (1997: 244) captures the essence of this "double movement" when she observes that:

> As the market organization of society expands, groups begin to act collectively in a return movement, seeking ways to channel and restrict market impacts through the creation of new regulations, laws or social institutions.

Drawing on Polanyi's idea of a double movement, one could contend that the expansion and excesses of the world market economy would evoke some reaction from society and different groups will react to the encroaching expansion of the free market economy. Seen in this light, the global social protest movement inaugurated by "the Battle in Seattle" in 1999 appears to support Polanyi's concept of a double movement, representing the return movement by society.

Relying on Polanyi's framework, one could argue that economic globalization (along with its market ideology that is a dominant force in all our social and economic lives) creates not only a growing process of social exclusion within and between nations, but also the social action that will contest it and seek to democratize it (Munck, 2002). In this regard, world social protests against globalization, neo-liberalism and transnational corporate power (a leitmotif in recent international protests) should be regarded as a form of anti-systemic resistance that is evoked by the forces of economic liberalism.

One would expect the return movement to be both institutional and spontaneous. If the expansion of welfare institutions and legal mechanisms after the Second World War in the advanced industrialized countries represents the institutional approach to the de-commodification of labor, then the massive global social protests since 1999 constitute a much more spontaneous resistance movement.

RELEVANCE OF "DOUBLE MOVEMENT" ANALYSIS

The use of a Polanyian perspective advances our understanding of worldwide resistance to encroaching globalization and transnational corporate power. Protests against globalization are a form of resistance as well as an attempt to "re-embed" the economy in social relationships.

The Polanyian analysis is illuminating on the nature of global protests in several ways. Admittedly, the challenge of "neo-liberal globalism" has considerably weakened the state as an instrument to regulate international corporate power. Thus, some are pessimistic that there is no alternative to neo-liberal ideas and a global marketplace. In this regard, Polanyi's analysis offers the poor and vulnerable some cause for hope to oppose the hegemony of neo-liberalism that often plays an overbearing role in their lives. His analysis of the market economy over the centuries serves as a call to societies to build their capacity and power to resist market forces.

Second, his analysis of the counter-movement is grounded in historical analysis of resistance to the erosion of social protection. It must be acknowledged that Polanyi belongs to the community of early analysts who warn against the subordination of societies and cultures to the accumulation of capital. Polanyi's *Great Transformation* is about the subjugation of social values to the imperative of the market (Pescard, 2002). Although these concerns were somewhat put to rest under post-World-War Two welfare capitalism, they are now re-emerging stronger than ever in the aftermath of economic liberalization in the 1980s and the concomitant erosion of the welfare state.

More importantly, Polanyi (1944) argues that different individuals would be affected by the expansion of the market economy in many different ways (Barham, 1997). Their responses would be varied but they would "find it natural to cooperate, although at first glance there seems to be no reason for them to do so." The course of the worldwide reactions to globalization and neo-liberalism since the "Battle in Seattle" indicates that individual responses are indeed diverse (deriving from such wide-ranging interests as the environmental protection movement, the movement toward sustainable agriculture, the labor movement and action groups against world poverty and inequities). These protests *in toto* symbolize the attempt to realize Polanyi's vision of a re-embedded economy. According to Polanyi (1944: 251), a re-embedded economy is one in which "the economic system ceases to lay down the law to society," and in which "the primacy over that system is secured." Re-embedding would demand the decommodification of labor, i.e. "to take labor out of the market" (Pescard, 2002).

In essence, Polanyi (1944) argues that a counter-movement could successfully protect society from the detrimental consequences of the market. As long as the market remains the basic organizing principle, interference with the market mechanism could only exacerbate the contradiction between the economy and society, creating strains that ultimately culminate in crises.

CONCLUDING THOUGHTS

It is premature to assess the actual impact of global social protests on poverty, income inequities and other social issues. Some academics view the prospective impact in a positive light. For instance, Smith (2001) argues that since the Seattle protests international organizations such as the IMF and the World Bank have been forced to bolster the case that more trade is needed to address the needs of the world's poor. Along similar lines, Thomas (2000: 15) argues that global protests have eroded the "façade of legitimacy and universality surrounding global governance institutions and their policies."

Despite the intensity of global social protests, some commentators voice a cautionary note. Some analysts pertinently question the durability of transnational alliances and global protests (Ayres, 2001; Block, 2001). Other criticisms touch on the long-term goal of building a global civil society (Scholte, 2000). While one of the ways to rein in transnational corporate power is to strengthen civil society, some critics go so far as to challenge the belief that impediments to the development of a global civil society can be overcome. Thus, Rootes (2002) argues that such a global civil society is only an aspiration. On the other hand, Kaldor

(2000) is more optimistic. He contends that what happened in Seattle is an expression of global civil society. It is still too early to predict the course of this particular form of civil society as it depends on the political alliances that are constructed and the extent to which global civil society can represent the voices of the victims of globalization.

Other writers like Tabb (2000) alert us to the possibility of a "tactical repositioning" or "a retreat to a token openness" on the part of world corporate powers like the WTO, IMF and the World Bank in the face of anti-globalization protests. As a matter of fact, pro-market writers have come to the defense of neo-liberalism and the market economy. Recently, *The Economist* (September 11, 2002) described the market as "the best means for reducing poverty," noting that "when companies, properly regulated and acting within the law, pursue profits, they end up increasing prosperity. This is not a theory but an easily observable fact."

Admittedly, the dominance of neo-liberalism and market ideology has evoked various powerful responses. Most notable is the ideological critique of the market economy from the French philosopher Pierre Bourdieu. Bourdieu (1999) has been vocal against what he calls "neo-liberal imperialism" and is critical of the tyranny of the market that makes money the sole criterion of social value. Bourdieu (1999) proposes that all collectives, unions, states and supranational state should come together to counteract the destructive impact of neo-liberal ideas.

Bourdieu's powerful intellectual critique of neo-liberalism is timely. But some form of political activism against the dominant neo-liberal thinking is equally and urgently needed. As Mann (1999: 761) observes, "For without social movements, they [progressive professionals and intellectuals] are reduced to social critics." More importantly, social movements help to keep alternative visions of social order alive in the collective memory (Boyd, 1997). The emergence of global social protests poses another forceful challenge to neo-liberal dominance and its neglect of world poverty (Brecher et al., 2000). If the Polanyian analysis of the ills of globalization and the market economy is firmly grounded in historical contexts, then the potency of a contemporary counter-movement against world poverty and inequities should not be lightly discounted.

REFERENCES

Adam, B. D. (1993). Post-Marxism and the New Social Movement. *Canadian Review of Sociology and Anthropology*, 30(3): 316-337.

Ayres, J. (2001). Transnational Political Processes and Contention against the Global Economy. *Mobilization*, 6(1): 55-68.

Barham, E. (1997). Social Movements for Sustainable Agriculture in France: A Polanyian Perspective. *Society and Natural Resources*, 10(3): 39-49.

Bleiker, R. (2002). Activism after Seattle: Dilemmas of the Anti-globalization Movement. *Pacific Review*, 14(3): 191-207.

Block, F. (2001). Introduction. In K. Polanyi's *The Great Transformation*. Boston: Beacon Press.

Borosage, R. L. (1999). The Battle in Seattle. *Nation*, 269(19): 20-21.

Bourdieu, P. (1999). *Acts of Resistance: Against the Tyranny of the Market*. Stanford, California: Stanford University Press.

Boyd, S. B. (1997). *Challenging the Public/Private Divide: Feminism, Law and Public Policy*. Toronto: University of Toronto Press.

Brecher, J., Costello, T. and Smith, B. (2000). *Globalization from Below*. Cambridge, Mass.: South End Press.

Castles, F.G. (2002). Developing New Measures of Welfare State Change and Reform. *European Journal of Political Research*, 14: 613-624.

Clark, B. (2002). The Indigenous Environmental Movement in the United States: Transcending Borders in Struggles against Mining, Manufacturing, and the Capitalist State. *Organization and Environment*, 15 (4): 410-442.

Cockburn, A. and St. Clair, J. (2000). *5 Days that Shook the World*. London: Verso.

Cooper, M. (1999). Street Fight in Seattle. *Nation*, 269: 21.

Crossley, N. (2002). Global Anti-Corporate Struggle: A Preliminary Analysis. *British Journal of Sociology*, 53(4): 667-691.

Davis, J. and Rowley, P. (2001). Internationalism against Globalization. In Yuen, E., Katisaficas, G. and Rose, D. (Eds.) (2001). *The Battle of Seattle: The New Challenge to Capitalist Globalization* (pp.25-28). New York: Soft Skull Press.

Dhruvarajan, V. (2003) Feminism and Resistance to Globalization of Capitalism. In Y. Atasoy and W. Carroll (Eds.) *Global Shaping and Its Alternatives* (pp.179-195) Aurora, Ontario: Garamond Press.

Economist, The (2002). *Why Naomi Klein Needs to Grow Up*. September 11, Volume 365, Issue 8298, p.70.

Ericson, R. and Doyle, A. (1999). Globalization and the Policing of Protest: The Case of APEC. *British Journal of Sociology*, 50(4): 589-609.

Foster, J. B. (2003). A Planetary Defeat: The Failure of Global Environmental Reform. *Monthly Review,* January.

Giddens, A. (1999). *Runaway World: How Globalization is Reshaping Our lives*. London: Profile Books.

Gill, S. (2000). Toward a Post-modern Prince? The Battle in Seattle as a Moment in the Politics of Globalization. *Millennium*, 29(1):131-140.

Godement, F. (1999). *The Downsizing of Asia*. New York: Routledge.

Gramsci, A. (1959). *The Modern Prince and Other Writings*. New York: The International Publishers.

_____ . (1971). *Selections from the Prison Notebook*. New York: The International Publishers.

Grundy, J. and Howell, A. (2001). Negotiating the Culture of Resistance: A Critical Assessment of Protest Politics. *Studies in Political Economy*, 66 Autumn: 121-132

Hewison, K. (2002). Globalization, Inequality and Governance. In R. Chan et al. (Eds.) *Development in Southeast Asia: Review and Prospects* (pp.241-256). Aldershot: Ashgate.

Howard, J. (1999). The Lessons of Seattle for Social Development. *Development*, 43(2): 91-93.

Kaldor, M. (2000). 'Civilising' Globalization? The Implications of the 'Battle in Seattle.' *Millennium*, 29(1): 105-114.

Kanbur, R. (2001). Economic Policy, Distribution and Poverty: The Nature of Disagreements. *World Development*, 29(6): 1083-1094.

Lambert, R and Webster, E (2001). Southern Unionism and the New Labour Internationalism. *Antipode*, 33(3): 337-362.

Levitt, K. P. (1995). Toward Alternatives: Re-reading the Great Transformation. *Monthly Review*, 47(2): 1-16.

Lorna, M. (2000). *Breaking the Neo-Liberal Consensus: The Multilateral Agreement on Investment and Its Links to the Seattle Protests against the World Trade Organization.* An American Sociological Association (ASA) Conference Paper.

Machiavelli N. (1944). *Machiavelli's The Prince.* Chapel Hill: The University of North Carolina Press.

Mann, E. (1999). Radical Social Movements and the Responsibility of Progressive Intellectuals. *Loyola of Los Angeles Law Review*, 32: 761-791.

McMichael, P. (2000). *Development and Social Change: A Global Perspective.* London: Pine Forge Press.

McMurtry, J. (2002). Why the Protestors are against Corporate Globalization. *Journal of Business Ethics*, 40(3): 201-205.

Melucci, A. (1989*). Nomads of the Present: Social Movements and Individual Needs in Contemporary Society.* Philadelphia: Temple University Press.

Midgley, J. (2000). Globalization, Capitalism and Social Welfare: A Social Development Perspective. *Canadian Social Work Review*, 17:13-28.

Mittelman, J. H. (1998). Globalisation and Environmental Resistance Politics. *ThirdWorld Quarterly* 19(5): 847-872.

Morris, A.D. and Mueller C. (Eds.) (1992). *Frontiers of Social Movement Theory.* New Haven, Connecticut: Yale University Press.

Munck, R. (2002). Globalization and Democracy: A New "Great Transformation"? *Annual of the American Academy of Political and Social Science*, 10-21.

O'Connor, J. (2001). On Populism and Anti-Globalist Movement. In E. Yuen, G. Katisaficas and D. Rose (Eds.) (2001). *The Battle of Seattle: The New Challenge to Capitalist Globalization* (pp.359-370). New York: Soft Skull Press.

Orsini, M. (2002). The Politics of Naming, Blaming and Claiming: HIV, Hepatitis C and Emergence of Blood Activism in Canada. *Canadian Journal of Political Science*, 35(3): 475-498.

Oxfam (1999). *Loaded Against the Poor: World Trade Organization.* London: Oxfam Policy Paper.

Peschard, K. (2002). *Accessibility Crisis in the 'Age of Access': Antiretrovirals, Transnational Aids Advocacy and Resistance to Neoliberal Globalization.* Unpublished MA Thesis, University of Northern British Columbia.

Pigman, G. A. (2002). A Multifunctional Case Study for Teaching International Political Economy: The World Economic Forum as Shar-pei or Wolf in Sheep's Clothing? *International Studies Perspectives*, 3(3): 291-309.

Polanyi, K. (1944) [2001 edn.] *The Great Transformation: The Political and Economic Origins of Our Times.* Boston: Beacon Press.

Rootes, C. (2002). Global Visions: Global Civil Society and the Lesson of European Environmentalism. *Voluntas*, 13(4): 411-429.

Sandbrook, R. (2000). Globalization and the Limits of Neoliberal Development Doctrine. *Third World Quarterly*, 21(6): 1071-1080.

Scholte, J. A. (2000). Cautionary Reflections on Seattle. *Millennium*, 29(1): 115-125

Seoane J. and Taddei E. (2002). From Seattle to Porto Alegre: The Anti-Neoliberal Globalization Movement. *Current Sociology*, 50(1): 99-122.

Shakespeare, T. (1993). Disabled People's Self-Organization: A New Social Movement? *Disability Handicap and Society*, 8(3): 249-263.

Smith, J. (2001). Globalizing Resistance: the Battle of Seattle and the Future of Social Movements. *Mobilization*, 6(1): 1-19.

Steward, G., Shriver, T., and Chasteen, A. (2002). Participant Narratives and Collective Identity in a Metaphysical Movement. *Sociological Spectrum*, 22 (1): 107-135.

Stiglitz, J. (2001). *Globalization and its Discontents*. New York: W.W. Norton.

Tabb, W. K. (2000). After Seattle: Understanding the Politics of Globalization. *Monthly Review*, 52(3): 1-18.

Tang, K. L. and Midgley, J. (2002). Social Policy after the East Asian Crisis: Forging a Normative Basis for Welfare. *Journal of Asian Comparative Development*, Winter.

Tarrow, S. (1998). *Power in Movement: Social Movements and Contentious Politics:* Second Edition. New York: Cambridge University Press.

Teeple, G. (1995). *Globalization and the Decline of Social Reform*. Toronto: Garamond Press.

Thomas, C. (2000). *Global Governance, Development and Human Security*. London: Pluto Press.

Thorbecke, E. and Charumilind, C. (2002). Economic Inequality and its Socioeconomic Impact. *World Development*, 1477-1495.

United Nations Development Project (1999). *Human Development Report 1999*. New York: Oxford University Press.

_____ . (2003). UNDP Webpage. Accessed January 29, 2003 from http://www.undp.org/

Vahabzadeh, P. (2001). A Critique of Ultimate Referentiality in the New Social Movement Theory of Alberto Melucci. *Canadian Journal of Sociology*, 26(4): 611-634.

Williams, M. (1999). The WTO Social Movements and Democracy. In A. Taylor and C. Thomas (Eds.) *Global Trade and Global Social Issues* (pp.151-170). New York: Routledge.

Wills, J. (2002). Political Economy III: Neoliberal Chickens, Seattle and Geography. *Progress in Human Geography*, 26(1): 90-100.

Yuen, E., Katisaficas, G. and Rose, D. (Eds.) (2001). *The Battle of Seattle: The New Challenge to Capitalist Globalization*. New York: Soft Skull Press.

CONTRIBUTORS

Sammy Chiu is an associate professor at the Department of Social Work, Hong Kong Baptist University. He was educated respectively in Hong Kong and in the United Kingdom and was qualified as a social worker at the University of Wales at Swansea. After working some years as a social worker, he entered into social policy and obtained an MA in social service planning at Essex University and a PhD in social policy from Sheffield University. His recent research interest is on East Asian social policy with particular focus on the issue of legitimization. His published works include *New Social Policy* (Eds.) (The Chinese University Press, 1999), *Youth Work and Empowerment: Theory and Practice* (Eds.) (Hong Kong Policy Viewers, 1999) and a number of articles which have appeared in various international journals, such as *Ageing and Society, International Social Work, Social Policy and Social Work*, and *European Journal of Social Work*.

Glenn Drover is an adjunct professor of social work at Dalhousie University and Carleton University in Canada. He has taught in several universities in Canada and Hong Kong and has published extensively in the areas of social welfare, social policy, social work, and political economy. He currently is undertaking research on the privatization of public pension plans and the history of social welfare in Canada.

Xin-Ping Guan is a professor and head of the Department of Sociology, Nankai University, China. He holds a BA in Philosophy from Sichuan University, a MA in Sociology and a PhD in Economics from Nankai University. He was a visiting scholar at Birmingham University in the UK in 1991-92. His main academic interests are social stratification, poverty study, and social policy in China. His main publications include *China's Urban Poverty* (1999), and a series of papers about poverty and social policies in China and comparative social policy. He is also the author of several reports about social welfare policies in the areas of health service, social security and poverty alleviation for the Chinese Government. He is a social work educator and the vice-secretary-in-general of the China Association of Social Work Education.

Arlene Herman is an assistant professor of social work at the University of Northern British Colombia, Canada. She has been in the field of social work for the past twenty five years and has lived, worked and taught in the US, Australia, South America and Canada. Throughout her social work practice career Arlene has been involved in the development of single issue and multi-issue coalitions focusing on a broad range of social justice issues. She has also been involved in the development of specialized services for women, particularly in the area of re-entering the job market and re-entering education. Her current research interests focus on the impact of neo-liberal policies on the experience of immigrant and First Nations women in Canada, globalization and social movements and women's leadership roles in community development.

Meegon Kim is the head of the Primary Security Research Team at the Korea Institute for Health and Social Affairs in Seoul. He holds a master's degree in welfare economics from Konkuk University in Seoul. His academic interests include poverty and public assistance. He has authored many books and articles. They include: *A Study to Estimate the Minimum Cost of Living* (1994); *Supplementary Benefit Policy related to the Needy* (1995); *Measuring a Poverty Line and Policy Implications* (1997); *A Proposal to Revise the Livelihood Protection Law during the High Unemployment Periods* (1998); *A Study to Estimate the Minimum Cost of Living* (1999); and *A study on the Enforcement Method of the National Basic Livelihood Security Law* (2000).

Sunwoo Lee is an assistant professor at the Department of Social Welfare, Inje University. He was a research fellow at the Korea Institute for Health and Social Affairs in Seoul. He holds an undergraduate degree and a master's degree from Seoul National University. He obtained his PhD in social welfare from the University of California at Berkeley in 1995. He previously taught social welfare at Seoul National University. His academic interests include welfare for disabled people, social safety nets, and research and statistics. He is the co-author of the book: *Statistics in Social Welfare* (Seoul, Korea: Nanam Publishing Company, 1997).

James Midgley is Harry and Riva Professor and Dean of the School of Social Welfare at the University of California at Berkeley. He has published widely on issues of social development, social policy, social work and international social welfare. His most recent books include: *Social Welfare in Global Context* (Sage Publications, 1997); *Alternatives to Social Security: An International Exploration* (with Michael Sherraden, Greenwood Press, 1997); *The Handbook of Social Policy* (with Martin Tracey and Michelle Livermore, Sage Publications, 2000); and *Controversial Issues in Social Policy* (with Howard Karger and Brene Brown, Allyn and Bacon, 2003).

Yuki Sekine is an ILO official specialized in International Labor Standards, and is currently attached to the Japan Ministry of Health, Labor and Welfare. She studied law in Brussels where she was born, then specialized in Social Security Law at the University of Tokyo, with an emphasis also on Labor Law. Her main fields of interest have been the application of international social standards, in particular workers' basic rights and human rights. She has published some articles on workers' rights, particularly in the field of discrimination, within and outside the ILO.

Kwong-leung Tang will soon become a faculty member of the Department of Social Work, the Chinese University of Hong Kong. He is currently professor and chair of social work in the College of Arts, Social and Health Sciences at the University of Northern British

Columbia, Canada. He received a Master of Science in social planning from the London School of Economics and Political Science and his doctorate from the University of California at Berkeley. He is the author of *Social Welfare Development in East Asia* (Macmillan and St. Martin's Press, 2000) and *Colonial State and Social Policy: Social Welfare Development of Hong Kong 1842-1997* (University Press of America, 1998). His academic interests include East Asian social welfare, law and social policy, human rights and international organizations and comparative social policy analysis.

Kate Yeong-Tsyr Wang is associate professor of the Department of Social Wok, Fu-Jen Catholic University, Taiwan. She teaches courses in social welfare, program evaluation, human rights for minorities, and advanced statistics. Her research and publications are in the areas of unemployment, poverty and inequality, policy evaluation, social work ethics, and welfare rights for ethnic minorities. She has been a board member of the Taiwanese Association of Social Workers (TASW) and chair of the Social Work Department at Fu-Jen Catholic University. Dr. Wang received her PhD in social work from Washington University in St. Louis, United States.

Chack-kie Wong is a professor in the Social Work Department, the Chinese University of Hong Kong. He holds a bachelor degree in social science and a master's degree in social work from the University of Hong Kong, and a PhD in social policy from the University of Sheffield. He has published substantially in the areas of comparative social policy, welfare attitudes, poverty, and welfare reform issues in China. His recent researches are on citizenship and social development, social welfare attitudes, and China's health care reform.

Mui Teng Yap is a senior research fellow at the Institute of Policy Studies, a public policy think-tank in Singapore, where she specializes in demographic and social issues. She has written and published on Singapore's population policies, population ageing and related issues, as well as on labor migration policies. She is the editor of *Social Services: The Next Lap* (Singapore: Times Academic Press for the Institute of Policy Studies, 1991). Besides her research work, she has also served on government committees and is currently the chairperson of the Feedback Group on Elderly Development, Ministry of Community Development and Sports, Singapore. Dr Yap has a PhD degree in Sociology from the University of Hawaii.

INDEX